Advance praise for
LONG TIME PASSING

This is a valuable book; it is really about human relations and the universal quality rather than a book just about lesbians. I want people, all people, to read this book. It shows how people grow.
— May Sarton

I enjoyed *Long Time Passing* a lot. The stories are entertaining and absorbing, and provide valuable insights into both age and a time of more repressed conditions for lesbians. The spectrum of class and professional affiliations also affords a certain comprehensive view. This should be an enlightening book for everybody, not just lesbians.
— Jill Johnston

I read *Long Time Passing* with great interest a few weeks ago. Jill Johnston called around that time and she too had read it; neither of us had expected to be so absorbed, saddened, encouraged or moved. Jill was all for the "Jock" sports passage. I was intrigued by the life of the woman doctor, the soldiers, the hiding, the enormous loneliness of earlier lesbian lives. And most particularly their terrible solitary courage...
hope, dignity. And I loved the stor...
year-olds, the sheer vitalit...
aging women, whether alo...
in the sea of a brand new l...

Long Time Passing
Lives Of Older Lesbians

Edited By
Marcy Adelman, Ph.D.

Boston : Alyson Publications, Inc.

This is a paperback original from Alyson Publications, Inc.,
40 Plympton St, Boston, Mass. 02118.
Distributed in England by GMP Publishers,
PO Box 247, London, N15 6RW.

First edition, December 1986

Library of Congress Cataloging-in-Publication Data

Long time passing.

1. Aged lesbians — Psychology — Case studies.
I. Adelman, Marcy.
HQ75.5.L65 1986   306.7'663   86-17285
ISBN 0-932870-74-0 (pbk.)

1 3 5 4 2

Contents

Acknowledgements

My friends and family have been stalwart supporters over the past two years' work on this book. Bref French, my lover, deserves special thanks. Her help, humor, encouragement and support were essential in making this book a reality. Our relationship has been a continual source of love, adventure, and amazement. My love and gratitude to Marny Hall for her profoundly generous and challenging friendship; her helpful introductions and suggestions greatly facilitated the completion of this project. My heartfelt appreciation to Abby Abernanti for her wise counsel and support; her editorial suggestions and assistance were invaluable. Christa Donaldson, Carmen Bergen, Victoria Galland, and Ellen Eagleson read, listened, gave helpful feedback, and warm support. My affection and thanks to each of them.

I want to thank my mother and father, Bennett and Julie Adelman, for their love and generosity; and my sister, Beth Adelman-Krantz, for her encouragement and constant support. The love and understanding of my friends and family sustained and nurtured me throughout this project.

Meredith Maran's editorial contribution to this book was pivotal; her organizational wizardry and editorial experience enhanced and enriched this project. Her daily messages on my phone tape kept me on track and taught me a first-class lesson in editing.

Ann Heron transcribed mountains of taped interviews and her unflagging enthusiasm and encouragement spurred me on through the sometimes long and difficult hours

I want to thank Emmanuelle Meynot for the constancy of her heart and for her continual search to find new ways to create and express herself which has been an inspiration to me.

Sasha Alyson, my publisher, believed in this project from the beginning. I am grateful to him for his faith and his patience.

Michelle Sumares worked skillfully any time night or day at the computer. Vera Ferris suggested important leads to several people interviewed and, B.C., before computer, typed and transcribed several tapes.

Thanks to Fred Minnigerode who ten years ago asked me to join him on the National Institute of Mental Health grant proposal on gay aging which started my work in the field.

For helpful conversations, my appreciation to Isabelle Lyle, Mateil Poore, Mildred Feiner, Lu Chaiken, Rev. Janey Spahr, Jan Faulkner, Marilyn Murphy, Carol Becker, Kate Rosenblatt, Betty Shoemaker, Muriel Fisher, Dotty Fowler, and Rosemary McCaslin.

Richard Hall listened to my problems with the title and with his literary acumen and experience suggested a superb selection of titles to choose from. His generosity and experience is very much appreciated.

On short notice three people helped me put the cover together: Sean Reynolds lent her expert photographic skills; Frances Lorraine lent her style and flair to the photo session and kindly permitted me to use her picture; and Kim Settle and her company, Red Shoes Slide Service, provided the professional technical assistance to produce the layout.

Finally, I want to thank all the women who graciously allowed me to interview and tape them and who trusted me with their stories.

With love,
to Bref French

Introduction

This book was conceived, appropriately enough, while my lawyer and I were in the process of writing my will. Just before we finished, she looked at me and asked, "Is there anything else you want to make arrangements for? Anything of value to yourself or others that you haven't mentioned?" After a moment it came to me; I thought: "Oh yes — the box I tap with my toe as I sit sipping my tea every morning at my kitchen table..." That was the box full of computer printouts and questionnaires: the results of my research on lesbian aging.

I'd been involved in gay gerontology since the mid-1970's, when I co-directed a National Institute of Mental Health grant on the subject. The grant funded a study which compared heterosexual men and women to gay men and lesbians over 60 years old, in terms of their adjustment to aging. This research formed the basis for my dissertation on "Adjustment to Aging and Styles of Being Gay," which was finished in 1980.

Before I did the research all the old women I knew were heterosexual and had children or grandchildren. I knew my old age would be different from theirs, but I didn't know how. The only picture I could conjure up was based on the stereotypical view of old gay people as bitter, lonely and miserable — and of old women as sexless, quarrelsome, humorless hags. The lesbians I met in the community were all my age or younger; our lesbian elders were dispersed and invisible. Our community seemed to have sprung up from thin air, suspended in time without any sense of continuity. How could we envision our futures if we didn't know our past and never saw people like ourselves old until we ourselves were old?

Doing the research gave me a way to look into my own future with a confidence and clarity I'd never known. Throughout the next several years of developing a private therapy practice, I shared the results of my study. After a while, I found myself thinking about how much I wanted to share the results of the research with the wider community and to do some more work in the field of gerontology. And then I was approaching 40, sitting in a lawyer's office composing a will and again wondering about my old age. Suddenly determined to bring the issues of lesbian aging to public attention, I headed for Old Wives' Tales, a San Francisco women's bookstore, to see if any such books already existed. To my surprise there was only one. I decided that day that the box in my kitchen had been underfoot long enough: I would put together a book on lesbian aging.

Instead of compiling an assortment of academic opinions, I chose to record the voices of women like those I'd interviewed for the study — to let them write about their own experiences in their own words. So I sent out a letter to acquaintances in the lesbian community, asking them for their personal reflections on their own aging process. The letter was followed up with phone calls and visits during which I explained the project and asked for their help.

Almost immediately I realized that it was going to be more difficult than I had imagined to get people to write about aging and lesbianism. I had envisioned my mailbox overflowing with articles on housing, retirement, age discrimination, spirituality, and sexuality; instead I received a steady stream of apologies. Many women said that the subject was interesting, but that they hadn't given it much thought. Some said that there was nothing to report; they were having no problems related to aging. "I couldn't have known how unready I was to write about aging and lesbianism until I truly tried," wrote one 65-year-old woman.

Clearly, I discovered, the taboo against discussing aging and old age is just as strong in the lesbian community as it is in mainstream society. Despite this obstacle, women did come forward who were eager to contribute. A few were able to write; most felt uncomfortable writing but volunteered to be interviewed. Over the next two years I solicited manuscripts and conducted about 200 interviews, most of which were then transcribed, edited, and in some cases turned into chapters by the interviewees.

As the pile of completed manuscripts grew, I began to realize that my original goal — to bring to life the findings of my gay gerontology study — was being surpassed. These women's descriptions of their later years and lesbian life before the emergence of feminism and gay liberation were compelling in a way that no academic or political tract could be. They shatter the homophobic stereotype of old lesbians as invariably depressed and alone. The stories also substantiate the findings of my own, and other studies, all of which point to one key conclusion: the most important factor for determining psychological well-being in lesbians in later life is the level of homophobia in society and in ourselves.

The fact is all people — gay and straight, male and female — face the aging process. All people face the issues that can become clustered in the later years: loneliness, physical health, and financial problems. And all people who live in this age-segregated, youth-oriented society face the prevalent mischaracterization of later life as a drastic and sudden decline in mental and physical ability. But in actuality, for most old people changes occur gradually, allowing for adjustment and accommodation. And statistically, 95 percent of people over 65 are in good health and live outside of nursing homes.

Many chapters in this book illustrate the ways in which the harshest effects of aging are felt by women and minorities, because they are generally the poorest. The conditions of older lesbians are determined by the conditions of older women; among all people aged 65 or older, twice as many women as men are below the poverty level; 40 percent of women and 15 percent of men live alone; 45 percent of women make $6,000 or less (U.S. index, 1983).

As lesbians age and mature, we confront the same developmental challenges as do heterosexuals (acquiring competency, self-esteem, etc.). Society's negative attitude towards lesbians, however, can make these challenges harder for us. To cope with hostility, most of us closet ourselves in some or all of our life settings: family, friends, work, church. Particularly in the pre-liberation era, disclosure invariably meant rejection, loss, and the accompanying damage to self-esteem. Those who did not disclose were rewarded with opportunities for career advancement and with social acceptance. Passing protected us by making us invisible. The closet provided comfort within a hostile environment.

And so we see that what is unique about the aging process of lesbians is the stigma and discrimination we face — and the repertoire of creative solutions that we develop to cope with it.

The histories of the women in this book tell the story of the building of our community upon a foundation of such creative coping. They describe what it was like to be a lesbian in the pre-World War II era, when marriage was the only socially and practically viable option for women; when few jobs were open to women; when moving about as a single woman was in itself both unacceptable and difficult. They describe the impact of the war on lesbians: for the first time, they could meet in the semi-public, mostly-male gay bars that sprang up in areas where military personnel were concentrated.

Lesbians who entered these early gay bars 40 years ago found a world of drag queens and bull dykes, a world of first names only in which kissing or even hand-holding were forbidden. One interviewee in my study spoke of that era. "I was 22 when I joined the scene in the mid-1940's after World War II. It was the beatnik era. You had musicians, artists, gay people and communists hanging out together. It was a raunchy scene and the bar where I hung out, the Black Cat, was a symbol of it. It was a dangerous place. There was the danger of being caught in a raid and publicly shamed. There was physical danger from roving bands of soldiers and rowdies. Other gay people were dangerous too and not to be trusted. A lot of gay people were into drugs and alcohol. I saw a lot of lesbians that were nice people turn into prostitutes and drug addicts. For several years I lived in that dangerous underworld. It seems hard to believe now, but really — what choice did I have?"

For many lesbians, the bar scene — the only visible lesbian community — was too alienating and frightening. These women met each other over backyard suburban fences, at work, at PTA meetings. Whether she went to bars or not, though, each woman made her way alone through a hostile environment. The other lesbians she met were as frightened and unknowing as she was. Lesbian feelings were not acknowledged to gay or heterosexual friends. Without benefit of community, the extreme isolation experienced by these lesbians forced them to draw on their individual resources to create such adaptive solutions as passing and butch-femme roles. They were unprotected; they were vulnerable to external and internal homophobia, to self-hatred, to mistrust of each other, and to drug and alcohol abuse. The dangers of being out were so great that few could risk it; many didn't come out even to themselves until late in their lives.

The closets of pre-liberation provided safety, but they also made gay women invisible to each other. Isolation from each other was the terrible price we paid for our safety. For this generation of lesbian elders, gay friends were difficult to meet and even harder to replace as time went on. Opportunities to meet lesbian peers decreased over the years. Many older lesbians adapted to this peer isolation by choosing much younger women — the women they met in the lesbian bars, cafes, concerts and bookstores of the seventies — for friends and lovers.

Today's generation of lesbian elders grew up in the post-Freudian era, when the dominant view of gay people defined them as deviant and deficient. Because there was no visible or viable gay subculture to help offset this homophobic view, gay people were vulnerable to internalizing it: attributing these values to ourselves and each other. Without benefit of mutual support, avoiding identification with other gay women was a way for lesbians to salvage their self-esteem. Edith, whose story appears in this book, remembers: "I had one good friend in LA who was gay. But we never really associated with gay people. I wanted the children to have as normal a childhood as possible."

For these elders, the struggle for self-acceptance was a painful and solitary process. Self-acceptance as a lesbian and coping with stigma was not accomplished in a day, or during any particular time in life. Rather, this is a lifelong, active process which coincides with the changing needs of the individual and the changing social environment in which she lives. Whatever their adaptations: marriage, celibacy, the closet — most old lesbians spent a long time passing.

The succeeding generation of lesbians grew up in a more supportive environment — one in which the lesbian community has provided an alternative to invisibility and isolation. In the past decade, gay people have become a visible and viable political force, which in turn has improved our social status. As lesbians we no longer view ourselves as deviant outcasts; today we recognize ourselves to be members of an oppressed minority group. This recognition brings us together; our self-esteem is elevated, not devastated, by disclosure and identification with other gay people. The ways in which we think about ourselves and each other — and society — has been radically changed. These changes have also altered our development across the life cycle.

The aging process of lesbians who came of age in the post-gay liberation era is sure to be different in many ways from what their foremothers experienced. Today, a lesbian who seeks out other lesbians for the first time may enter the subculture through any number of well-marked entry routes. All of them — gay churches, lesbian softball teams, gay liberation organizations — are socially and personally affirming of her gay identity. The lesbian friends she makes will educate her; books, articles and gay service providers are available to further guide her passage. Coming out in what is still, today, a homophobic society can be traumatic but the gay and lesbian community absorbs some of the toxicity.

As I collected the stories of this long passage I often wept with these women as they recalled their hardships and their losses. I rejoiced with them as they told me about their loves and their triumphs. Their spirit of adventure and their courage to love in an era much more difficult then my own made me proud. Their vitality and strength in later life taught me that things we fear most — illness, separation from lovers and friends — can be survived; that death and dying are just another part of life.

Most importantly, my contact with these elders provided me with the context I was searching for — a sense of a past and a future. They showed me the continuity in their individual lives: the lesbian mother whose child is taken from her, only to return eighteen years later as a loving gay son; the lover of twenty years who leaves and then becomes a best friend ten years later; the 65-year-old who falls in love as intensely as she did at 25; the death of a lover of twenty-five years, followed by the growth of a new lover relationship.

And we shared the gift of lesbian continuity, which is reciprocal between the generations. We provided each other with a context to understand ourselves as part of a greater whole. This is a fluid relationship, not a fixed one. We are at once, generation to generation, each other's future and past. Disconnected from each other, we lesbians are held prisoners of heterosexual society's perception of us. We are unable to shape our own community and individual identities. But aware of our past and intergenerationally connected we can better interpret and understand ourselves in the present — and we can better shape for ourselves and those who follow a more secure future.

MARY FLICK

Good Friends

I'm going to be seventy in January. I dated boys when I was in high school. Then, during my first year in college at the University of Wisconsin, I was involved with Mimi, who lived in my dorm. We were in a double room second semester and became involved sexually. It seemed to me we weren't very discreet about it. We weren't openly lesbian, but we were affectionate among other women in the dorm. We didn't hide it a lot, but still there was an element of hiding.

Mimi came from a rich family; she joined a sorority and moved into the sorority house after that year. Otherwise we might have stayed together. I was on a very limited budget so I moved into a rooming house. I met Jane because she happened to be living in that same rooming house and we got acquainted. I started to talk to her on my nineteenth birthday. I think the attraction was mutual almost immediately.

This was really falling in love. Intense. We didn't want to get involved physically, or at least she didn't. She held back a lot. We looked for a room and we found one. We wouldn't sleep; we'd lie there in adjoining beds wanting to be close to each other and not giving in to it.

Finally I said, "this is ridiculous. We want to be together, we are together, we have a room together." At that point, Jane had been going with the man she eventually married. She wrote to him and told him she was in love with someone else. She told me she was going to terminate the relationship with him.

I don't think either one of us ever expected that we were going to live together forever. After college we both moved to Milwaukee from Madison. We rented an apartment there. Hal, the guy she married, lived in Milwaukee, so she began to see him again. She was always attracted to him. The three of us would do things together and it was really horrible because she was having sex with him. He'd come over and I'd either go in the bathroom and take a bath or I'd go out. But he'd never stay. Then she'd have sex with me after that.

After a year, Jane decided that she wanted to go to law school. The campus was in downtown Chicago so she moved back home to Chicago, and I moved into a girl's rooming house. I gave up our apartment; I couldn't afford the rent. I just kinda gave up. I didn't know any lesbians living together, and I think I just accepted the fact that it wasn't to be. It never occurred to me that we could have worked out a way to live together.

Within two years, we'd stopped being lovers and we were both married to our husbands. But we were still close . . . it was hard sometimes not to be sexual. I remember one time we drove to California with her parents. We had to sit in the back seat because her parents were driving. We had to sit right next to each other and it was just murder. But eventually it wasn't so hard. We talked to each other pretty near every day on the telephone and told each other how things were going.

We didn't have any kids for a while, so we saw each other as couples all the time. We spent our holidays together, our vacations together. And even though there wasn't any sex between Jane and me, we were close to each other.

Jane and Hal bought a house and we moved into the house they had been renting. My husband and I were always kind of trailing along behind. We lived there until we adopted a little boy.

I was at the hospital when Jane's daughter Penny was born. It was a very difficult birth for Jane. Penny had an unusually large head and when she came out her head was deformed from the birth process. But she turned out fine . . . I was involved with Penny from the very beginning. I would come over and take care of her. I was pregnant and taking care of Penny. She still is a wonderful young woman. She's a therapist now, a family therapist.

I think I fantasized a good deal. I fantasized when my husband was making love to me. I sort of became asexual, less and less sexual with my husband. I think I sublimated in many ways. I had kids and I stayed very busy.

When the four of us were living next door to each other, Jane and I weren't affectionate very often. It was dangerous. It was important to stay married and it was important to keep our families and we couldn't risk sleeping together and so we never did.

I still see her husband. They were divorced eventually. He lives here, and I see him and play bridge with him weekly. It's so ridiculous. He knew.

In the end, he threatened to divorce her, and it freaked her out so badly — she didn't want to divorce him — that he would bring that out into the open, that he would name me in court.

Her mother, who is still alive, and of whom I'm very fond, she's very fond of me — never suspected that there was any lesbian relationship. I'm sure she didn't. She just considered us good friends.

Eventually Hal, her husband, separated from her for a year. That was in the early fifties. Then he decided he wanted a divorce. That was when he said he would name me.

I called up Hal when she told me and I said, " That was the most dastardly thing I've ever heard of anyone doing. To think you would do this to Jane, you've loved her all these years. You know, we haven't had a relationship in a long time." Which we hadn't. But he knew the feeling. The feeling was there. So they were divorced.

My husband died in '65 . . . He had turned into an

alcoholic and the last five years with him were just sheer hell. He began doing such erratic stuff that I finally had to commit him to a mental institution. He never forgave me for that; he never came back home. He moved away. Finally my lawyer said, "You've got plenty of grounds for divorce," so I divorced him.

We were divorced at the end of March; at the end of July, he died. Jane, in the meantime, was living alone. So I sold the house my kids and I were living in and I moved into the next block in the suburb of Milwaukee where she was living. Penny had gone off to college. I rented an apartment with my son just a block away. By this time, Jane was not well at all. She had terribly high blood pressure. It just got worse and worse.

I'd gone to her apartment every month and paid all her bills, because she didn't even have the strength to write out the checks. I would do her shopping and she would just sign the checks. I took care of her; I took care of everything.

She started going away with her mother during the winters. The year she died, which was '68, she and her mother went to Ft. Lauderdale. On the way back, she had a lung hemorrhage and was taken to the hospital. They knew she was terminal. They called Penny at college. And Penny called Hal. But she didn't tell me. All I knew was that Jane was ill. Penny called me and said, "Mother's in the hospital." And then she called me after and told me Jane had died. I never saw Jane again. Penny and I have talked about that. I said, "I would have liked to have seen your mother." And she said, "It never entered my mind. I just thought about Daddy." It certainly was hard. It was terrible to not be able to say good-bye to her.

And all the while she was in Ft. Lauderdale, I had one postcard which I still have. That whole winter. I was writing, but she couldn't; she didn't have the strength to write back. My daughter had gone to France for a year. She was gone. There's just that gap, that ocean and long distance calls are so awful. Jane was in Ft. Lauderdale and I didn't talk to her or anything. It was an awful, awful winter.

After she died, her mother and her sister came from her

apartment — it was just up the block from me — from going through her stuff and marking what should be saved and what should be thrown away. They said that they had just read Jane's will and she had left me some money. The will started out, "I give five thousand dollars to my friend, Mary Flick." right on the first line of the will. I said, "She always said she wanted me to go to Europe and she was going to give me enough money to go to Europe." So I went to Europe. My daughter, Alice, was already over there, and I decided that my son Pete and I would meet Alice and we'd spend that money. We did, and it was wonderful.

I got into the gay world when I came back from Europe. There was a young woman working with me. She said, "You seem awfully distressed about your friend Jane dying." I said, "I am. She meant the world to me. She was the closest friend I ever had." And she said, "You sound like you might be gay." And I said, "I guess I am."

Jane's wonderful daughter Penny lives out here and she's part of my family now. I used to come out to California and my daughter Alice was always living with a guy and never had room. Penny was always living with women and she always had a bed where I could stay. So I always stayed with Penny and I was just as close to her as I was to my own daughter.

Penny had been having a relationship with a woman whose name was Barbara and she came in to talk to me about it. I was in a bedroom there and she said, "I don't know if you understand, but Barbara and I have been lovers and we're breaking up and I'm just distraught about it." And we started to talk about it and she said, "Were you and my mother lovers?" I said, "Yes, we were." "I've always thought you were," she said. Then she asked, "Does Alice know this about you?" "No," I answered, "I never had nerve enough to tell her but I think she must suspect." Penny said, "I think you should talk to her about it." I agreed, and the next time Alice came over, I told her about it. Thanks to Penny. And it was fine. Alice said, "That's OK, Mom, it doesn't bother me."

Now Penny has two wonderful little boys and a great husband. When I told Penny I was coming out to live in San Francisco, she said, "Come and stay with us. We have a basement until you find a place to live." I lived there for ten months and had a wonderful time. I spent all my holidays with them. In fact, I was going to go up and see my daughter, Alice, at Thanksgiving time and Penny said, "You can't do that. You always spend Thanksgiving with us. Go see Alice any other time." I think Alice has always been jealous.

Jane stands out as the most primary relationship in my life. It's wonderful to think that I'm practically a grandmother to her grandchildren, whom she never got to see because Penny was not married or anything then. And it's also strange that Hal is still around and I'm playing bridge with him. I don't think he even remembers that he threatened to sue Jane for divorce. Maybe he's just blocked that out.

I used to tell Jane that she needed to talk about our relationship, to get it out in the open. I think one reason her blood pressure was so high was that she was keeping all this inside of her and not letting it out at all, not telling anybody about it. Penny thinks that too, that she should have been able to talk about that aspect of her life a little more. It was a terrible secret; if her mother found out or her sister found out . . . that kind of feeling was just terrible.

I'm now at age 70 in a really loving relationship with a woman a good deal younger than I am. She'll be forty-nine in August; she's twenty-one years younger than me. But we seem to be peers in every way. Her political philosophy is pretty much the same as mine. We're into the peace movement and anything that has to do with what used to be called the liberal philosophy.

I think it's easier being gay now. Heterosexual women now can be friends with lesbians. I was talking to a friend this morning who is not gay. She was kind of kidding me — "You've been gone all week down at Big Sur; what was it? Some kind of honeymoon?" And I said, "Yeah, that's exactly what it was." So there she was acknowledging my relationship, joking about it and thinking it's fine.

Having an affair with a younger woman doesn't necessarily make you feel young. The women in my family live into their nineties. If Ginny and I were to stay together, I'd get into almost an aging parent role, rather than a lover. I'm a little worried about that.

I have no sadness that it wasn't easier to be gay when I was young. I really wanted to have children. I got married to have children. But I think for the women who didn't take my path, the women who really wanted to live with other women and be with them, it was very hard. Unless you were wealthy or very prominent, you could be discriminated against. Not everybody was Gertrude Stein and could broadcast and get away with it . . . even she couldn't.

I don't think about aging much. I'm with a lot of young groups — they treat me as a peer. I think if you're treated as a peer, you don't think about aging. People have such a mistaken idea about how old people should behave. When I'm marching down the street in a parade, people say, "You're seventy? I can't believe that." Like it's unheard of that you would be doing these things. I think there are a lot of seventy-year olds and older that are doing the same thing I'm doing.

ALMA ADAMS

If You Live, You're Going to Get Old

I was born in 1910 in Elgin, Illinois, where they used to make watches. My cousin tells me they've torn the watch factory down and there's some senior citizen housing there now. My mother worked at the factory. My dad worked at the factory. If you weren't at the watch factory you were at Moody's Publishing. Or you worked at the Elgin State Hospital. Elgin was one of the Underground Railroad stations. It has quite a history to it. We celebrated Emancipation Day. It was a good place to grow up.

Until I was about six years old I thought that I was Jewish. The Fishers lived down the street. I played with their kids — Sylvia, Ann and Irving. I ate at their house all the time. Mrs. Fisher made good stuff and she was always inviting me. At Easter time, it was Seder. Fridays, Mr. Fisher would have his cap on to start the Sabbath. I spoke a lot of Hebrew. And I thought that I was Jewish. Nobody said anything about me being anything else. Nobody said anything about being black or white; they talked about being Jewish, Italian and Irish.

So, even though I was black, since I associated more with Jewish children I became Jewish. I went to synagogue. My mother never said anything about religion although she was an ordained Methodist Evangelist minister. We had to go to Sunday school, but she didn't mind me going to synagogue. She and Mrs. Fisher hung over the back fence and talked about their children. Mr. Fisher pushed a vegetable cart. My dad drove a coal wagon. Everyone was friendly. There was never any animosity. There was never any bickering. But that came all too soon.

When I was eleven we moved from Elgin in northern Illinois to Columbus in Southern Illinois and it was full of rednecks. You had to go to the back door of restaurants to get your sandwich or your coffee. We weren't called "black," we were called "colored folks." We were driving one time and this little kid said, "Hi, colored folks." I didn't know what they meant. My sister said, "I wasn't dipped in a pot of dye."

One day after we had moved, we went to the movies and we couldn't watch the show for seeing all these colored people. Well, come to find out, it was a colored theater. It was in the black section of Columbus. I couldn't watch the show for seeing all these colored people — I'd never seen so many colored people in my life. I didn't know there was that many in the world. I was simply amazed. When we saw all these colored people in the streets, my sister and I didn't say anything; we just had our mouths hanging open. And we talked to each other at home. My sister said, "Where did they all come from?" I said, "I don't know. I wonder do they all live here or did they just come here like we did from some place where there's just a few."

It made me laugh, it was such a good feeling to see all these black people. At school, all black kids. In Elgin, there weren't a half a dozen black kids. It blew my silly little mind. I walked backwards looking at all these people. My uncle had this Flint — it was a great big, beautiful, ugly car. Now I know it was ugly, but then I thought, "Gee, my uncle is rich with this car." There were black people with cars! At home *no one* had cars, only a few rich people. There were no street cars either; you walked in Elgin.

Later my mother worked in a frat house and we moved

down near the university. There weren't so many black people out there in the north end. East Columbus was where the blacks were.

I didn't realize then that I was gay, but there was this woman — my mother's best friend — and she was doing these things and I didn't mind it. She was my mother's age, in her early thirties. She'd have me over for cookies and to help her count the canned goods in the basement. She always lifted me up so I could count the ones up there and she always held my little butt so I wouldn't fall. And she'd always squeeze my little butt. I didn't mind it at all. If she was going to give me cookies for a squeeze, it was all right. It didn't upset me. As I can remember it, I jumped and ran. I knew she was going to do these things and it was pleasurable. I'd run to her when she called me. Boy; zing — right over! "Yes, ma'am." She went down on me when I was twelve and it was nice. It was pleasurable and I didn't mind. She gave me extra money to go to the show. My mother only gave me enough for popcorn and the show. I got used to her and then they moved away. We'd been neighbors for about four years.

When I was about fifteen years old, my friend Zenobia and I cut school. We didn't know what else to do after we ate everything in the house, so we decided to experiment with each other. We went to bed and we tried sex. 'Course neither one of us knew how to do it. But we fooled around and she decided that we needed a candle. So I said no, that Mrs. —— (Oooh, I can't think of her name) never used a candle. She never used anything but her fingers and her tongue. Well, we decided we would see what we could do with our fingers and our tongues. We tried it for a long time, I mean weeks and weeks.

I continued to fool around. When I was nineteen I was with Kay who is now a police officer in Chicago. Kay really initiated me and made me aware that this was where it was at. I was really hot for her. She lived in Aurora which was twenty-two miles away from Elgin. I made that trip so many times! But we found we were both girls and it didn't work. We tried it for a while, but two girls don't make it. I never have been the boss. I have been agreeable or disagreeable, but I've never been the boss. There wasn't anybody there taking control with Kay. It wasn't hard to leave Kay. I was filling in for the love of her life. The girl she loved was in the Penitentiary for killing someone, but she was going to be paroled in nine years. And Kay said, "You understand when she is paroled, it's over because I love her and I always will. My body can't wait for her, but I'm waiting for her." So I knew that I had to go on with my life. She lives with that woman today. Anyway, my longest relationships were with little boys — you know; butches. Sometimes I'd experiment with femmes.

I got raped when I was thirteen. I think that's one of the reasons that I decided completely that men weren't for me. They dragged me. For years I had scars on my backside where they dragged me. That was in Portsmouth, Ohio. One of them sat on my face while the other one raped me. Took two of 'em to do it though, by God. One of them's sister wrote to my mother and said her brother was ill and that it would help the parole board if my mother would write to them. When Mama told me, I said, "Well, what are you going to do, Mama?" And she said, "Well, I forgot she wrote." Both of the rapists died in the penitentiary. Dirty old bastards.

My mother knew about me and girls because I told her when I was in high school. I asked her, "Mama did you ever like to kiss girls?" And she said, "You mean kissing? We always kiss." I said, "I don't mean like at church. Did you ever feel like that you like to kiss a girl?" She said, "I never thought about it honey. Why do you ask?" I said, "Well, I feel like I like to kiss girls. Did you ever French kiss a girl, Mama?" She said, "Oh, no." I said, "I did." She said, "What did you think?" I said, "I liked it." She said, "Oh my Lord . . . So what else did you do with the girls?" I said, "Well, things that I don't do with a *boy*." She says, "Oh my Lord, oh my gracious Lord."

She didn't get angry. She just kept saying, "Oh my Lord." I think she said it a dozen times. She kept looking at me. I said, "Well, what?" But she accepted it, just like she accepted me not going to church. My sister was baptized, taught Sunday school, sang in the choir, prayed and all that stuff. Married and children. And there was just the two of us. We were all very tight. But Mama never got through saying, "Oh my Lord."

I lived with a gal in New York for six months when I was in my early twenties. She was something else. Mercy. I had to leave New York to get away from her. She was too much woman for me. She was a sex fiend. She was a fanatic. There wasn't anything to do but go to bed. I'd want to go to Hyde Park. She'd want to go to bed first and then see. If I did it good, then we'd go. She never went. But I did. She had lived in New York for twenty-five years. She'd never been across the George Washington Bridge or seen the Statue of Liberty. I left her. She wouldn't do anything but screw. Whoo! I was just hanging around in New York, having a ball. But I didn't get the ball much with her around. I left New York and went back to Elgin. I wasn't going to gay bars or anything.

I didn't go to gay bars until I got to San Francisco. There were a couple of places in Chicago — sort of secretive places where you run the risk of getting beat up. Not very healthy places to go, but when I came to San Francisco, Jesus God! That was in '54. There were about twenty bars here. It was almost a year before I got into the swing of things.

If it wasn't for my mother, I wouldn't have learned all these things. I brought her out here. My mother came out to cook at the convent. Sister Mary Ann, our superior in Elgin, had come out to California and asked Mama to come out here. The Father asked me if I'd cook for the priests; I stayed three years cooking for eight priests. And in staying I discovered San Francisco and the girls. You know how I discovered it? Through the Red Cross!

I volunteered to drive for the Red Cross and one of the drivers asked me what else I did on my days off and I said, "Nothing. That's the reason I'm driving for the Red Cross. There isn't anything else to do." She said, "Do you go to San Francisco — to the bars?" I said, "No, I can't go to the bars by myself." She said, "Why don't you go with me sometime?" I said, "Okay." I always bless the Red Cross. That's where I got started.

I said, "Oh God, this has been here all this time and in the three years I had only had two or three little old pieces that I bought. I bought 'em in Oakland. I wouldn't buy them again in Oakland, boy. Back then, though, it was pretty safe. I knew where to go. It never occurred to me there'd be any trouble. There wasn't the trouble then that there is now. There wasn't any dope and pimps. I guess there were pimps but the two gals that I went with didn't seem to have anyone. They just did this in their spare time. They taught. Both of them were school teachers. And they just liked to do it in their spare time.

I was nervous the first time. I didn't know how this was going to turn out. One of 'em asked me if I was into dildoes and I said, "No way, love. Just old-fashioned, down to earth, let's get it on." That was the only two pieces I ever bought. Not bad at all. With them it was a business, but they enjoyed their business. Both of them gave me their number to give them a ring sometime. But by then I had found somebody that I didn't have to buy.

I'd keep on seeing people. You don't say that you're going together but anytime you feel like it, you connect. Maybe you go to a party and "Do you want me to drop you off?" or "Did you come with anyone?" We knew how that was going to end up. I'm not going to drop you off; I'm going to take you home with me. I was just having a good time. I was going to see how much I could get.

Gerry was my longest relationship. It lasted eleven years. Gerry is a very jealous person. We couldn't have any company. She'd get mad and go out and walk for hours. And if it was male company — oh boy! We used to go out with some fellows to the leather bar and we used to take this boy in a wheelchair with us. One night he asked me instead of Gerry ... and we couldn't take him any more after that. She was a very giving and loving person, but very peculiar.

If I would decide to go somewhere, I'd go by and ask Gerry if she wanted to go. But if she wanted to go somewhere, she would say, "Let's go to so-and-so." Or I would say, "Do you want to go?" And if she said no, we didn't go. It worked that way sexually too.

I got involved in the gay movement because it was the thing to do. Oh my God, I was so happy to find all this stuff here. It was down at the Nude Beach at Half-Moon Bay. It was Moonlight Night and I was laying on the beach. I met this guy and we started talking. He asked me if I'd heard of SIR [the Society for Individual Rights, an early homophile organization]. I made some smart-ass remark, "Sissies in Retirement?" He said, "Why don't you come to a meeting sometime?"

Anything I'm invited to, I go to. I went to DOB [Daughters of Bilitis] and to their parties and to their open meetings. I went and I joined that night. Gerry was going to DOB so I went to SIR. I said that I was going to go, but I didn't say that I was going to join. She was not very happy about it. And she was the kind of person that stayed unhappy for days and days. You were always afraid that you were going to do something that would upset her. And it's a strange thing. I don't know whether it's the same with everyone else. She would never let me go down on her. I knew that there weren't nothing there that was different than I had ... but that makes it all right to me. I wouldn't choose to be in a relationship with her today although we have had sex several times. I enjoy her but I wouldn't want to belong to her again.

You didn't see too many black lesbians in the bars. A few gay black men. There was a leather bar that the boys used to invite us to after bowling. There were no blacks. Gerry and I were the only blacks in the bar the several times that we went there. There was no friction. No feeling of not belonging. The feeling was that you were with your own people. More than if you *were* with your own people. I never went to the black women's bars. I went down to Redwood City one time to a girl bar and they scared me there. They were diesel dykes. And the diesels were scary. A butch only five foot five was five foot ten the way she walked around and rubbed her crotch. I just left — quietly.

Every year Gerry and I would go to the Witch's Christmas here in San Francisco. It was on Halloween. There'd be a big dance. Gerry had a tuxedo; we were Lord and Lady. We were presented and had pictures taken. The last one we went to was in '69.

One night when I came home, Gerry told me she was seeing someone else. I said, "Oh?" Gerry is short. She said it was another Mutt and Jeff thing. We continued to have sex for three weeks and then she said, "I'm going to move Thursday evening." Just like that. After eleven years.

We'd broken up once before. That first time I was heartbroken. But when she left that second time, it wasn't as bad. I didn't care as much. I figured why let myself be hurt time after time? Since it's cut, let it dry.

You try to placate your partner without giving up everything. But in a lot of ways, I did give up a lot. It was too extreme. I see her fairly often now; we're friends. Her sister had this barbecue every year and it's gotten so it's practically all gay.

We've had sex many times since we broke up. She's a great lover. At my house, motels, out in the forest. I enjoyed her, you know. The first time we broke up my poor mother was living. She said, "Baby, dear, what is the matter? Tell Mommy what's wrong." And I said, "Gerry and I have broken up. We're not friends anymore." She said, "You'll find another friend. I'm sure you'll find another friend. And maybe you and Gerry will go back together again." Oooh, I snapped at my mother. I went off to the bowling alley drunker than a bitch wolf. God, I must have been a mess. I don't know how they still liked me. I was really a pitiful mess.

You know that you're going to get older. If you live, you're going to get old. In my situation, I don't have any children. I have a cousin in Chicago. He's gay. He's fifty-two years old. I think I'm the first one that he let know that he was gay. My sister is seventy-two. Certainly if anything happens to me, she's not going to be able to take care of me.

I'm in good health — not excellent, but good. My blood

pressure is 125 over 80, which is excellent. I have no problems. I swim eight lengths without tiring. When I go down to the health club with my sister, I swim three times a week in an Olympic-size pool. I do the machines too. I wish I had that sit-up board at home because when I'm trying to do sit-ups, I can't keep my feet down. They're big, but they sure are light!

I'm surprised to find that I'm seventy-five years old. Where are all these seventy-five years? Where are they all gone? How could I possibly be seventy-five years old already? All of a sudden it's March the fifth, 1985 ... baby, you're seventy-five years old. Seventy-five big ones! Jesus, Mary and Joseph ... How did it happen? I marvel every day that all these years have gone. It's amazing. I look at my birth certificate — it's true, it's true. There can be no doubt about it.

I don't know if I feel seventy-five. I don't know how seventy-five is supposed to feel. Maybe I don't get as many wide-ons as I used to. But I think about sex all the time. Sex really hasn't changed over time. I've kept up — I keep doing these things. My sister is seventy-two and her ex-husband comes around and when she feels like it, she lets him get in there. My mother married her fourth husband at sixty-seven. I have sex whenever these days — and I don't depend on Gerry for it.

When I had my dog, I found a gal up in Hillsborough who had a dog. We get together occasionally. I call her or she calls me. We don't go together. We don't go anywhere together but to bed. That's been going on for seven years. She's younger than I am. She's seventy-one.

I'm a research specialist for a research company ... we do snooping. We snoop with tape recorders and cameras. It's a private investigation firm. There are people who don't pay their bills, who skip out, who are in hiding. We track them down. I do a lot of work out of my car. I work on an on-call basis. I like it. I move around. Like Monday — I'm going to Sacramento. I'm going to sit in my car and see if I can take some pictures of somebody. We got to find out where we can locate him. I like the work.

For forty years I was a pediatric nurse. Then I decided to get out of pediatrics and get into geriatrics because anybody will help a baby, but there was a need for someone to help old people. What I was going to do at first was Red Cross again. They wanted volunteer drivers so I volunteered to take a couple of ladies to dialysis three times a week and pick them up. I got into geriatrics from there. Now I just do volunteer work in geriatrics.

I worked in Oakland in the fifties and sixties as a nurse in the Veterans Hospital.

There isn't much I can tell you about age, because I don't recognize age as such. I have covered insurance that is paid for. You keep it fifteen years. I can retire any day I want to and I will get five hundred dollars a month from that. I will also get social security when I retire. I could get it now, but I'm working. I don't want to get social security now. I'll take the chunk — when you decide to take it, they pay you for all the years in between that you didn't take it. You get a big chunk. My mother decided to take hers all of a sudden at seventy and so she said, "Alma, look at this check I got from Uncle." I looked at it and it was six thousand dollars. She said, "Do you think this is real?" I said, "I'd try it Mama. It got government all over it. Try it and see." Of course it was all right.

I have no plans for the future in terms of retirement. Today's Saturday, right? Okay, I'll take today. And if I should be here tomorrow, I'll take it. I think I've always had that attitude. One day at a time. Long before they had the television thing.

I live alone. If there was one thing I could change in my life right now, I wouldn't live alone. I'd like to have a roommate. I would have a larger place with two bedrooms and have a roommate. It's a little late now, but the thing I would change is that I wouldn't live alone as an old person. An old person alone — an old *gay* person alone, an old lesbian alone — is very sad. You are afraid of younger people. In San Mateo there are a bunch of young women — lesbians — who have moved on me. I'm afraid of them. They're children to me. They're in their twenties and thirties. And I don't think that I need that type of connection. They see me as a person financially secure, living alone, taking Caribbean cruises — I must have some kind of money. They know that I'm gay. They see me as a touch. I know they're going to use me, if I let them.

It's hard to find women my own age. It seems like I'm the only one who's old. There's Chris who lives in Emeryville, she's 60, old Navy. We've been on trips together. Chris and I are friends, but we could never be lovers. I think we're both ladies! I haven't made any friends in the last ten years that are my own age. There's no one as old as I am. I was talking to my sister. I said, "Do you suppose that I'm the oldest living lesbian in the world?"

JEANNE ADLEMAN

Falling and Rising in Love

I. Before

There had been bargains, bargains I had made with life.
That is, with myself. A few were conscious, most were so unconscious that I only now recognize them as bargains — only
now that I don't need them. What were these bargains? At-
tempts to be satisfied with less than what I crave.

Examples: Loving is more important than being in love.
Romance is delightful but begets desperation, so might as well
settle for pleasant sex with loving friends. Anyway, I don't
really need more sex in my life. I've had a sexually plentiful
and vigorous life already, but never enough tender love, so I
might as well settle for nonsexual loving intimacy. Good
friendship can substitute for the connubiality I desire but fear.

More: I've built a satisfactory life based on living alone.
Probably nobody would ever be able to live with me because I
always want things my way in the house. It would be too
much like my marriage — I'd be so afraid of being called "impossible to live with" that I'd probably sacrifice my integrity
and assertiveness to avoid proof of my impossiblity. My
unlovability.

Especially: I don't know any more how to live with a

lover. If I'm not going to live with her, why bother seeking and making adjustments? True, I don't want to live alone as I grow older, meaning much older, meaning really old — but I can always join a communal lesbian household. Can't I?

I seem to be craving romantic passionate love while disbelieving that such will come my way again, that I can either inspire or experience it at my age. Clearly I am too old to fall in love. The best I can hope for is mature love: reasonable, affectionate, understanding, caring, pleasurable. Mature.

Sigh.

II. 1984 — May

A woman comes along at a time when I'm preoccupied with other concerns. She and I are at a committee meeting at my house, awaiting the arrival of a third woman who's supposed to be present but phones to say she can't make it. Never mind what the committee is about — it could have been about almost anything. I am alone with someone I scarcely know. There's a charge in the air, but I'm task-oriented so I ignore it. We do as much of the committee's work as we can, and make a lunch date for two days later to finish it.

Before she leaves, this woman makes it plain that she has been interested in me since we'd met at a conference months earlier, and that she's interested in more than committee work with me now. (This, then, is what the charge in the air has been. Taking the initiative has been difficult for her.)

I'm a little hesitant, but essentially receptive. Intrigued but cautious. My impression is that she's someone easily hurt, otherwise known as vulnerable, and I worry that I'm a hurter of others. As usual, I overlook my own vulnerability.

We say goodnight, kiss and hug tentatively. It's awkward. She seems to want to linger, but I'm feeling more nervous than desirous.

Two days later, the lunch meeting is at a restaurant in her community. I'm impressed (and turned on) by the obvious respect and pleasure with which several people greet her. She's clearly Somebody.

This revives my lifelong intermittent fear of being a nobody. However, there will be time to think it all over. I have my tickets and reservations and am leaving in four days for a week's vacation. We finish our lunch, finish our committee business, and make plans to get together on my return. I'm high on anticipation and fearful of expecting too much.

Next morning I wake from a night full of thoughts about her, too impatient to wait. I call to invite her over for Saturday evening, the night before my departure, and she sounds happy to agree.

My memory's unclear as to how long after she gets here, how long after our trembly embrace on her arrival, how long after we sit down on the couch and look at each other and away and back again — how many unmemorable things we say — how long it takes until I'm welcoming her to my bed. Probably not very long.

Certainly not as long as we spend in bed.

I find myself surpassingly excited by her body, unprecedentedly thrilled by our skin-to-skin-all-over closeness. Our fleshiness. The differences in our bodies, the similarities of our bodies. Kissing, caressing, kissing, clinging, riding, plunging, biting, kissing, kissing — I feel wild, passionately out of control, then I feel strong, in charge, then swept away, swept away, swept away. Feels like vertigo I experience when looking down from great heights: my thighs tremble, my legs seem to melt. Feels wonderful, feels frightening. Like flying and falling, but oh, such a soft warm tired spent landing.

What happens next? Do we eat, drink, celebrate? No time for all that. She has to leave so I can calm down enough to pack, sleep a bit, be at the airport at six next morning to start that vacation.

I send her postcards. One wonderful card is a depth-seeming vista of a famous valley, taken from an angle which reminds me of the view of her legs, thighs, pubic area and belly when I had looked up from her intimate private valley while we were together. I buy a duplicate card to keep for myself.

All the time I've been away, she's been in my thoughts, absorbing my daytime hours, occupying my dreams, while I try to remind myself that I may be building up to a big letdown.

III. June

I arrive home Sunday evening, am back at work on Monday, and Monday evening she is here. It's nine days since we've been together. I'm nervous all over again. This time I'm the one who's shy but, characteristically, won't give in to it. Back to bed! Is it possible the second time will equal the first?

Yes.

I begin to acknowledge how very involved I'm becoming, though I don't recall giving much thought to how little we know each other. We have been carried along by this intense sexual attraction so fast that we haven't become friends yet.

Later that week we are together again, and it's even better.

This is a stunning sexuality such as I haven't experienced since my early twenties or thirties. And now begins a time when not only do we arouse and satisfy passion in each other, we also read poetry, tell stories of our lives, and talk, talk, talk. With this intensity, intimacy is building.

About two weeks after my return, we: two mature women, she fifty and me almost sixty-five, are acknowledging to each other that love is what we are feeling. That love is what we are in. We begin to recognize the potential — and, with it, new fear.

We talk seriously. What is it in me that so draws her? What is it in her that I so love? This is hard to put into words, even though I'm a person who loves words, which are like music to me, like art, like dancing.

I recall saying something like, "Well, for one thing, I think you know who you are. I think you respond to my real self more than to my flash or occasional charisma. I think we're not young enough to have the illusions that it will be easy. And I love your body."

I seem to recall her saying that she loves my mind, and that she has been drawn to my gentleness. This helps me to cultivate my gentler side, which I've been known to neglect.

Yes, it is hard to put love into words.

Can we trust the feelings? Intellectually we know it won't be easy, but we want it to be. Easy as magic.

For me, becoming enamored means that I'm in constant danger of blowing it, of losing her, of wrecking the relationship by doing something stupid. But, when I sometimes do stupid things the relationship does not end.

We spend more time talking about our lives, our professional work, our community activities, and we discover that there are many people we know in common although we ourselves met so recently. Most are women closer to one of us than to the other. We discover that we have the same primary care (lesbian) physician. We talk about whom to tell "about us" and when, and who will do the telling.

My urge is to climb the rafters and shout. Hers is to keep things quiet a while longer. Here we are uncovering one of the differences which will recur between us: I am very out; she is very selectively out. I dislike what I consider secrets — she has strong convictions as to what is and isn't other people's business.

Early on, the following scenario: I am due to have breakfast one morning after I leave her with a colleague friendly to both of us but closer to me. A few days later I'm to have lunch with another friend who is closer to my lover. I want to be able to "tell about us" but she doesn't want me to, and I agree not to. With each of the friends, however, I'm unable to contain my happy excitement. They inquire, probe, tease, press — and I tell. Then I'm ashamed, distressed and scared. I make them promise not to tell her that I've told them. Me, who hates secrets. I can't wait to confess and be forgiven, which does happen.

Because I feel so caught, I beg her to hurry and tell our secret to friends who deserve to hear it from her, so that I won't have to try again, and fail again, to be discreet.

We decide to go to a major dance as a couple. It has been

just four weeks since we "got together."

Now begins what I've come to see as the lesbian equivalent of becoming engaged. We go to several women's and lesbian functions, gaining recognition *as a couple* among friends and acquaintances. I am so elated at such times that I feel cling-y and intoxicated. I feel as though I want to spread my joy like a rainbow over everybody.

We also go to some "straight" functions together, where we behave circumspectly and apparently provoke no questions.

Friends who get the word on the grapevine start phoning one or the other of us and tell us we're a great match. We agree that I can tell our mutual physician at my next visit, and she beams at the news. I bask in the sense of community support. I love seeing my friends light up in response to my happy face. I get loads of goodwill from my family too. Offspring, cousins, aunts — all seem happy for me that I'm so in love with this fine woman. I can think of a few people I do not tell, a few who might not be supportive, but my happiness really does seem to win people over.

IV. August

Euphoria has faded into anxiety and my face is often cloudy, with tears trembling at my eyelids. I'm walking on eggshells, fearful of displeasing, terrified of losing the love I want so much. The feeling is disturbingly familiar. I've begun to repeat some of the negative patterns of my marriage. The more I want this woman to be permanently in my life as my lover, the more timid I become. The more timid I become, the more despairing over our differences, the more trouble I create.

As I approach my sixty-fifth birthday I'm fearful she'll no longer want me. I lean more on my lifelong best friend to help with the giant party I'd planned long before. Not at all the kind of party my lover would have chosen, possibly not the kind I'd have wanted if I'd expected to be in a relationship. A community party and fund-raiser, with about a hundred folks expected. A party designed to help me dance my way into my sixty-sixth year, defying society's view that sixty-five is the beginning of *old*.

The edge of fear remains (defiance being one response to threat), but in reality the party has further secured our couple identity, and I can breathe easier for a little while.

V. September

The next round of anxieties begins when some of her emerging wants remind me of my ex-husband. Someone who feels deprived if she doesn't watch Monday night football? In addition to Sunday games? Someone who turns on the television set as soon as she enters her house, and leaves it on even when she isn't watching. Her pleasure in televised football reminds me of miserable hours with a husband who'd sit silent in front of the set, who'd become enraged if I spoke to him during a game, who'd keep the sound so loud that it dominated the household. And I'm reminded of myself in those years — too afraid of losing him to stand up for my rights in that house.

It takes me a long time to understand that my lover can read and talk and carry on, have fun, all the while with one eye on the game. She actually gets annoyed if I don't keep up my end of all this. On the other hand, she frequently interrupts herself, or me, to react with a yell to something in the game. Then she says, "Go on, don't stop, I'm listening," and doesn't seem to understand why I'm put out.

Some discomfort over differences is unrelated to my past.

. . . My lover has a religious affiliation and practice; I am thoroughly non-religious, almost but not quite anti-religious.

. . . It's been years since I used cosmetics or scent. She uses both, and enjoys them. Says she likes to "look and smell good," which makes me wonder how I can look good or smell all right to her without them.

. . . I become physically uncomfortable when there's much cigarette smoke in the air around me. I wish I didn't but I do. My lover thinks it would be an appalling failure of hospitality to ask a guest not to smoke in her house.

. . . She is an observer of injustice, whereas I want to take action. What I mean is, she notices more of what is right to be angry at, and gets angrier than I do, and faster, but seems content to just point it out to me. I, though slower, want to *do* something about the offense if possible. Make a statement, teach another way, express the anger, make a demand, or a request, or even just a "liberal" suggestion.

. . . And there are others. Not insuperable but problematic stuff. Some of it is like daily irritation, and some we're finding ways to deal with.

One issue does rake up past connections and anxieties. My lover and I use alcohol differently. Neither of us abstains entirely, but when she says she can't imagine a party being fun without drinking and smoking, I feel my heart contract in fear. I was married to a man who drank more than he could tolerate, and drank, I think, because of everything he couldn't tolerate. In those days I knew nothing about "co-alcoholism." Now I do. I also know my lover is not a replica of my ex-husband, but I fear replicating my old behaviors, fear that I haven't learned what I need to have learned.

But at least I haven't lost my ability to learn. I try to use my worries to raise my consciousness. Each time I feel that contraction of fear, I respond to it slowly, taking a deep breath and using my head to think past the moment's crunch. One, they are not the same person even if they have some characteristics in common. Next, I review what I've learned in the years since that marriage ended: how to assess my own wants, to propose them, to listen to another person's wants without imagining I must meet them or be a bad person; avoid attempting to read the mind of the other, to guess the unexpressed wants; to negotiate for mutually satisfying outcomes when possible, or compromise when necessary. Occasionally, to just plain give in, but as a last — not a first — resort.

I do believe that if, out of moral cowardice, I walk out of this relationship, I'll probably regret it the rest of my life. I hang in with my fears, and take fifty percent of the responsibility for my reactions. With time, those fear-spasms are fewer, and much further apart.

VI. November

Money!

We talk about how we were brought up differently about money, about the ways our respective families dealt with monetary insufficiency. That isn't so hard as talking about the ways they thought, spoke and taught money to us.

Once, I mention to her what I expect will be my income in the current year. She says she is reassured, having been concerned that because I am entirely self-employed, I might not be earning as much as I might need. I now assume that she will talk about her income, but she doesn't, and I interpret this as her not trusting me, which hurts. Another time, when she seems to be counting pennies, I ask if she is OK financially and she answers curtly that she is fine. "I'm not that flaky!" she says, sounding insulted. But flakiness was nowhere in my thoughts.

For her, having had to buy "day-old" baked goods or produce in her childhood makes it easy to continue doing so today. For me, having had to do the same in my childhood makes me unwilling to do it today, when I don't have to. Similarly, she loves garage sales and flea markets and bargaining, and I hate all three.

What now seems clear is that we are each frugal in some areas and extravagant in others. Fortunately, or unfortunately, we are frugal or extravagant in opposite areas.

Money is still hard to deal with, but we're better able to cope. The relationship is not presently in danger over differences in self-disclosure about money.

All the while, and right alongside the troubles, our "nevers" keep collapsing. She would *never* get involved with a woman with children. (My children are adults, but very much factors in my life.) I would *never* get involved with a woman who wasn't completely out. With someone who hadn't raised children and wouldn't be able to understand some of my concerns and pressures. I will *never again* stay in a relationship in which I feel guilty almost all of the time.

But here we are. We have, we did, we are. She is. I am.

I learn to risk getting angry at her. She learns that if I'm angry it's about something going on, not a sign that I'm ready to leave her. When she gets moody or seems to be withdrawing from me, I no longer start looking for my running shoes to prove to myself that I can survive if she leaves.

Having made public declarations of coupledness, having broadcast in my community that I'm so in love, helps me through some bad times. Public knowlege is a kind of glue. How embarrassed I would be if I had to tell all those well-wishers that I was giving up! Perhaps I shouldn't be embarrassed, but I would be.

When things are smooth or high between us, we talk — playfully? — about wanting to be married. If one of us was a man we'd be talking seriously of marriage at this point. If one of us was a man? This wouldn't be happening. Neither of us, I think, would be willing to engage so deeply with a man, or to give up so much that had seemed essential parts of a known Self. The real glue is that we're both women, with underlying similarities that provide a cushion of trust, support for dealing with and accepting our differences.

How hard it is to recognize them as differences, rather than moral issues with one of us wrong, the other right. To begin with, each of us has unexamined assumptions about what's right. Then, in addition, there are the carefully worked-through and thought-out decisions each of us has reached about right and wrong. Now here comes someone we're mysteriously bonded to, who is or does otherwise. Wrong? Or merely different? Values and judgments are bumped up against and need reconsideration. At sixty-five, I can do this better than I could when I was younger.

At sixty-five some things don't hurt as much as they used to, but other vulnerabilites appear. When my lover mentions the age difference between us, I react, internally, as though she is under the illusion that she is twenty-five and I am one hundred years old. (I wonder how centenarians deal with age differences.) Or when she says, "People your age . . ." I feel a snarl inside that I try to hide. I've chosen to see us as essentially contemporaries. That is, I've considered her a significantly younger contemporary. Am I fooling myself? If so, why? It takes a long time, and an incident with another lesbian couple, to bring this up with her.

We're at a restaurant having dinner with the other couple, both of them in their thirties. Good talk, excellent food; the chief topic is the pleasure of being in love. One of the younger women is a long-time friend who would not knowingly do anything to hurt me. Yet she says to my lover, "Is this the first time you've been in a relationship with an older woman?"

From then on the dinner party is not quite the same for me; but it takes hours before I understand why or feel able to talk about it with my lover. First of all, I have been objectified. No longer is it "Jeanne" who matters, but my age that is of interest. Next comes a feeling of shame: how could I have been so stupid, not to know that this is how people see me? What kind of denial have I been practicing?

Bringing this up with my lover helps me, probably helps the relationship. She is, I think, more thoughtful of my feelings after that, more attentive to how she expresses herself around this particular issue.

To help me consider the implications of our different ages, I sometimes think back to myself at fifty. The last fifteen years have been among the most change-full in my life. A new career, years of studying, a profoundly changed relationship with my mother (who is now eighty-six) — and reaching the decision to declare and affirm myself as a lesbian. Nobody made me do any of this. One by one the changes came because of life's circumstances, and because I saw them as possible.

Beginning an intense relationship at this time of life is good in many ways. Neither of us has needed to idealize the other. How wonderful to know at all times that the loved one is a whole person, with a few bad habits, an imperfect disposition, some hang-ups, and with well-developed likes and dislikes — a whole person, not a fantasy image, and not a reflection in a mirror.

Coming together at this time — given past experiences,

successes, distresses, all of it, we know to value not only each other but also the relationship itself. We plan delights, and we accept the need to make accommodations. She likes to cook for me. I like to send her little love notes, and flowers. I warm my house for her till it's warmer than I'd like. She cools hers for me.

At *our age*, I think we've learned that even when things aren't going well, even when everything seems hopeless again, *something can be done*. That running away is not the answer. Even just staying with it may help. Letting time take care of it.

VII. 1985, January

What's interesting is that because we've reached a level of commitment now, things which used to eat my innards are relatively innocuous now. Football. Her self-containment that seems to me so secretive. The differences about money. Other things I haven't even mentioned here. The concern over whether we can ever live together when our wants and needs seem so different.

The differences haven't melted. I am simply not threatened by them. She watches the Superbowl at her house while I read or write letters or articles at my house. She wishes I liked opera or football or her kind of movies, and I wish she liked jazz and my kind of movies. But none of this means we don't love each other enough.

Sometimes, now, we go to bed and talk. Sometimes now we go to bed and are asleep almost at once. Not always! Something turns both of us on and passion flares up fast. Or one of us is stimulated and the other is willing. We grow less fearful of shocking or overwhelming the other, and we become more daring, more sexually adventurous with each other. Sex is still one of this relationship's assets.

The bargains I'd made with my life about love are irrelevant at present. I'm moving from unconscious bargaining with myself toward conscious negotiation with a real live woman. Here I am with hopes-wishes-plans-desires, all rising. Fearful of saying it for cold print, but believing that this love is growing.

Friends tell me I look "radiant."

I'm happier than I've been in years.

I intend to keep this glowing going, to do what's in my power so both of us stay happy. To hold on when we're not. To work at it till we get happy again. That's what I intend. I want this to last for the rest of our lives if possible. If that turns out not possible, I want to be able to look back and see this time in my life as a time I can treasure.

VIII. August

I'm not glowing, nobody tells me I look radiant, I'm frequently discontented and anxious, often feeling like a sulky kid, scuffing my shoes and feeling sorry for myself because I can't have what I want. My thoughts clash against each other, contradictions running in circles:

I want us to live together, I don't see how we could live together, I've got to hurry up and plan my future with or without her, live in the moment, I hate when we're defensive with each other, we're never going to make it for real all the way, things were never better, oh yes they were right at the beginning and they get better again when I relax, but she keeps setting up tests for me to fail . . . I'm tired after twenty years of mostly living alone but I'd be better off alone, but if she doesn't want to live with me I've got to hurry and find someone who will want to . . . I'm afraid to talk sometimes about some things on my mind (my mother, my children) for fear she'll either be overwhelmed by my problems or tell me I'm in the wrong, and either way will make me less lovable . . . When she's the age I am now I will be eighty-one, a thought which overwhelms me, not that people of eighty-one don't have loving relationships but I tend to think that age similarity may be increasingly important in advanced years . . . Probably we'll never live together but maybe we can find a way to sort of live together . . . Circles of contradiction.

Many, many accommodations seem to be working well these days. I've promised to go to a football game this fall, and I am planning to enjoy it. She doesn't keep the television on while I'm at her house unless we're watching something together or agree to do different things. I've bought some cologne and sometimes remember to wear it. As I predicted last year, we have grown to like pretty much the same house and room temperature.

A very important recognition surfaced a while ago. I recognized that my lover is quicker to react to overt or covert insults to *my* ethnicity (Jewish) than her own. This has enabled me to re-define my earlier perceptions of how she reacts to injustice in general.

However — new differences arise and disturb what might be peaceful. She hates to plan ahead, or make reservations for dinner at restaurants, or fasten her seat-belt, or do anything else that provokes in her a feeling of being confined. As a recent convert to seat-belts, I have a convert's zeal for urgency about others in a car being similarly protected. Restaurants aren't too important, just irksome, but the structure of my life seems to depend on planning ahead — often far ahead.

Recently I proposed that we experiment. Each of us gets a month-long chance to have both of us do things her preferred way or mine. Alternate months for a while. Maybe we'll find we like the other one's way if we give it a fair try?

I also proposed a different experiment recently: that without giving up our present separate living places we spend every night for a month in one place, together, and then the next month in the other's place, starting with her place if she wants. She flinches, says she doesn't know if she can stand to come home to someone every night. Well, I don't know if I can stand it either, but that's what makes it an experiment.

To these and other suggestions my lover rarely says No, rarely makes substitute suggestions, rarely offers to negotiate, but even more rarely says, "Yes!" or "Let's try it!"

She seems to like things the way they are. Does that mean we've gone as far as we can go? I see us at a standstill. Does that mean I'm pushing too hard or too fast?

She seems to like best the comfortable side of our relationship. I like best the exciting times.

What is it I want that I don't have at the present? More fun and playfulness between us. More involvement as a couple with other friends. More of the intangible called support. More freedom to differ and to argue. More dancing!

How much of this stems from who I really am, and how much if any is connected to my age concerns? At this writing, I seem unable to relax vigilance on the issue of age, though I don't want anyone else to bring it up. My sense of olderness is like an exposed nerve in a tooth which my tongue repeatedly reaches for, both to test for pain and to provide comfort for pain. Age is a screen I hide behind when the relationship is difficult, and it's also a real factor. I get caught between "one day at a time," which is a valuable concept for a worrier like me, and "time is running out on me, take care of the future, now, now, now before it's too late."

On the other hand. That postcard picturing a dark valley still hangs on my bedroom wall and still turns me on. And my lover is making a party for my sixty-sixth birthday, the first time since I was a child that I haven't felt I had to make my own party.

True, nobody has told me lately that I look radiant, but they do say I look well, sometimes pretty, sometimes "great." My lover has told me how, sometimes after we've spent some close sweet time together and she goes out into the world again, strangers behave differently from how they usually do, are pleasanter to her — or people she works with make comments on how well she's looking.

I think I'm learning as I try to get inside her perceptions of the world, learning not to rely exclusively on my own.

It's time to end this story and turn it in for publication, but the story hasn't ended. Trying to find a way to wrap it up, I suddenly recall a book I read maybe fifteen years ago, in which a woman muses about the last time she ever made love with her lover. If only I'd known, she thinks, that that would be the last time, I really would have made it wonderful.

I look to this to resolve some of the stress of paradox. Resolution comes not from either/or but from both/and. To make love as if it may be the last time, *and also* as if we have all the time in the world. To love one another as if today is all we have *and also* as if tomorrow and the future are unconditionally guaranteed.

Elenore Pred

Healing Group

In 1981, I was diagnosed with breast cancer. I had to have a mastectomy and chemotherapy. I had eleven positive nodes . . . which is a hell of a lot. My mother had died a painful death of ovarian cancer in 1972. I was really scared of being in pain and going through what I had seen my mother go through to die. I was scared of dying and scared of pain.

That experience, as awful as it was, led me to one of the most positive experiences of my life. I "did" my illness in a way that I would never repeat. I learned a great deal from that encounter with cancer and have a much different idea of how I will do any future serious illness or my own dying. My experience led me on a journey to what I call a healing group.

A month before the cancer was diagnosed, I'd gotten back together with Cela, my lover of five years. She really wanted to be there for me and I really needed her to be there for me. It was very difficult for us to deal with anything besides the fact that I was very ill and needed support. She was scared to death that I was going to die. It was very difficult. It would have been less difficult had there been a group of people around us. Cela has never wanted to share me; that was true even when I was ill. She wanted to be everything, to do everything herself. And I'm the same way so I understood; both of us are very possessive.

At some level, I wanted her to be everything to me and to do everything for me.

I became totally dependent on Cela, which was a disaster for us. If she got angry about anything and wanted to withdraw, I was left without support. For example, I was scared about spending the night alone. I really wanted to have somebody there at night and her way of withdrawing, quite often — we were living in separate places at that time — was to go home to her house and it was terrifying to me to be left alone. Even though I might have preferred having her there to other people, if I had been able to accept what was sincerely offered to me by others, I would not have felt abandoned.

Given the nature of our relationship, it was pretty impossible to avoid conflict. So there were conflicts and there were times when I just felt abandoned.

Being so isolated with Cela didn't continue. When I got sick, I had a lot of friends who wanted to be there for me. It created more problems between Cela and me. When I was in the hospital, a friend who had moved to L.A. came up to see me and brought flowers. Cela got very angry — what was going on that Lyn had come all the way from L.A. to see me? I felt terrible about it. It was very upsetting. I was sick and I really appreciated the kindnesses of friends. It was an inappropriate time for jealousy as far as I was concerned. And there was nothing I could do about it. I didn't have enough strength or energy to deal with it. It was a mess. And it made things difficult for some of my friends.

I'm not sure how much the experience with Cela affected my joining the healing group. I'd read some Elizabeth Kubler-Ross . . . and I also felt very positive about alternative healing after my own experience getting through chemotherapy. I did some visualizations while I was sick and I felt — and still do — that sharing my own experience was a positive thing for me. I think it was probably a combination of wanting to learn something and feeling that I had something to offer. I wanted to learn about what was possible for a group of people with that intent.

* * *

The healing group had been going on before I ever met Alvah. Alvah was a fifty-nine-year-old artist with a rare form of cancer, and around her was a wonderfully supportive group of friends who formed the healing group. Cela and I were both invited into the group by Alvah herself. She and I had spent some time together because I was available, and she needed some help going to the doctor. I'd had some of the same experiences that she had; cancer and chemotherapy. So she invited both of us to participate. I was excited. I really wanted to see what that would be like because when I was sick I had read about alternative healing and it was a way of putting into practice some of what I had read.

So both Cela and I went to the group. It was a group of very diverse women including Alvah's lover, Jill, and some of her friends; Alvah's daughter, and a couple of straight women friends. It was held in Jill and Alvah's home. We dealt with how Alvah was feeling, not just physically, but any of her concerns. We'd sit in the circle and just talk — any of us who had anything to say. Alvah would begin.

Almost as much attention was paid to Jill's needs as Alvah's lover, as was paid to Alvah. They would give a check-in about how they were feeling and what their concerns were and what had been happening since the group had been together last. A couple of women in the group were very spiritual, very close friends of Alvah's and Jill's. They often had clarity and advice. Sometimes we just sat and held hands and passed energy, tuning in on having energy flowing to Alvah or among us. The meetings of the group were not that long, maybe an hour. Then we would eat together.

I particularly remember dealing with issues between Jill and Alvah. Jill's problem was that she wasn't able to get her needs met because she was trying to meet Alvah's needs at the same time; she was trying to keep Alvah engaged with her around things that their relationship needed to resolve. Jill dealt with her feelings in an ongoing way. Of course, it was difficult as Alvah got sicker because she was dealing with her own illness. After a while, she was in pain much of the time and that became her focus. Jill still wanted to keep Alvah engaged in trying to deal with the relationship. I'm not in the least bit negative about that; I think it was a wonderful thing.

Sex was not an issue. They had not had a sexual relationship for some time — since Alvah had gotten sick a year before. Jill and I have talked about it since. Jill was quite able to forego dealing with sex because Alvah just wasn't able to deal with it. But Jill wouldn't let go of her other needs. She felt it was OK to hold onto her other needs but not her sexual needs. One strong thing was not wanting Alvah to die and not being willing to let go of her, even when it became pretty evident that Alvah was going to die.

In the beginning we thought Alvah was going to get better. It was very sad for everyone because Alvah had struggled so to live. She really did her damnedest to get well. She tried everything — the healing group, visualization, and a positive attitude. The hardest thing for everyone — the group, for Jill and for Alvah herself — was to have to say "No matter that we did it all the way we were supposed to or not, Alvah's not going to make it." It was hard. I'm still very confused about all the responsibility that has been put on us for our own health, that something inside in our attitude is responsible for being well or ill. I have a hard time with that. It's a real burden. I still get angry with the attitude. "You made yourself sick, so you can make yourself well."

For me there was that same old question about the pain. Why does anyone have to suffer in order to die? I still don't know the answer. The best that came out of going through that process with Alvah was, "I don't know the answer, but struggling is not going to make it any easier and probably the best way is to integrate the pain the way one does with anything else in life." And then you can get past it and that's not all there is.

My mother had a very painful death. I watched part of it and I ran away for most of it. But I was there for Alvah. Being in the group helped me with this because I took in other people's attitudes. That was a very special group of people. Everyone there for the most part was very accepting of death being a process of life. They weren't immobilized by it and that helped. Everybody did what they could to help. The group organized itself to be there part of each day to do things that had to be done. The function of the group changed when it switched from a healing group to a dying group.

When we got together, Alvah could talk about different things: preparation of food, shopping, physical needs, bathing . . . it wasn't just the relationship with Jill. My image of people who were dying — who were ready to die — was of people who were much more fragile or less physically capable than Alvah seemed to be even at the end. Nevertheless, she was on morphine and was sleeping a lot of the time and couldn't do a lot of things. Movement was painful for her. She needed to have things done for her. Jill was there at night. When we met once a week, everybody would say what they could do that week — "I'll be here Wednesday to prepare lunch for Alvah." Everybody just flowed into the spaces that needed to be filled.

One night Alvah was in a very different frame of mind from where she had ever been before. She was a very gracious lady and that night, she did not want anything on below the waist. She had taken the covers off. She had taken her pants off and didn't want anything on. There was some banter about why, and she said something about wanting to shock Kay who was her old, old friend — a straight woman. Alvah was pretty drugged but lucid. Her mischievousness put us all in good spirits. That was the last time I saw her. Her death later that day was a surprise to me. Perhaps death is always a surprise to the survivors.

I think Alvah was ready to die except for Jill not wanting her to, because Jill was fighting against letting Alvah go. And I think people are held by other people. We tried to support Jill's needs, too. Her needs were emotional, not physical, and she had a therapist, but in some ways the group was just as much therapy for Jill. It was a safe space for her to deal with her feelings.

Many of the people in the group were very close friends to begin with. Jill called them her family. They saw each other a great deal, not just at group. Some other people's feelings got taken care of outside the group. But the group was always open to anybody talking about what was going on with them and in fact this was at a time when Cela and I were separating. The group helped with that.

The group met a couple of times after Alvah died. First we met the day she died. We met to grieve together and to plan what passed for a funeral — a celebration. She'd had some things to say about that before she died. And then we met a couple of times after that to wind up and to see where we wanted to go with it. There was some talk about writing something about our experience, but we didn't do it.

And then Jill was moving to the country. She and Alvah had been building a house up near Yosemite; Alvah's one big dream was to live there before she died. Jill felt like she needed to live that out, so she moved very soon after Alvah died.

I'm not sure how everybody else felt about the group disbanding. Some of them were very close and were going to continue seeing each other anyway. I was really sorry to have that finish. I guess I always felt like if I needed that kind of group, I hoped that they would be there for me. Jill and I are still close. She's the main person that I've stayed connected to from the group.

If I needed a healing group, I can't think of anything that I would do differently. If I could have, I probably would have continued that group just to see what else could be gained from continuing that experience. I tried on a couple of occasions to suggest the possibility to other people who have been ill. One of the owners of my company died of AIDS and another owner is dying of it. Everybody in my office is involved with AIDS and death and dying but nobody wants to talk about it or to do anything about it. I've suggested we form a group, but no one is interested. What a lot of denial!

The group took care of me; it was a very redemptive experience. The part of me it took care of was a lot of guilt about not being able to deal with my mother's death. We hadn't been close since I was sixteen. I never was able to find a way to be close to her. I'm still not sure why that was. When she was sick I could not face the fact she was dying. I did not want to realize the terrible pain she was having and that it was terminal. She lived in another part of the state and that was a good excuse not to be there. I felt terribly helpless and did not know what to do.

I am glad that my own denial has been broken. I know for myself, as awful as the experience was at times, I am glad that in the future I have options to the silence of denial. I feel that this "lesson" has carried over into the rest of my life as I now work to create a "family" of my own. As lesbians and gay people we may have to work harder at this, to create our own families, but I now know what is to be gained.

ALISON

"It's Not Any Worse Than Alcoholism"

I stopped being me at the age of fourteen when I started wearing dresses. A boy I liked was more attracted to a friend of mine. I thought it was because she wore dresses and I wore pants. Not being able to bear the feeling of isolation, I decided to conform.

My first sexual experience had occurred when I was eleven years old. I fell in love with a sixteen-year-old boy who was a handsome football player. I cared about him, but his interest in me was only sexual. The result was guilt and a feeling that I must have done something very bad. After that, I went with guys, but I wouldn't let them touch me until I was twenty-three years old and I met Carl, whom I later married.

I had my first real love affair when I was sixteen. I fell in love with another girl in class. I'd never felt so excited being around anyone before. I didn't know what it meant. I didn't have any name for it. I just knew it was wonderful. We never talked about it but I knew she felt the same way. We'd go on double dates together with the guys we were going steady with. I'd stay overnight at her house and we'd sleep in the same bed. We did a lot of hugging, and I think we kissed once or twice. It just felt so wonderful, all the butterflies. I was really in love.

I didn't know the name lesbian then. We didn't use that word in 1942. I had never heard the word homosexual. But I knew that Sandy and I had to be very discreet about it. We played the game of dating boys. I thought no one else in the world felt the way I did. I felt quite different. I wasn't excited about boys as other girls seemed to be. They just lived and waited for Saturday night. The only reason I dated was that I was very active in school.

Sandy and I planned to go to the University of Illinois together, but she got accepted to Smith. The separation was very painful for me.

At college I was attracted to other women. I walked around with a split personality: dating guys, but having strong feelings for women. I remember feeling that I wanted to fit in. I didn't want to be identified with women like the two women in my house who were lovers. My inner conflict between my emotional desires and the need to conform to society continued.

Meanwhile, Sandy and I were corresponding. She was getting involved with a religious group at Smith. After I'd been in school for a year, I had to go to work. I got a job in Seattle and then became engaged to be married. But we broke it off. I just couldn't go through with it.

After breaking this engagement, I started going to the library every weekend. I thought that by reading philosophy I could find something to hang on to. I just didn't feel that I fit in anywhere. All my passion was for women. I didn't know what to do with all that. I was trying to find myself. I was reading Gandhi and Christian philosophy. I went to a religious study group through the college, still searching. There I became involved with another woman.

The guilt from being involved with a woman while being in a religious group led me to believe that I must be mentally ill. I talked it over with Sandy, who had recently come home and gotten married. "Why don't you go talk to someone?" She recommended that I contact a Jungian therapist she'd heard of. So I called the therapist and made an appointment. I remember the first time I walked into her office. I was terrified. I sat down and in this very tiny voice, I said, "I think I have this homosexual problem." And she looked at me and said, "Oh, don't worry. We'll cure that in about six months."

I was enormously relieved. I'd revealed the hidden pain and guilt of all these years to someone else, and I had not been rejected. It was like going to confession.

Jane, my therapist, suggested that I take courses in Jungian theory, which I did. In the meantime I started seeing Carl, the man who later became my husband. He was taking the same courses and was also one of Jane's clients.

When Carl and I were married, Jane would not work with both of us as clients. For therapeutic reasons she chose to work with him. I understood, but I still felt rejected.

Being married made me feel as though I fit in. I no longer felt left out. But the truth was, I never was as excited with my husband as I'd been with women. I knew that all along. I told him before we got married that I'd been attracted to women. I had to tell him. It didn't seem to bother him. He said, "Well, psychologists don't take it very seriously."

After being married about thirteen years, I found I was miserable and lonely. Carl was gone a lot. We had two children, a boy and a girl. Our son had brain damage. Carl avoided dealing with that by going to meetings all the time. He wasn't home very much. I spent a lot of time gardening. I blamed myself for our son's brain damage and for the condition of my marriage. I felt that if I'd only been more of a woman, we'd have a better marriage. I took it all on myself. I felt that if I'd been more feminine, if I'd been a real woman, I could have hung onto my husband. He now was interested in another woman.

That summer, I took some more psychology classes, and in one of them I met Susan. We fell in love. There was hell to pay for that. My former therapist, Jane, who was working with Carl in therapy, asked me to come see her one day. When I walked in the door, she said, "Now don't lie to me about how much time you and Susan are spending together because Carl tells me how much time you're spending." That's how she greeted me. She was furious. I'll never forget what she said then. "What are you doing to your daughter; you're going to ruin her. It's not any worse than alcoholism, but it's on the same level." This was an attitude held by most psychologists in the 1950s. "Look," I said, "if this is the best love of my life, I will feel terribly grateful."

I was still trying to hold my marriage together because that was the right thing to do, but it was falling apart. Jane called and said, "I think you should go work with Don Beachum. I think you should be working with a man."

I worked with Don, a nice guy, but he had no understanding of what it means to be a lesbian. He really was not too sympathetic to homosexuality, but he was good in some ways. He said, "I think you and Tom have a sick situation going on between you." I asked, "Do you feel it's destructive for Susan to be around the children?" He said, "Not if there's love between you. Why would that harm them?"

I decided to separate from my husband. Don's being a little bit supportive gave me the tiny nudge I needed. I thought that this was my chance to get out of the marriage. Carl was having an affair; I wanted out. I didn't even talk to him or anyone about it. I simply said to a friend, "I need a lawyer. Do you know one?"

I started divorce proceedings. And Tom had a fit. He said, "It's all because of Susan." I said, "Carl, it's not true. This is no good for either one of us." For two years our lawyers were fighting and we were fighting. Carl was going to expose me as a lesbian and take the children away. He was furious to have to pay alimony and child support.

I went to a business school to brush up on my typing and shorthand. After I'd been there a few weeks, they hired me as the director of the school. I went back to college at night and got good grades. The successes I was beginning to experience gave me a renewed confidence in myself.

The first year with Susan was fantastic. But after that she would rarely have relations with me. But I stayed. I think it was because I had so little belief in myself, and I still thought there was something wrong with me because I wanted to have physical relations with her. I still felt that what Jane had said was right, and this continued to depress me. There were other things that were positive about our relationship. Susan had been a grade school teacher and she loved my kids. Her mother had a place on a lake which we visited every summer; we often took the kids with us.

It wasn't until I was fifty, and still with Susan, that I first began to identify as a lesbian. I met these two lesbian women, and they were my introduction to the women's community. They also helped me self-identify. Susan didn't like them. She said, "I wish they wouldn't put their arms around each other in front of people." I said, "What's wrong with that?" I thought it was wonderful.

Susan and I had been together for ten years. She then became involved with another woman, and our relationship started falling apart. She wanted to continue both relationships, so I walked out.

I had spent fifteen years in a marriage and ten years with Susan. My marriage was over and my relationship with Susan was over, but I was beginning to feel my own identity — beginning to feel good about being a lesbian.

My daughter was married last August, and after the wedding I received a letter from Jane, my first therapist, whom I'd not heard from for several years. I recognized her handwriting, and I thought, How nice, she's writing about my daughter's wedding. Instead the letter bawled me out for not inviting her to the wedding. She felt bitterly rejected. I was surprised and felt bad that I hadn't invited her.

I didn't answer that letter for a couple of months because I thought about it for a long time. This was my chance to say something to her that I needed to say, and it related back to what she'd said about my ruining my daughter. I've not forgotten that. I wrote and said that I had not meant to hurt her. "I've thought about this a long time, and I want you to know that the woman I have lived with and loved for seven years now had a seat of honor along with me at my daughter's wedding. I don't know if you feel this way anymore but I still remember the deep hurt that I felt when you said that I was ruining my daughter. And knowing that my lover and I would be seated together at the wedding, having you there would have made you uncomfortable and would have made us uncomfortable too. And on an unconscious level, I think that's why you weren't invited. I don't know how you feel now about women loving women. I hope you've changed."

She never responded to that letter; I don't think she ever will. I'm sorry I haven't heard from her, but I'm not surprised. Nevertheless I'm glad I sent it. There was, for me, unfinished business between us, and her letter gave me an opportunity to affirm myself.

I think about what it would have been like if Jane had been accepting instead of telling me loving a woman was sick and neurotic like being an alcoholic. I would have been a very different person now. I wouldn't have gotten married. I would have been freer; I just can't imagine. I would have liked myself. I would have been one person.

I can still feel the pain of being in the closet. Anyone who has to be in the closet needs pity, not condemnation. It takes a hell of a lot of courage to be out. But it's much more freeing. At least you're yourself to yourself.

ANONYMOUS

Admissions of Mortality:

The pleasures and problems of lesbian athletes

If you had viewed them in some club lounge, wedding rings enunciating their heterosexuality, expensive sports attire color-coordinated, you might have identified them as upper-class housewives engaged in a giggly gossip session over a few drinks. Because — just like upper-class housewives — some were pretty and feminine, others loitered along the ill-defined boundary of masculinity, while a few were quite ordinary in appearance.

But these women were not upper-class housewives. They were lesbian athletes representing a variety of sports, who were gathered several years ago during a major competition in one of those sports. Some were entered in the contest; others were there to cheer their friends on. They were now socializing in the luxurious condominium of one successful couple.

"And now tell me!" demanded one charmer of the group, in a heavy Australian accent. "Tell me how any of you first discovered you were gay!"

---

* The author of this piece, while she is self-described as "quite out," believes integrity dictates that she not reveal her friends, past and present sports figures who prefer to remain closeted. Thus, she has submitted her memories and observations anonymously.

I responded quickly. "And how many of you can remember the exact date you discovered it? I do: it was the night I won the national championship for the first time."

* * *

That date is now some near-half century past, but the night of the celebration remains as vivid as the performance which merited it.

Women groupies are inevitable peripherals at any women's sports event. Among mine during that national competition was an exceedingly wealthy woman who herself had been an outstanding athlete in several sports in the 1910s and 1920s, decades during which an unmarried woman athlete was merely regarded as "eccentric." She brought with her to my performance a younger friend, an outstanding amateur competitor in the same sport as me.

The woman of wealth (we'll remember her as "Amelia") invited me to her estate in an adjacent suburb for a celebration dinner, and to spend the night before I headed home to my then-husband. I accepted, primarily because I felt some as-yet undefined fascination for Amelia's handsome, intelligent, and cultured young friend, Anne.

I was unfortunately not completely aware of Amelia's greatness as an athlete, so absorbed was I in what I then perceived to be my own. I realize now the incomparable opportunity I flubbed — an opportunity to explore the obscure heritage of women's sports in America through the eyes of one of its greatest champions.

But I was more enthralled with the popping corks of the vintage champagne, with the simple elegance of Amelia's stone-walled mansion, with her retinue of servants — and with the glacier-blue eyes of Anne, across the table from me.

Amelia, then in her sixties, excused herself and retired early, leaving Anne and me to share the euphoria of my victory.

Anne had been discreetly assigned a separate guest room by Amelia, as had I. We eventually proceeded to our rooms, ostensibly to prepare to retire, but somehow we reconvened in Anne's room and lay on her bed. We recalled the critical moments of my competitive triumphs just past, and contemplated my future as a housewife-athlete of the 1940s, an era when housewives were expected to epitomize The Second Sex.

"Why, oh why, did you ever get married and relinquish your right to compete?" Anne asked, aghast when I confessed to her that by pre-nuptial agreement I would play in competition for only another four months past the wedding date, which was now four months past.

I recounted how my mother, as mothers of women athletes do even today, sat with other mothers on clubhouse porches and whispered in hushed tones about how athletics deformed some of its female participants, how younger and unsuspecting women could be recruited into lives too immoral and unnatural to contemplate. My mother determined, by some mysterious deductive process prevalent in the 1940s, that if she could only coerce me into marriage to the first remotely attractive young man interested in me, the possibility that I would become one of "those women" — and mothers did not then speak the name — would be eliminated.

No force in my life propelled me more assuredly toward women than did my repressive and unrewarding marriage.

My mother persisted in repeating for my benefit the oft-whispered clubhouse rumors which inevitably swirled around our competitions. "They say that Mrs. Berry is married in name only," she announced, coating the slander with a veneer of discretion. At eighteen, I had little comprehension of that pronouncement's meaning. Mrs. Berry had been friendly to me, sharing with me the benefits of her superior athletic experience when I was yet a rookie.

Yet Mrs. Berry did not recruit me.

Mother had eager assistants in her rumor-mongering.

"Didn't you know," I was warned by one older, straight athlete, with a pretense of maternalism, "that Betty Gage is a lesbian." Betty Gage (a fictitious name) was then the No. 1 performer in my sport. So, I thought in my youthful naivete, Betty is a lesbian? And what is wrong with being a lesbian?

I was to learn, through a brutal series of lessons, what our society deemed was wrong with being a lesbian, or more accurately, how society exploited the label "lesbian" to brand any woman who engaged in activities threatening to men. I was to learn as well about the firing line on which an unmarried woman athlete placed herself simply by being an athlete in an era when women athletes were societally unacceptable.

* * *

I treasure close friendships with many lesbian athletes who are currently competing, twelve of whom were sitting in that sun-flooded condominium with me, engrossed in a conversation which ranged from knee-slapping humor to poignant expressions of psychic pain.

And I had to say to them, "You must know that the personal corners of your lives are only slightly more habitable than was mine two, three, and four decades ago."

* * *

Her stern image remains vivid, 44 years after our encounter — the city librarian seated primly at the information desk, graying hair forced tautly into a bun, thin, unembellished lips sealed, unsmilingly thwarting all evil, hands clasped in the stereotypical clench of morality's guardian.

I rallied all of my courage to whisper, "Do you have a book called *The Well of Loneliness*? By Radclyffe Hall?" Grant Wood's portrait of a middle-America farm wife was raucously joyful in contrast to that defender of my city's virtue.

"We do not," she announced, lips barely parting, "allow pornography on our shelves."

Later I surreptiously acquired the now-classic fiction by special order at a sleazy back alley bookstore. And I had to smile at the librarian's judgment of pornography as I read the novel's most lascivious line: "But the moment passed, and the two women drew together. . . ."

* * *

As I glanced around the room filled with those magnificent women, I concluded there has been only one major change in the lives of lesbian athletes: They have come out to each other en masse. They now feel free to gather in groups, as we did in that sun-country condo, and hold lively rap sessions on the problems and pleasures of lesbian athletes. A gathering exploring that theme could never have occurred 30 or 40 years ago. Then we discussed "it" in groups of two. The prospect of going to a women's bar was terrifying to us; most of today's athletes are unembarrassed to make the public statement implicit in a bar appearance. Today lesbian athletes enjoy strong and empathetic support groups. I do not know how we survived without them, almost half a century ago. I do not understand how we coped with the trauma of the rumors, the pursuits of married groupies, the male inquisitions, our crippling existences in our labyrinthian closets, and the trauma of competing against our lovers — without support groups. Indeed, it was remarkable we could exist as lovers at all in that explosive environment.

Tragically, except for the heightened willingness to come out to one's peers, the environment for the lesbian athlete today is very little changed.

* * *

Now I am an aging lesbian athlete.

For women, "aging" is a term conveniently associated with the cessation of ovulation, a concept I find rather amusing. (I have learned that if I can be amused, the anger is tentatively put aside.) In fact, the aging process begins at birth.

Over the past half century I have observed countless young athletes battling an assortment of physical ailments through their teens, twenties, and thirties. How ironic it is that we fear the infirmities of old age, when in fact it seems miraculous that we live to celebrate (or lament) our fortieth birthdays.

Aging only means that the emphasis shifts to whatever deterioration we are attempting to prevent, to erect defenses against, or to cure.

I personally embrace the theory that chronological age is a non-measurement. I believe that we need to adapt a physiological indexing system to evaluate ourselves more realistically. There are senile 30-year-olds; there are youthful

80-year-olds. There are 20-year-olds who can never remember where they put their car keys; in 70-year-olds such forgetfulness is attributed to Alzheimer's disease.

I recently asked several lesbian athletes in their twenties and thirties to state their most immediate gut-level response to the question, "What is the first thought you have when you are asked, 'What frightens you most about aging?'"

"Alzheimer's!"

"Being in a wheelchair."

"Losing my sexual desire."

"Being incapacitated and dependent upon someone else."

"Paying the price for all of my indiscretions," was one answer, accompanied by a small giggle.

To this Medicare card-carrier, aging means freeing!

Aging has produced freedom from those awful "What if's?" of my years of stardom. What if my business manager learned the rumors about me were true? What if my fans found out? What if my respected coach learned the truth about my sexual preference? What if the parents of the junior athletes I coached knew?

Aging means remembering, with a small smile engendered by the glee of retribution, how I learned the business manager was gay, that the most raucously-cheering of my allegedly straight female fans were actually in love with me, that several of the mothers of my junior stars would have instantly forsaken their offspring for the chance to bed down with me.

Aging means the voyeurs are no longer curious about my sex life because they believe that women over 40 have little if any interest in sex. (That gross under-estimate merits the "Myth of the Year" award.)

So aging means freedom from hiding behind that facade which many young lesbians must continue to carry.

Aging means freedom from playing the "fool the males game" — freedom from borrowed engagements rings, from contrived male lovers, from the intense social pressures to act out the traditional female role.

Aging means the freedom which comes from learning that being loved — by lover, parents and family, friends — is not contingent upon the quality of my athletic performance.

Aging means freedom from that gnawing compulsion to win, because I have at last learned that there is more joy to be derived from the physical movement of my sport than there is from its consequences.

EDITH AND SARAH
We Have Each Other

Edith: We met in 1962 when we both were working at the post office. I was 28 or 29; Sarah was 18. We met, we liked each other, we became very good friends. She had a friend named Webster. I was separated from my husband, and I started going with him.

Sarah, to me, was a baby. I felt that there were a lot of things I could tell her. I used to try and tell her how to dress, what she should do and what she shouldn't.

Sarah: How to comb my hair, how to put on make-up, and things like that.

E: She was my babysitter. She was very good to my children and she was very good to me. In fact, Sarah was the first one that had ever given me a gift for no reason — a very nice gift. I still have it — a wine set from India. It's silver, a beautiful set. I just couldn't believe it. I said, "This should go to your mother." And she said, "No, I want you to have it." So I took it.

S: I'd almost forgotten about that.

E: The first Christmas, I'd taken ill — shortly after I'd met

· 71 ·

Sarah. Being separated and just starting at the post office, I didn't have much money. So Sarah and Webster, between the two of them, more or less helped me over the hump. I didn't have the money. My husband wasn't the type to pay child-support. The first Christmas, Sarah went out and she bought all these gifts for my children. The tree was loaded.

I gave her a birthday party when she turned twenty. She moved in with me on Sixth Street — still a friend. At that time, everybody started saying, "You know, something's wrong with that girl. She's funny." I'd say, "Funny, what do you mean funny?" They'd say, "You watch her." My aunt used to say the same thing. Sarah's sister, who's gay, used to tease her all the time. She'd say that Sarah was in love with me.

S: I don't think everybody knew that I was in love with Edith. When they were saying "funny," I think they meant that I was mental . . . The other part was not that I was gay, but that I was a bull-dagger, and therefore you had to be careful and watch out. The mental part was that I had a lot of struggle being around other people; I was a loner. I was an introvert by choice. So if people were around, I wouldn't talk to them. I used to have this rocking chair. Her friends would come in and I'd sit and rock.

I knew what I was feeling, but I couldn't figure out how to go about getting it across to *her*. I knew I was in love with her off the top when I first saw her. The only problem I had was with Webster since we were buddies. I remember the first time I saw her at the post office — I said to Webster, "Oooh, look at her! What's her name?" And Webster said, "I don't know." And I said, "Well, I'm going to go ask her." He said, "No. You can't go over there like that." I said, "Yeah, I'm going to go." So I just walked by and Webster said, "You got her name?" I said, "Yeah." At lunch, I said, "Webster, why don't we ask her to sit at lunch with us?" So Webster was my go-between at first. And that S.O.B. starts going with her.

I knew I was gay since I was twelve, but I didn't call it gay. I didn't call it *anything*. I got love letters at twelve years old from little girls and stuff. I knew that I didn't like little boys. But at that time, in the late fifties, you had to go along with the game, so in order to go out in the evenings and stuff I had a lot of male friends. They were really just buddies but other people sometimes thought we were going together. I only knew one girl at the time that was openly gay ... and I knew I wasn't like her; she had a motorcycle. I knew I didn't want to be like that. You go out and everybody points at you. Or calls you names and wants to jump on you and fight. That's one reason me and my girlfriends would only go so far. We'd go to a certain point — emotionally — and then I'd leave them alone. I'd get close to them and then I'd have to back away.

But when I saw Edith I was nineteen and I was making money. I was still living at home, so I had money. I felt just as grown-up as anyone else. But then one time I went by her house and she was serving drinks and she told me not until I was twenty-one. And then I realized she was thinking of me as the younger sister she never had so I just played the younger sister part. I did a lot of lying. I told her I didn't know how to iron so she ironed my clothing. I told her I couldn't cook. She was saying, "Oh my God, what's wrong with this girl's mother? This child needs help." At first I don't think she caught on. She had her room and I had my room. My room was right next to the kid's room. Her room was right in front. She used to have boyfriends in. She was being wild.

E: I was separated from my husband. At that time, I guess I was trying to prove a point — that the marriage hadn't worked, but I *could* hold men. But these men did not come up to the standard. I was a mother with three children and I needed help. So I just got help from various ones. Sarah was probably seeing me as this bad woman.

S: I can tell you the exact day that it hit you. And at that point, you were fighting it in yourself. It was Thanksgiving of '64. I was twenty. You had a party. I got a headache and went to lie down in my room. When you noticed I was gone, you came to find me. When I came out of my room you were pretty high, and you said, "What were you doing in there? Who were you with?" And you got mad and started slapping me. When you did that, then I knew. And the whole atmosphere in the house changed.

E: Maybe subconsciously, but I had never questioned that part — whether I liked you sexually. I always was surrounded by men. I mean, a *woman*?? Heaven forbid! The thought never entered my mind. Honest to god. I never made the association between me and another woman being together. Then she went into the service and she was getting on the plane. Her mother and I drove her to the airport. When she was getting on the plane, she looked so tiny up there on this huge plane. We were standing there and I had the loneliest feeling and she hadn't even left yet. Then she would call and I would call her. I had a tremendous phone bill. Her sister kept saying, "You love Sarah. Why don't you admit it?" I decided then, that I had to do something. I wasn't giving attention to the children like I should because when you're partying constantly, you can't. I knew that I had to straighten my life out. I quit the post office and I moved to Los Angeles.

S: I was stationed in Indiana at the time. We were talking on the phone one night. It was right before the Watts riots. Edith was living in L.A. And Edith said, "I love you." And I said, "I love you, too." Before we hung up, I said, "Why did you wait so long to tell me that you love me?" And then I went upstairs to my bunk and I cried all night long. She waited until I was way out there in Indiana to tell me.

E: I moved to L.A. to get away from everything. I was lonely. I moved to change the way I was living — drinking and different men.

S: I was scheduled to come on leave when the riots came. When the riots came in L.A., though, they cancelled everyone's leave. I became increasingly worried as I couldn't reach Edith by phone. I finally got to see her a couple months later, in November. I went down to L.A. and we consummated the relationship then.

E: It was hard. We had to wait until the children were asleep. It was uncomfortable because children can sense things. Just when you think everybody's asleep, somebody comes out, "Mom, can I have some water?"

I don't think we ever had a comfortable time in our sexual relationship unless we went away from the children. Sometimes, we'd say we were going out of town and we'd go rent a motel or something in the area. It was very rare that the children were all away at the same time. If two were going, one stayed behind . . . like a sentry — on guard all the time. I realize now that the children did know that something was happening, but they really couldn't put their hand on it. They always seemed to monitor us. It went on the whole time the kids were living with me.

I didn't want to think of myself as gay. I bought every book that they ever printed about gays trying to sort out my feelings. The reading didn't make me feel any better. I felt being gay was going against the Lord.

My whole life took on a different perspective when I finally admitted that I loved Sarah and wanted to make a life with her. But I had to go against everything to do it. I had to go against the way I was raised as a Baptist, against my family, against everything I'd ever heard.

S: After we consummated the relationship, I had to go back to Indiana. We were together for a week and then we did not see each other again until the summer. I saw her in November of '65 and then in July of '66 and then I was overseas for the next two years. I had affairs with men while I was gone.

E: I would have liked to strangle her. We were in constant contact — we always wrote or called. We never made any long term plans. We just let it happen.

When she got out in '68, she came to Los Angeles.

S: I always knew what I wanted. There was a lot of little crooks and stuff in the way, but I knew what I wanted. And when I got out of the service, my first phone call was to try to reach her in L.A.

I was stationed on Okinawa. At one point before I left I was thinking of staying there. I was offered a job doing the same thing I was doing, but as a civilian. There were lesbians there. It was like being king of the hill. I never denied what I was doing; I used to keep Edith posted. I'd write her and tell her everything I did. I was doing everything I could! The whole time I was there I slept with two women.

We had a code. The barracks was like eighty percent straight, twenty percent gay. Most people think it's the other way around, but it's not. There's more straight women in the military than gay. There was like an unwritten code that the gay women did not try to convert anyone — you didn't mess with the straight women. When I got there most of the people in the barracks did not know whether I was gay or straight because as soon as I got there I ran with a guy I met earlier — we became buddies and ran around together.

Every now and then Uncle Sam would go through and try to weed out those women who were gay and give them discharges or threaten them with a discharge unless they told on everybody else. The team of investigators with the military took all the pictures of our softball team and they took one girl and had her sit there and point out everybody on the team that was gay. She did it. I was on the team, but nobody thought I was gay. It was scary. The group I hung out with was always mixed with married couples, heterosexual couples, homosexual couples. Some of the guys were gay, so if we had a party we'd have six men and six women, even though two of the men were going together and two of the women were going together. That was our protection.

What saved our neck was that the white girls were the

ones that were always pointed out and put out. I guess they figured that since black people are so hot and sexy, when they'd see a black woman with a black man, they figured that we were getting it on. For some reason, Uncle Sam was very stupid like that. Any time there was an investigation — they used to call them "sweeps" — we would get word that they'd be getting ready to do a sweep. We'd know that for a month before the sweep was due they'd be sneaking around taking pictures. I never saw any black get swept. It was always the whites. We used to tell the whites, "Hey, you're stupid. Why don't you mix it up?" We actually had both black and white in our group. The white girls that hung out with us never got swept.

We didn't talk much about being gay or our rights, or getting kicked out. We talked about "being stupid". That's the way we put it. There was one white girl. We used to pass her up in the hall. She used to wear a "dilly-dally" — a dildo. When we got off work, you could wear civilian clothes. She'd put a little dilly-dally on and put her slacks on. Then she'd go out into town. We'd tell her, "You're stupid." We happened to run into her at one of the clubs. She asked if she could sit with us. We said, "Hell, no. You sit somewhere else. You're stupid." She was asking for trouble.

E: You got to keep in mind they were in Okinawa. People were getting killed. From her letters, they weren't thinking, as gays, "We're being oppressed." They were thinking more about living.

S: Being gay was secondary. In the states here there was a lot more discussion about it. But over there, it wasn't as important because we were at a jumping point. Every now and then I would go temporary duty to Vietnam. Our concern was survival. We *lived* to get back home. Our concern was, "Will we live to get back home?"

E: When she finally got home, she'd have nightmares. She'd shake and bump her head against the wall in her sleep. The first time she did it, it scared me to death. It was from an experience where one of her friends was killed.

S: A lot of our guys got killed and they got killed with U.S. weapons. Our guys had old M-14s and the Viet Cong had brand new ones. There was nowhere you were safe there. You couldn't trust anybody — kids, women, anybody.

During the Tet offensives, there were big med-evacs and they would use you whether you were a medic or not. It was awful. They were bringing in guys — some of them were dead by the time you got to them. So our group drank. A lot of others got high all the time. Being gay seemed pretty secondary.

After the offensives calmed down — *then* the military started with the sweeps. They didn't bother before. Sure they used us. But it didn't bother me as much as them using me because I was black. What I saw on the front line was all the young blacks. Even on Okinawa, when I'd walk down to town, I saw half of my high school class out there. I'd ask about friends: "Oh, he got wiped out last week." or "He got killed last month." But very few of the white guys were there. The white guys I did run into were in the office on Okinawa; the black guys were in Vietnam getting killed. We talked about that more than we talked about being gay.

At one point I considered re-enlisting; I had this offer that if I did, I could go to officer's school. But then I said, "Hey, the brothers are getting killed and the white guys are sitting here. What the hell am I doing? To hell with Uncle Sam." The military was so prejudiced that they would bring in a new white lieutenant from school in the states and put him over a total black platoon. These guys had been out there for six months already and here'd come this white guy with no experience. That's why so many white lieutenants were killed.

But all of them weren't killed by the commies; some were killed by the group. There was this one white lieutenant who was a real bigot; he wouldn't listen to this black sergeant who had been there and knew how to survive. One day he said, "Let's go take this hill." The brother said, "No, it doesn't make sense to go up that hill." The guy said, "I'm the lieutenant. Let's take the hill." The brother said, "Okay." They started up the hill and the brothers stayed in the bushes. When the white lieutenant got half way up the hill, the Viet Cong showed their face and he looked around and realized there was nobody behind him. The Viet Cong wiped him out.

There were other incidents where a mixed platoon — black and white — would be doing search and seizure. The Viet Cong surrounded them. They killed all the white guys. They told the black guys to lay their guns down and go; "We're not fighting with you." That happened quite a few times.

I got one friend who has no legs. They were going through fields and they were often booby-trapped. His white lieutenant told him to go and he wouldn't. The white guy pushed him and he landed on a mine.

So we weren't concerned with gayness.

E: We've kind of always known that we needed more than the freedom to be gay as opposed to equal rights. Gay rights? We just want *human* rights. Once we get the human rights, we can deal with all the rest.

S: No one walks around with a sign on them that says, "I'm gay." But there's a sign on me that says "I'm black," and I can't come home, put on a dress, change my walk and nobody know it. What I have done with the blackness is that I have become me. While I was overseas, the whole Black Power thing was happening over here, but we were in another world. One girl showed up there with an *Ebony* magazine. There was a picture of an afro. At that time we were all in perms. And I said, "I want my hair like that." So I waited till my perm grew out. I looked in the magazine and they showed a pick. There was no pick over there so I used a fork from the mess hall. I used to comb my hair with a fork. I did this on a weekend. On Monday morning we had formation. I was in uniform with this natural, and my hat just right. The sergeant said, "What the hell is wrong with your hair?" I had to go and report to the CO. I told her it was a new hairstyle that I'd seen in a book. She said, "Get me the book." I went and brought her the magazine and she said, "As long as you keep it down underneath your hat, you can wear it. If it comes out from underneath your hat, you can't wear it." So we just took a towel and patted it down real tight. I was the first woman over there to do it. Everybody kept saying, "Oh Sarah, you're going to lose rank. They're going to bust you down."

I kept trying to find out what was going on with black power. Anyone who came in black from the states, we would just eat them up. "Tell us what's going on. What you guys doing over there?" The word that we got was that they were rioting and burning down houses. For a while there they had trouble with us. We got a black group together. Our white friends were getting afros.

E: Sarah got out of the military and she moved in with me in Los Angeles. We were there until 1970. Then we came back up here and bought a house.

S: I had a military cot in the same room where you had a double bed.

E: We had an extra bed in the bedroom and Sarah was supposed to be sleeping in it. Then we would close the door — we bought these locks for the door — and she'd get in bed with me. We used the locks because my children would knock and come in. They didn't knock and wait. So we'd be in the double bed together and if somebody knocked, she'd get in the little bed. Then in the morning, Sarah'd run and jump and get in "her" bed. Then when we moved, Sarah had her own room. But that didn't work too well, so we took to saying it was a study and the beds were in the bedroom. My son Robbie comes here now and he knows now that we sleep together and he's okay with it.

S: Yeah, but that just started a couple of months ago. He'll be thirty-two next month. In March, he'd come in and we'd be in bed watching television and he'd just come in and lay across the bed. He'd never done that before, but he does now.

E: For twelve years while we had the kids we never kissed or held hands in front of them. It was hard — very hard. We don't want to offend anyone so we still do the same thing for her mother. It is easier now that we have the house to ourselves.

S: I don't think it bothered me as much at first. But when the kids got up to size — junior high and high school — I went through a period. When I came out of the service, I was totally open. So if someone were to ask me something then, I'd just blurt it on out. Except to my people and to the kids. I don't attribute that to a problem with being gay; it was the way I was raised. You respect your elders. It was respect for my mother and I didn't want to do anything that would not give the kids a full shot.

I feel like I put a lot of energy and thought into those kids and did not get it back. I think deep down, the kids love me and I think, even deeper, they hate me. I think the kids and me have a love-hate relationship. I think it's because of their mother that they show respect. But anytime that Edith is not present, the respect sort of leaves.

I feel hurt about my relationship with the kids. Now that the two of us are getting older, I miss having the family type relationship that we had when they were kids. I think it's due to their resentment that we don't. I know the youngest child hates my guts. The daughter. But at this point, it's something that they have to settle for themselves. I feel maybe that if anything got real bad with me, they *might* come. They might come. I'd be there if anything bad happened to them, sure.

E: I feel bad because the children know about the relationship now. I guess they feel like I was afraid of them; I was afraid to tell them all those years. But now they're adults and what I would like for them to do is accept the relationship. On the other hand, I can understand. How can they tell their children,

"Well Grandma doesn't have a husband because she had a lady-friend." That's kind of hard for them to have to explain.

There's three children. It's the youngest one that has the problem with our relationship. I can understand that it isn't easy for her. Society says we are unnatural, but we've put twenty years into this relationship. We should be considered for our whole lives not just what we do in bed.

Regardless of whether they accept her or love her, whatever they have is because of Sarah. She was there for them. She put in her time mentally and emotionally. And she put in her money. She gave all these things to them when they were in school. We still support them. Anything happens, she's the first to say, "Well, you want to drive down or do you want to get a plane?" No questions. It's sad, they don't come up often for holidays. Sometimes, but not often.

I had one good friend in L.A. that was gay. But we never really associated with gay people. I wanted my children to have as normal a childhood as possible. Our whole life centered around the children — their home life, their school life, the weekends. I'd give them projects . . . The kids would talk to Sarah about things they didn't talk to me about. The kids asked her to take them shopping. They'd call her upstairs to talk and they'd all be gone for two or three hours.

After seventeen years, we told Sarah's family about the relationship. They all said, "Oh we know that." But they blame me because I'm older. Sarah's mother does not believe that Sarah is gay. She doesn't believe the sister's gay either and she's wearing leather . . . If I had to do it over again, I'd do it different.

S: If I had to do it over again, I wouldn't do it with anyone who had children. That would be the first question; "Lady, do you have children?" They say, "Yes"; you say, "Forget it."

E: You have the option. You *still* have the option.

S: It was hard. Lot of time, you wanted to choke the kids. You couldn't say anything and if you caught 'em doing anything wrong and she was upset, you couldn't say, "Well that child's wrong." You couldn't say anything. You *still* can't say anything negative to her.

E: So why did you stay?

S: I don't know. To tell you the truth, there were some days back then I really don't know why I stayed. Once we had a temporary separation. Don't remember why.

E: It was because you always went home to your family on the holidays — Christmas and Thanksgiving. Even though I would not come out and say that I was gay, I felt we should be a family on the holidays. You know I had to work hard against all odds to keep this relationship.

I wish my mother could hear this tape. I wish my children could hear this tape — the things we had to go through in order to just be ourselves.

E: First we're black people. Next we're two women who live together. We deal first with the black. Then we deal with the other stuff. We don't get into a lot of gay activist stuff. Sometimes I might have a little tinge of guilt because I think I get more or less of a free ride. People out marching for my right to express something and I didn't do one thing to bring it about.

S: I don't feel that way.

E: I just feel I have so much else to deal with. We have white gay acquaintances who are financially less well off than we are, but over all they're in better shape. Reason being they get better interest rates for financing. You may find that hard to believe but it's true. Better insurance rates, too.

S: I feel differently because I feel that I have contributed to gay rights because I took all the punishment in the sixties. I took the beat-ups and all that. Coming off that military base in Arizona, first they'd jump on you because they were demonstrating against the war. You learned that and then you stopped coming off base in uniform. The second problem was if you came off base and you went into a gay club, there was likely to be a carload of males when you came out of the club. I saw one girl get her head split open. I got hit once.

E: At work, I can't tell them about my weekend and say, "Oh me and Jim did such and such." I'll tell them, "Me and Sarah did such and such." I don't tell them we're gay, but they know we live together. I've never said anything that indicates that we're gay.

S: All in all, this is the happiest time in my life. The kids are grown. We own this house and we have each other. Yes sir, there has never been a happier time in my life.

E: This year's the twentieth year of our relationship and the lady's still with me.

SANDY BOUCHER

Half of a Map

Party. Kitchen. I'm sitting up against a high counter behind a collection of Calistoga and wine bottles, looking out into a room where women, dykes like me, stand talking. Two of them have sat down on the floor to compare shoes. One wears those soft brightly-colored laced shoes that are fashionable this year. The other arches her foot to show off a pair of brown and white Spaulding saddles that she found in a secondhand store. Immediately I recall how absolutely crucial it had been, when I was a high school student in the early fifties, to wear Spauldings. And I realize I am the only woman in the room over thirty. Usually I don't notice ages, but now as I look around I see the firm cheeks, the slim — or if not slim, resilient — bodies, the clear eyes and particular freshness of very young women.

They examine the laces in the shoes, thick ropes of pink and grey. And I find myself talking, my words astonishing me. "When I was young," I say, "the boys wore charcoal grey flannel suits with pink shirts."

The women in the kitchen barely glance at me. There is a small jerky pause, and then the woman with the Spauldings says, "Oh yeah, charcoal grey, I could get into that. I could see it — and a pink shirt, hey I bet that'd look hot."

When I was young . . . I am numb, sitting there staring at a wide-hipped greenish bottle of chablis. I can't remember ever uttering that phrase before. It has pointed to a chasm that I never imagined to exist: between that presumably distant and unreachable time *when I was young*, and now. Now . . . what?! Now, according to the logic of the phrase, I am *not young*. Then am I old?

I look around the room. Any woman here under that age, say, of 27, is young enough to be my daughter. That spiffy dyke over there with the crewcut and the three earrings in a little row up the curve of her ear: I imagine her as my daughter. What an arresting thought. As it is, I am free to enjoy her loud laugh and the swagger of her thrust-forward leg, her tanned arms crossed over her silky shirt. How differently would I feel about her if she had suckled at my breast, had tested me with the demands of her growing up, had given me the delight of her developing mind and body, had loved me and then rebelled against me and finally condescended to me or maybe become my friend.

But she *could be* my daughter, and this fact stuns me. She has only heard and read of the Second World War, whereas my childhood took place under its shadow; the fifties exist for her as "Happy Days" on TV, while I lived that complicated decade as a high school and college student; there is so much that formed me that she knows nothing of.

Another woman, lounging near the doorway, draws my eye. She wears shorts, and her legs are flawlessly smooth. I am reminded of the picnic in 1979 where I first noticed the changes in my own legs. I happened to glance down at my thigh beneath the hem of my shorts, and saw a little swelling under the skin. What is this? I wondered. And then I noticed on the inside of my calf a lumpy snake of bluish vein crawling toward my knee. Once I saw it, it began to ache. Later I remembered my father's legs, on the rare occasions when he wore a bathing suit, his calves clutched by the bluish crooked fingers of vericose veins. So the hereditary weakness arrived. Having lurked outside the door like a shy friend, now, noticing my body's (only beginning) loss of resilience, it came furtively in to bestow its gift.

In 1982 the letters on the page of the book I was reading began to blur if I read by anything but intense sunlight. If I moved the book away — ah, there, it's better — I could find just the narrow range in which my eyes could focus. Soon my arm was not long enough to manage this. One of my students who was near my age told me I could buy magnifying glasses at the Emporium for twelve dollars. I did so, and use them now when I must.

Yet my picture of myself lags behind the actuality. For many years I thought of myself as a big rangy girl, an Irish- setter type person, long-limbed and supple, flopping about good-naturedly. That image had little to do with the constricted ladylike creature I most certainly appeared to be through my teens and twenties. I came closer to it in my thirties after I became a lesbian, with all the freedom that choice brings, to be oneself. Still, people tell me I was often remote, and intimidating when threatened. Now sometimes I sense a person's conception of me when she looks at me, and if I am seen as an "older woman," someone weighty with years, dignified, to be deferred to, I feel like snorting raucously at the deception. No, no, I want to say, you're not *seeing me*. I'm as vital, as "experimental with my life" as you. Then if I am tired or in a position where I need to get something done, I use the deception. The deference becomes a lever to get what I want, the deception works in my favor and I let it, while knowing that this erodes me morally.

But I am only 48 years old, at the very beginning of this journey. When I think of my Aunt Helen, who is 83, who can barely see or hear, who walks with two canes and is so twisted by age that to cook a meal in her kitchen is a slow, torturous and even dangerous endeavor that requries tremendous energy and inventive skill — when I think of Aunt Helen still insisting on cooking meals for my mother and me, I experience the vacuum of my knowledge about age. Standing at the stove, Helen shakes her head and says with the brevity that has always characterized her utterances, "Don't get old."

But my body has begun speaking to me differently than ever before, and so I am brought to these thoughts, this investigation that Helen has been engaged in for thirty years or so. I'll know more when I'm eighty, but that's no reason to keep my mouth shut now.

* * *

In the summer of 1982 I was driving across the Midwest doing a promotional tour for my book *Heartwomen*. Alone in the car, I would drive for six, eight, ten hours, arrive at a town, be interviewed by the newspaper and the radio station and that evening give a reading and slide show at a university women's center or a women's coffeehouse or bookstore. Then I would sleep over at someone's house, get up the next morning and drive six, eight, ten hours to the next specified town. Perhaps because this schedule was so strenuous, my period was delayed, and for weeks I endured the swollen breasts and belly, the irritability, the increased emotionality that precedes my period. In Iowa City, I happened to examine my breasts and found several distinct lumps, and even though I knew that before my period my breasts always show such changes, I decided that cancer had finally struck. The next morning, my birthday, I awoke in a strange bed in an empty house, with a thunderstorm raging outside, and my first thought was, "I'm forty-six, I'm over the hill." That noon I went to lunch with a young woman from the Iowa City Women's Press, who, noting my depression, asked delicately, "Are you tired?" I glanced up at her, gauging whether I could lay this burden on her, but she appeared so dewy with youth that I felt the way I did in the kitchen at the party when I noticed how young everyone was. Lonely. And not able to speak of what bothered me, because I would have to start at zero and so it might take all day and even then she might not understand. "Yes," I said, "I'm tired."

Here I am reminded of an encounter with Elsa Gidlow. Several other younger women and I drove Elsa, who is in her seventies, home from a poetry reading. As Elsa is a lesbian poet of a time so remote from our own, we were eager to talk with her, and asked her many questions. Elsa responded with tart half-sentences or monosyllables, her strong lined face set in an expression of restraint, until finally we gave up and drove in silence. When she had left the car, my friends wondered whether Elsa had not been feeling well or if something in our questions had been particularly annoying to her. But when I thought of it, it seemed to me that perhaps Elsa simply despaired of communicating to us a reality so different from our own, of doing this in one short automobile ride, with women she did not know and might never see again. Remembering her in the front seat, small and sinewy and elegant, her grey hair bound with a purple headband, her narrow shoulders swathed in plum-colored suede, her back resolutely straight under the barrage of questions, now I feel her loneliness.

On my return to Oakland from my promotional tour, I discovered that the cancer scare had been a false alarm this time. But a week later my period arrived with a violence I had never experienced. I was not bleeding, I was hemorrhaging. All strength left my body, and a great heat entered to take its place. I lay in bed, my flesh burning. When I did manage to get up, I was shaky and sweating, and poised on the edge of tears. I had never felt so vulnerable. All my life I had experienced regular periods with little pain. I had looked forward to my periods as a time of folding in, of taking care of myself and listening to myself. Now what I heard when I listened was a rampage. Odd how predictability brings the illusion of control, for obviously my periods had never been under my direction, and yet because I knew what to expect from them, I experienced that order that feels like control. Now my body was running riot. I had read about hot flashes, of course, but nobody had said that one's body might burn with a deep heat from one's very center for two days without relief.

In this condition I craved the comfort of my lover's understanding and acceptance. Although she is much younger than I, she could sense how unprotected, how at the mercy of my body I felt. She tucked me into bed, brought me ice cream, stroked my head. I welcomed this special treatment. And as I lay in bed I understood something I hadn't before: that the deference paid to old people comes, when it is most genuinely offered, not just from respect for their years of experience but from the recognition of their vulnerabiltiy. They are not so insulated as we by our strong bodies and sharp sensory capacities. They become more and more fragile, prey to accident, to disease, to emotional distress.

I think of the photographer Imogen Cunningham, who had just turned ninety when I met her. My lover at the time was shooting a film about Imogen, so we spent whole days with her and often went out to dinner with her. Now and then I came along. On one occasion we were all to go out to a Chinese restaurant in North Beach, but when we arrived we found Imogen in her bathrobe, and she told us she was experiencing the vertigo that sometimes came on her and said she couldn't go with us this time. Her hair hung in a long white swatch down her back, her tiny body in the flowered robe trembled as she went to get back into bed. Sitting against the pillows, she was like a gnome, her eyes blinking at us snappishly, as she shot questions at us, always in a tone of annoyance that was meant to be, and *was*, provocative. Her flame burned brightly, but it was a small flame, her presence light. It was her skin that struck me most, for it was so delicate as to seem transparent, in places ash white, with here and there a faint blush of rose, so delicately dry-seeming that it looked as if it would tear at the touch. So little protection between Imogen and the world: no wonder she felt the need to hold people at a distance with the scourge of her wit.

* * *

It was June 1983 in the makeshift camp next to the freeway which was being used as a jail to house the three hundred women anti-nuclear protesters arrested at the gates of Lawrence-Livermore Laboratories. On my first day of imprisonment there, seated on the ground at a meeting in the tent, suddenly I experienced the worst pain I had ever felt. A dagger plunged deep in my jaw. Stumbling outside the tent to hold onto a guy rope, I bent forward under this agony, tears in hot rivulets down my cheeks. Three days before I had gone through the first procedure for a root canal in one of my molars. The dentist had prescribed codeine for the pain he said might come, but there had been no pain at all, and so I had not even tried to sneak the codeine into jail with me. Now, clutching the tent rope, I longed for some relief. Mercifully, the pain lessened and disappeared after a short while. But it was to return each day for the first five days of our incarceration, and impale me for some minutes. After each bout I was exhausted and could barely function for a period of time.

In the warehouse I sat on my cot for the meeting of our "cluster," the Cosmic Elders. This grouping had come about because of Sarah, a seventy year-old indefatigable member of our affinity group who decided if she were going to jail she wanted more "white heads" with her. Here they were, in their sixties and seventies, the eldest 82. I felt privileged to be included in Cosmic Elders after a few of these meetings, for there was such accumulated political experience and wisdom in the elders that our group generally dealt with problems more efficiently than the groups of younger women. While they struggled to understand the significance of a particular move by the sheriff or happening in the camp, our veterans quickly put the event in a political context developed over years in the labor and peace movements. The elders knew what things meant and what our alternatives were.

I soon noticed, though, that it was not easy for them to be in jail with us. Conditions were harsh for everyone, with inadequate beds and blankets, constant wind and sun, wretched food, fumes and noise from the freeway, and the subtle harassment of the guards, but the elders brought with them additional hardships. Rose suffers from arthritis; I would watch her get up with great difficulty from her seat on the straw-littered ground. Marion has skin cancer; she wore a hat and rubbed sun-screen on her face and hands. Helen apparently has some form of neurological disease, for she often tottered and bumped into things, and her hands shook. Goldie's high blood pressure showed in her flushed cheeks and her dizzy groping for support when she got up quickly. Sitting with these women in our meetings, I rarely thought of these infirmities, for such steadfast energy came from each woman, but when I did notice something — a hesitation in speech, a shifting of stiff limbs, an attempt to shield the face from the relentless sun — I knew that my five minutes of excruciating pain each day were nothing next to this constant management of a problem, this continual dealing with discomfort or incapacity.

The elders probably did not understand before their arrests what their presence might mean to the rest of us in jail, but on the third day of our eleven long days there a crisis occurred that prompted us to call upon them, and it became clear that their contribution was essential for the cohesion of the whole group. On that day certain women made a decision, independent of the larger group, to go for arraignment. The three hundred of us had previously pledged to refuse arraignment in protest against the punitive sentences being meted out by a prejudiced judge. When these women acted against the interests of the whole group, my heart dropped; along with most other people I felt betrayed, and panic hit us. Suddenly we were in trouble, women who had been resolute and cheerful the day before becoming angry, confused and depressed. The feel of defeat was in the air.

Then someone thought to ask the elders if they would speak to us that evening. After supper, we gathered, women of all ages and backgrounds and political experience, in a giant circus tent. When everyone was there — a mob of bodies sitting, squatting, standing along the walls and at the back — four or five old women came to the front of the tent. From my place against the canvas drape of the side wall, I felt the waiting silence gather, its presence so intense that the roar of the freeway fell away. Soon the voice of a whitehaired woman in a red t-shirt and jeans filled that silence. She spoke of early labor movement struggles and how, often, just before success was to come, the strikers would feel most dejected. We must never give in to that, she cautioned. Another woman told of how she had not engaged politically with others until a few years ago, had been a staunch Republican individualist, but this threat of nuclear holocaust had brought her here with us, and she felt honored to be among us. Two more old women stood before the group, simply, unselfconsciously, to tell of the political battles of their lives and how they had managed to keep going when all seemed lost.

As they talked I could feel the mood in the tent and in myself changing. I was encouraged by these old women, I would *be them* one day, and if I could be as honest as they, as generous of myself as they were, then I could be proud to be old. A warmth, a cheerfulness began to grow in the tent. We trusted these women, we loved them for coming here with us; and in so doing we trusted each other again, began to believe once again in our collective strength.

* * *

I guess it was when I was about forty that I noticed that life is a long time. Most women over forty have lived several lives; the growing up and becoming a woman; the twenties and thirties of marriage, childraising, professional growth, searching, establishing one's lesbian identity, whatever occupied and fed us then; and the life that began when that earlier existence fell apart or drastically changed. Looking back I see that with the end of each period and begining of the next, I knew more, could dare more, and opened myself more trustingly to life. Now at this new juncture, I feel tremendous possiblity. And I know that the progress of each of our lives is not really so linear as we sometimes imagine. Elsa and Imogen, my Aunt Helen, the Cosmic Elders, the spiffy dyke with her crewcut and earrings, my 32-year-old lover, my teenage friend who has just started college: we stand not in a line reaching from the womb to the grave but in a casual group, like women at a picnic, lounging, resting after hard work, playing together, sharing our minds and bodies, living the present with all the joy and attention we can call up in ourselves.

This essay was first published in Sinster Wisdom 28 (Winter 1985)

NANCY ROBERTS

A Gift to Share

After twenty-two years of marriage, I felt like a stranger in my skin; I was emotionally empty. I'd been ignoring my feelings, year after year. Patching up a relationship in which neither of us was happy or satisfied. When I was young, I thought I could do it forever, though I knew it was a charade. Finally we were divorced. After being on "automatic pilot" all those years, I felt adrift and depressed. The four-year gay relationship I'd had before my marriage — the one that I thought I'd put out of mind — became an anchor point for me. The realization that my life was half over finally helped me accept my lesbianism.

One year later, in 1978, when I was forty-nine, I met Morgan. Morgan was real for me and our relationship deepened into love. With Morgan, all that I loved was already a part of her life: being outdoors, growing things, books, music. We spent much time in the country. Rainy mornings we'd stay in bed with books and breakfast and the cat. She played the recorder, I played the guitar. We had quarrels as well as joys, yet everything seemed to bring us closer together. In middle-age, I no longer thought that I had all the time in the world, and I valued my commitment to Morgan. Unlike my experience in marriage, autonomy was encouraged, and our separate yet complimentary work enriched our life together. In my struggle to be open and honest, I learned how strong love can be. In spite of quarrels, we were truly 'right' together.

And then came our hardest struggle. I kept a journal, and I will reproduce sections of it here for you so you can understand and share that time with me.

1/4/82: It's been raining for over 16 hours now; hard and cold, the wind bringing down branches, and I'm beginning to feel it *inside* me — cold and desperate and dark. I am fearing in my heart for Morgan and for me. So I write here the *worst* of my fearful scenarios to keep it from poisoning my mind, to keep this day *outside* me. Morgan has been having pain in her chest and trouble breathing for some time now; went to Kaiser Hospital for a check last Wednesday and ended up being there for six hours, being x-rayed, checked, etc. X-rays showed fluid in her left lung, which was drawn off, a rather large amount. They will test the fluid — let her know if it is "serious" . . . it "could be" TB (?) or pneumonia (?) or related to her cancer of seven years ago (mastectomy on that side) . . .? We must wait a week for results of tests, and of course it's hard. Morgan is tired, and I am too, and we have a quiet, restful time this weekend. A quiet New Year's start. I am glad of that, we are easy and loving with each other. I think the scare makes us both value what we *have* and we're (I am, I know) trying *not* to let fights spoil that . . . We've acknowledged the fear and put it away for a while. We both hate the *uncertainty*.

1/8/82: Series of tests on Morgan continue. Cancer evidence has been noted in the fluid drawn off the lung on the left side. Today she had a blood test and liver scan, and on the 12th she will have a bone scan. Then more can be known as to extent of the cancer and treatment procedures decided on . . . Radiation and chemotherapy have been mentioned. If there seems to be no cancer evidence in the bone, the doctors recommend Tamoxifan, until the cells become immune to the drug; then other treatments will be tried. Of course we're upset. Morgan said, "I really felt discouraged and angry when they said 'cancer'; I wanted to burst into tears..." She says this all matter-of-factly, and shows nothing outwardly of any upset. "Christian Scientist upbringing has something to be said for it," she said. "This can be viewed as a challenge." I've been anxious and fearful of unknown worsts, and for me, it helps me a lot to have straightforward talk. I have a tendency to imagine the worst, and I fear (with more intensity than necessary) that Morgan will die, that I will not be able to do anything to prevent it, that I will not know how to help Morgan in any way. Morgan says plainly that we will talk frankly, not be "obscure" with each other about our feelings, and that seems right to both of us. She laughs, "Maybe I lack the imagination to be worried!" I tell her imagination is a curse in this instance! "I've got an oversupply!" She seems strong and no-nonsense, and that's what is needed rather than the trauma-dramas *I* get into! Dearest one! *She* gives *me* courage when *she's* in the middle of a hard place!

We worry about how we can be recognized as a "couple" (!) if there should be hospital procedures. Red tape that may exclude all but "immediate family" — one's *spouse*, but not one's lover (lesbian)...(?) There are Power-of-Attorney papers we will sign for each other ... More and more I love her; she is dearer to me than I ever thought possible...

3/4/83: After work, I came home preparing to be by myself and Morgan was there! "I'm very down," she said tearfully, "I'm so tired and have no energy — and I *know* how it's going to be to be old. This is not going to change; I'm not going to get better and I have to realize that ... this is not going to go away." That strikes me to the heart — how can I answer? What comfort can I offer?

She talks of priorities, too. "I want *not* to put off what's important..." I tell her: "I know my number one priority, and that's *you*! It's what we share—" She says, "I think we must not put off making plans for how we'll live — sometimes I feel like chucking it all and going to live in a small town, a rural place. Could we do that, I wonder?"

3/30/83: Back from a lovely jaunt through the Foothill country, the landscape all clothed in vivid greens, even a clearing sky and bit of sunlight to warm us — we took our time, stopped when we pleased, and had no schedule to meet, both open to the beautiful world! I told her I felt like someone who'd been in a sensory deprivation chamber for months, and had just gotten out. Everything is wonderfully vivid and goes straight to the heart. It was a good time between us, both of us gentle with the other, teasing about some of our previous trips where we've had tremendous quarrels!

I'm aware of a different tempo. Morgan tires easily, and I can hear the breathing problem imperceptibly increase again . . . Her weight is down to 100 pounds. She is weightless in my arms when we curl up together at night. I refuse to let any of that take away from the dear sunny times we have (and the sun *is* out today!) . . . I feel as if all of my being is focused on the time we have together. Morgan seems to be in a different state — I feel her to be more trusting of me (and it touches my heart) trying to be more open to herself, to me . . . It seems to me that she is "allowing" herself to be more dependent(?) on me, there are things I can do, must do, will do — my love for her overflows, how intricately, how deeply she is woven into my being. . .

4/4/83: Stevie spent the day with Morgan and me after his overnight stay in the hospital for an ear operation. It's dear to have him — and hectic too. A five-year-old grandson can keep things moving! And I felt no time to be with/talk with Morgan. She is going to go out to a meeting at 7:30. I had dinner on for Stevie and his mom when she came to visit after work. I got a chicken and roasted it as the simplest thing to do, put potatoes in to bake for us all. Morgan is eating a special diet and is limiting herself rather severely. Broccoli is fine and we're having that . . . As usual there is a lot of hullaboo with my daughter and grandson visiting — and I felt Morgan got a bit testy with me — (ARE the potatoes in? Where's the broccoli? . . . The potatoes were in at 5:30, the broccoli ready to cook in the pan. . .) but I didn't really pick up on it until she was leaving. I see the all-too familiar expression of tightness, anger (hurt?) and I'm sorry, but removed . . . We've had too many a flap over food and I *refuse* to take *all* the responsibility for that! I hate to "wave" the food she can't have under her nose, but how am I to cook if I can't, on the one hand, fix what I'd like (guests would like) OR can't, on the other hand, fix what she would like because I don't know how?! She changes from one diet method to another and it seems I'm always out of synch with what is okay to eat, or the proper way to prepare it. . .

4/4/83: She says I don't support her when I ask about things. I know she wants to find organic, non-chemical treatments, and I cheer her for that. I admire that, and share her worry about *how* to do it — so much conflicting diet advice. I think it gets touchy between us when I ask her about treatments because she doesn't have any answers — and that's hard. It's hard when you don't know what to do.

4/14/83: How will it be for me when Morgan dies? Hard to write that. Hard to see that on paper. From the first mention of "cancer cells present" my fear was that Morgan would die; in day-to-day life however this not borne out; we/I want to believe that this recurrence will be controlled. Feels like "bad magic" to even think it . . . but that's crazy — How will it be without Morgan? Not imaginable — or rather more truly, not willingly imagined . . . Will housemates and I be able to stay in this house? Will it be sold? *Where* will I live? Oakland, my studio, somewhere . . . Could I live in this house *without* Morgan? She is in everything here, I cannot imagine the pain. We make plans for a party in July (fourth anniversary). When she's cheerful and seems "up", I am too. But then when she's down, tired, hurting, I am less optimistic . . . Right now she feels pretty good, *looks* pretty good and it is good to hope.

4/22/83: Went to therapy after exercise workout and I'm really tired. Had a lot to say last night and can't remember it today. Upset with Morgan, with myself. Feel anxiety around not getting needs met (especially sexually, and feel worse because I know Morgan's illness is partly to blame). Same old dynamic between us: I want more, she wants less. It's discouraging. Morgan says she's too fragile in body and I (must) accept that. I say to her, "Now there's a 'legitimate' reason. I hope you don't view sickness as an 'out' to be free of me pressing you sexually? She acknowledged that thought . . . and the conversation left me feeling bad: a part of loving I feel is *necessary* she sees as *pressure*.

5/8/83: An unusually good, close visit with Mother and Dad and sisters in San Jose. Mother talked about "being old"; she said it surprises her that in her head she doesn't feel old. We all say we want to feel that way too, when we get there ("old"). We admire the best in her and she is more lively and animated than I've seen her to be for some time. How good that is for us all. I came home to a weary, sun-burned but happy Morgan who had a good hard-working day with volunteers pulling water hyacinths out of the Delta Waterways . . . she says, "I would like to sleep with you out on the porch tonight, sleep, not "make love" (that I certainly knew) so I do; I like being out on the porch . . . But something is happening in me — writing this morning, I feel very sad — alone. It's not that Morgan is any different — she is as she is. I just have such a sense of loss, of emptiness. The feeling that Morgan doesn't have that warm needing, touching, caring, that I feel such a part of loving is what is hurting me so much — the feeling that she doesn't want to *share* herself with me (any more?) I feel that I'm hurt in some almost mortal (?) way.

5/11/83: Tamifoxin isn't effective any longer; Kaiser doctors are recommending chemo drugs which are painful to take and have destructive side effects. Morgan finds a new doctor; she is pleased with his program: EAT, he says, "never mind what you shouldn't" be eating. The first priority is to put weight on —

"you're not getting enough food, or utilizing what you *do* eat. *Eat* lots and rich and often! Morgan is delighted and so am I! Again, it's having someone *tell* you it's okay to do what you really *want* to — but fear to—? He's prescribing Laetrile and will monitor her weekly. We have new hopes . . . and I balance hope against worry/fear. I feel close to Morgan — she is sleeping in my bed, hugs me — I feel I can *see* ways out of our impasses and *see* how things are between us and it gives me a lot more confidence and patience. . .

5/26/83: A minor flap with Morgan tonight. We end grumpily and turn out the light on a bad note. As usual, my anger and disgust soon evaporates — (there's no need for me to be so damn insistent — Morgan is *hurting*, not knowing *what* to do. . .) and I turn back toward her saying, "It's stupid to be arguing. . ." but get no further. She says she's "not angry, just indifferent, which is worse." I feel the sting of that, and get up, take a book and go into my room to read. I really have no more "give" for this sort of thing. She wants a lot *of* me, *from* me but can give very little in return. What do I want from Morgan? I want her to know I care about her. Feeling helpless, feeling shut out is awful to me. I need to know how to take care of her. I need to know how to take care of myself. I know I must look to other friends for comfort. It's just a bad time to get through and a lot of things important to me are not being openly talked about. I feel like I have a low-grade fever, emotionally; I need something good to happen! I don't need Morgan to be so cranky with me over every little thing, even if she *is* sick. . .

7/13/83: Morgan has been feeling increasingly bad this past week and is discouraged, low in mind and, hardest for her to bear, feeling confused about the "right thing to do". . . We had a small set-to the other morning, in the same old Nancy-Morgan pattern.
    I find I'm unable to say clearly what's on my mind (death) and my indirect attempts infuriate her. She, hearing everything said as "non-support," becomes very angry. It blew up

over talking about doctors. Morgan has elected not to undergo chemotherapy. *And that's okay.* I keep telling myself: what do *I* know? It's part of *my* denial stuff to think that if she did X instead of Y, then it "would be better." She says to me, "Don't *worry.*" I ask, "How *not* to worry? What would *you* do, feel, if this was reversed?" She says, "I'd worry."

7/14/83: Dr. Smith will see her on Friday a.m. I offer to drive, but she will have none of it! "If you *don't* mind," she said, "I'd like to go by myself; you just confuse things." My concern is that she is going to Southern California in a few days, and her breath is very short... I wish she wouldn't go, but she is very determined and will not be deterred. I know she has to find out for herself what she can do — I can only watch and it's hard ... I know dying is coming and I don't know when...

7/15/83: Morgan returned from her appointment with Dr. Smith at Kaiser with a new awareness of the seriousness of her illness. She has been in such pain for weeks now that relief from that is all that can be thought of ... Dr. Smith says that 6–12 weeks of chemotherapy will show some slowing of tumor growth. Now it's the time to work hard, hands *on* — to hope that this will work. If it does not, I know I'm going to lose her ... it's been terribly in my mind for weeks now.

Maybe this is the beginning of the real fight to survive — I hope and pray she doesn't see it as a failure, having put all of her energies into nutritional, vitamin therapies, alternative methods of healing ... I asked her this. She said, "Yes, I feel 'down' about that..." I said I thought "maybe it is all part of some *larger* picture — now we only have separate pieces. In some way both chemo-drug and nutritional therapies may come together when we know what cancers are ... What you are doing is real, valid, a piece of the puzzle in some way..." It is terrible to see her so despondent. She *will* go to Southern California to see her old friend. She will not hear anything to the contrary. I'm worried that she will be so far from me. Sunday 7:00 a.m. she leaves ... 6–12 weeks: the end of August to the middle of October . . . (Dear God, let us have an *easy* winter.) Today is the anniversary of our meeting, four years ago . . . I know I'm going to lose her . . .

7/18/83: It is very hard for me to grasp that Morgan is dying. How meaningless it is to say, "we are all dying" . . . I called her in Southern California tonight and she said she's okay "tired, slept a lot . . . you're not to worry." (!) It's hard for her to talk on the phone, and her voice is very subdued, serious . . . slow . . . I'm just not able to think this is real. I'm *tired* of everyone saying how "hard" it is for me. I don't want to hear *idiots*. It's very lonely in this house without Morgan and I'm afraid that's what will happen. I can't stand the thought that she'd not ever be around, not walk into the room where I am, not hear her puttering around in her office. I don't even want to *imagine* it — and that's what my mind keeps doing, doing. Her cat Suki is hunting the house over for her, and gives me dirty looks. Suki, you will have to get used to it too. My hopes: When she comes home, she will be better. We will have *at least* another year together. I'm very tired.

7/20/83: Oakland Airport. I'm flying down to Southern California to get Morgan. She called, weak sounding, and said, "It's best if I come home" . . . and then, "It's thought best I not travel alone — I'm too wobbly — can you come get me?" I tell her I'll be on the next flight . . .

I have to keep steady and together, and be real help now in what is left. What time is left? How trivial all those quarrels over "insurmountable differences!" Differences that seem to be made of gossamer . . . She is so much to me, she has given me my *life*, a teacher of trust . . . Morgan is always with me. I write as if she's dead. I have "rehearsals" of loss in my head. I snap them off. I fear them. I can't give in to them now . . . I am just going to get her. She is not going to die today.

I have so many feelings, intimations of her dying *now*, not in the far away future. I want there to be *time* — there *is* no time anymore. There is so much yet to tell her, so much to say. I want to share some old photographs I have with her . . . I want to hear *everything* she says.

At last we're on the plane, Morgan beside me and we're going home. "It's been one of my more serious errors of judgment," she said. "I'm famous for things like that!" and she half smiled . . . She's weak, but smiling. I can't describe how good it is to *see* her, I tell her I am so glad she's coming home. It's been awful without her. . .

7/22/83: Morgan has resumed chemo treatments as a last hope. Now she is so weak and in so much pain that I know she is dying and there's nothing I can do about it. I cried a lot in therapy session this morning. I can't stand to listen to any rationales for human life, death, or any philosophizing to give comfort. The world *is* neither good nor bad; it just *is*. What conceit to think humans make any difference in the universe!

7/23/83: A hard week. Morgan is less well. We are looking for help, someone to cook and shop for food and be in the house between 10 a.m. and 3 p.m. each day. Housemate and I out working. Hard to see each step that diminishes. She, who was always up at dawn's light (often to my disappointment!) now hardly wakes at all. I've brought the comforters down and she rests on the living room couch.

Morgan asked me to get some books from the library; Sontag — *Illness as Metaphor* and Elizabeth Kubler-Ross *Death and Dying*, which I did. I sat next to her on the couch, teasing a little: "It's not *all* bad when I can sit close to my sweetie all day!" Her hand is thin in mine.

And at dinner — chicken soup which Jay made and sent over — we talked. She talked to me about death. She said, "I've found the 'five stages' one hears so much of — disbelief, anger, bargaining, resignation, acceptance—" I asked her what she felt and she said, "I have a lot of anger, I feel very angry. . ."

Now stairs are too much for Morgan to negotiate, and she is sleeping downstairs in the back bedroom. I have changed places with my housemate. She's upstairs and I'm downstairs in her space for sleeping in order to be near Morgan. It is very hard for Morgan to breathe ... a terrible thing; she's always had a horror of being smothered...

This is not a dream and I will not wake up.

Somehow I want to gather her up into me. Holding her hands in mine, I look into her eyes, trying to see, to keep her with me forever. She looks back at me (dear wide clear brown eyes), "There is a lot to learn," she says. "Let's learn it together," I say. Dear wonderful woman I love, we both know that *now* is all there is. When I go in to say goodnight, and sit a while together, she says, "I feel so close to you."

I have crazy fits of crying. Corky the dog is sleeping with me and I'm glad for her weight and warmth on the bed.

8/6/83: Dr. Smith prescribed and began Chemo treatments on Morgan on 7/15; Tamoxifen, Hydrocortisone, Aminoglutathimide. By August 3 she was not doing well at all, very weak, in pain, and "blue" about the lips. We went to the hospital again for another lung tap. They took her off the aminoglutathimide. August 4 and 5 Mary much better!!! and felt good enough to want to go out to the Marina for a bit of sun, so we did.

8/6/83: By early evening she was ready for bed, hugged me and said goodnight, and as I left the room, I said "Turn on your intercom..."

I have moved back upstairs to our sleeping porch space; it was too hard not to be in my room and so we bought the intercom so I could hear if she needed me. "I like these things!" she said. "Me too," I said, "I feel connected to you!" It's hot upstairs. I read for a while. For the first time in months, I feel sexual (!) and try making love to myself, but it's mechanical, intensity lost in tears knowing Morgan and I won't ever be making love again together ... This morning I weep and *don't want to believe it*.

8/20/83: Talked with Dr. Smith yesterday; he said Morgan must come in for IV if liquids are not being taken. I asked him about her outlook and he said statistically, 60% respond to treatment and of that, 20% have complete remissions. "That still leaves 40% unaccounted for," I said, "Of course," he adds, "she didn't begin treatment right away, so there's a problem of being run down..." I help Morgan into the bathroom, and she says, "I can't *do* this, Nancy" and she looks awful. I am in despair. I ask if she would like to stop the treatments and she says, "What else is there to do?" We see the doctor next Friday. *Monday* I'll call for home visiting nurse through Kaiser to give IV's. *Monday* I'll call Hospice again — does Kaiser insurance cover? *Monday*, it's 5 a.m. Time to get up almost. At least tears, grief have stopped. Just weariness, just ache, just tiredness.

8/21/83: Sunday morning early I went in to her and she said, "I don't think I can make it, Nancy..." and right away I called Kaiser Hospital in a panic. Dr. Smith said bring her in right away to Emergency. Slowly, slowly, carefully Morgan walked, not wanting help, to the car. She would go *dressed* (not in gown and robe) to the hospital and as best as we could, put on corduroy pants (body too swollen to close belt) and the easiest shoes (on swollen feet). I gently laced them (oh grief to see) and we got to Kaiser about 9:00 a.m., Morgan very weak and blue looking, not breathing well. Oxygen was administered through tube in nose, and IV fluids were given, and a thorocentesis again, very slowly draining the fluid, and they gave her morphine for the pain. Then it was found that a pericardial tap would also have to be done, so a Dr. B. (a woman) came and made an incision for tube in the chest cavity to drain the fluids. Much was explained to me and I learned what I knew/feared already, that Morgan was dying *now*. It was arranged that I should talk with a Hospice worker, Dr. Smith had "already placed Morgan on the list" ... Monday I will make the hospice arrangements and see that she gets full care — maybe at home with household help? Although now with pumps and tubes it looks very bleak.

Friends came, on hearing what was happening, to be company and stayed with me while the doctor worked on Morgan.

Morgan calls me to her bedside: "One thing I'm worried about — sometimes in the night I have pain and I wonder if I might be given something for it?" I assure her she can and will be given something. I ask again about calling her brother. She says, "No, I wish you wouldn't. Maybe tomorrow." I ask . . . ? She says "Maybe it's foolish, but they'd just worry and think they should visit." I try to reassure her that they will be able to handle worry.

She said, "I'm sorry I put you through all this and I said, "Morgan, I choose to be here — I *choose* you."

It is 6 p.m. The day has vanished in worry and grief, but Morgan is resting and breathing better. Finally in the evening I went home, Morgan saying, "I'm all right."

8/22/83: Early out to Kaiser and Morgan looking so wan. It's so hard to watch her emaciated body filling with fluids. She is sedated, and groggy. She can't swallow and is getting IV's. I pray for ease for her. I pray she is not hurting. She is going to die and it seems so awful. There is no easy way to die. I keep seeing her mother in my mind. I think I pray for her to come for Morgan. More friends came in and Morgan recognized them all and managed a few whispers and smiles.

I know she is going to die and I fear that too. Sitting here with all the apparatus around the bed and looking out of the window at a big sycamore tree dappled yellow-green, it's like being on a platform suspended between two places, the pause of some pendulum swing. Does one ever get used to death? Dear dearest Morgan. I don't dare allow myself to think.

She said to me once, "Sixty is the age *I* think is old! I just can't imagine myself at sixty!" She's 59; will she make it to sixty next spring? I remember when we were just beginning to know each other, when she told me of her mastectomy. I thought, "Am I coming to love this woman, only to lose her?" Not just because cancer scares everyone, but a real feeling of death, quickly dismissed.

8/23/83: Dr. Smith took me out in the hallway for a talk about

"Prolonging" (?). I asked, "What does that mean? Will she be able to read and write and talk to friends?" He didn't answer, just shook his head. Morphine will continue to be given. He said he was surprised to see how much she had "deteriorated." A friend had come and I was glad someone was there with me . . . I talked to Morgan and I know she could hear me. I said, I think, groping for words to carry my feeling, "Morgan, let's go for a walk" and she said, "Yes". I tried to speak of the woods around Lake County, the Redbud trees, the sound and scents, and she said "Stop." I did. I realized with shock those images were being *disengaged from* . . . She did not want to be touched. I said (I think), "It's okay. Go (Be?) easy." Something like that. Something like, "Your mother says it's okay to just let go." I said, "It's a hard passage." and she smiled at that. I said how much she was to me, how "right and enough" . . . "I love you," I said and she shaped, "I love you, too." with her mouth. I said, "We are going to be 'invisible' to each other again for a while. . ." So much I wanted to say, didn't know how. I was trying to *hold* her with words, trying to *be with* her. . .

After the tap, she was quite unconscious — her eyes turned away under closed lids. I talked and stayed quiet with her. Her breathing was deep and slow. I felt such a *focused* (?) feeling — all else around became non-existent. Her face became smooth and quieted and so beautiful. A transparency; all creases, wrinkles, tightnesses smoothed away; her mouth soft like a young girl. It seemed somehow good, and I could only watch. Her breath just stopped, and the pulsing vein in her neck closed, faltered, and stopped and she was gone.

5/18/84: 8 a.m. at Anna's Longbarn. *Happy Birthday Morgan!* Morgan would be sixty today, the birthday she dreaded. "I can't think of being sixty! That seems so very *old*. I just don't want to think of it!" Perhaps a knowing on some level — not the getting *old*, but the dying.

A beautiful morning! I wake to a flawless blue sky and a brilliant sun, it's going to be hot today. A fading moon low in the west. Some sparrows have nested under the eaves of the long barn, and such a commotion of birds, feeding young, chasing intruders and other would-be nest builders away!

This morning is as sweet and peaceful as last night was difficult and tear-filled. What a splendid day for a birthday! Dearest Morgan, I have nothing to give you for your birthday but my love, and that you've always had...

Thank you for this beautiful day — it is *you* giving *me* gifts! And that is very *like* Morgan!

* * *

I realize now that right after her death my own feelings of grief and despair kept me in a numb state of shock. I wonder how I ever got through those days. The same way, I guess, I'll get through the rest of my life. Just *do* it, and measure the day only against itself. As the memory of that time recedes, and though a sadness may be a permanent part of my landscape, I find it's *pain* that fades. Love remains strong, a wonderful gift of peace. Maybe at this late date in my life, I'm finally learning how to 'be' in the world. Not to fear loss and change and death, but to know it's all one with life, and I'm part of it too. It seems important to share this with you...

JUNE PATTERSON

How to Mend
a Broken Heart

I have lived most of my life outside the lesbian community. It was through taking part in a Women's Re-entry Program that I began to discover who I am and that there are others like me. I have been married, and have a son who had two mothers whom he loved equally. I am grateful to Operation Concern for the Disabled Women's program and GLOE (Gay and Lesbian Outreach to Elders), where I am now "at home." It is in these programs that I receive understanding, encouragement, and continued support through the recurring setbacks (hospitalizations, periods of confinement at home) in my struggle with chronic heart disease.

* * *

Today I danced *one whole dance* at a senior women's party! The woman didn't even ask me. I was sitting, plastered against the wall, watching the others enjoy what was formerly my favorite form of recreation. This woman stood in front of me, smiled, and held out her arms. I said to myself, "oh, what the hell," and got up on the floor. I explained, as we swayed there, that I had heart disease and that this was my first attempt at "bobbling about" to music in three years. I explained that I might not be able to finish. She was gentle and understanding. When the music stopped, I was overwhelmed with gratitude and joy. It was such a triumph!

Before today, I dwelled too often on the moment when I regained consciousness after my open-heart surgery. I would remember the sudden realization that I had survived, and I would weep. I thought it would have been so much better if I had slipped quietly into non-existence. Being alive meant I was alone and helpless. But now the time of my defeat is over. Today has opened a new door of delight.

I wish that my lover, Trudy, could have survived her time of defeat. Years ago, when Trudy discovered that she had cancer, she made sure she wouldn't endure the pain and suffering of the death that was ahead of her. I wish I'd listened more carefully when she held my face in her hands and wept, "I don't want you to suffer with me darling. I don't want you to be burdened with me." Despite my honest remonstrances that I wanted to care for her, to share her pain, she drove to the hills above our home early one Sunday morning and put a bullet through her heart. It pierced my heart, too, for it ended our eighteen years of life together. Because that life had been lived in such a deep, dark closet, Trudy's death caused me to close the door in denial of my lesbian feelings.

It took eleven years for me to begin to creep cautiously from the closet. I emerged by inches, peeking out and withdrawing; discovering at last a new and exciting freedom. I enrolled in a women's studies program at a local university, and "bravely" took a class in lesbian literature. Oh, wonderful, wonderful, coming out!

Not long afterwards, the nagging ache in my left arm suddenly became a heart attack, which led to emergency bypass surgery. I awakened from the anesthetic with the conviction that I did not want to exist any more. The doctors had saved my left leg, which had been in danger of amputation. They had saved my life. They saved everything but the "inner me" of me. I pasted a smile on my face that was impossibly dishonest. I "thank-you'd" everyone in sight for things they did and didn't do until one doctor threatened to throw me and my dishonest demeanor out the window. Of course he didn't throw me out the window, and that pasted-on smile remained on my face.

When I was released from the hospital, all was not yet well. I was disoriented, weak, and fearful. At home I kept smiling, though, even when I was alone. I was probably wearing that insipid grin on my face when someone found me unconscious on the floor two months later with scarcely a pulse. Sirens screaming, the ambulance rushed me back to the hospital. There it was discovered that I was allergic to my medication and that two of my four bypassess had occluded. I accepted the new medication better than I did the news that now my activities would be curtailed.

My lovely new lesbian life had been short but sweet. I could no longer attend classes at the college; since my heart was very weak I couldn't walk around campus, nor propel myself in a wheelchair. No more women's studies courses. Since I knew no lesbians other than those I had met in classes, the closet doors were about to swing shut once more.

When I returned to my house for the second homecoming, I found a basket of flowers on the doorstep. At first, I leaned against the front door staring at them and trying to guess who pitied me enough to send them. Curiosity led me to pick up the card. When I read the message, I knew that I hadn't lost my new life after all. The message was filled with love and courage — and told me to keep being my feisty self. It was signed by the young women of my lesbian literature class! Holding the card, and balancing the basket of flowers, I stepped into the house. This was my first hope since the operation. The card and the flowers did it! I was able to acknowledge to myself that I was an aging, disabled woman, and a lesbian. The card told me that the word "alone" would be *my* choice, not the choice of the lesbian community.

The basket of flowers sat on the coffee table long past the time when they should have been discarded. Petals dropped on the floor, and lay there till the new issues of the monthly womens' newspaper, *Plexus*, arrived. On the back page, I saw a small notice of a disabled lesbian rap group that had an opening for a new member. But the ad didn't say "aging disabled."

"Maybe I'm too old," I thought. "Perhaps heart disease is the wrong disability. I can't take rejection. Maybe I'm not lesbian enough, whatever that means." I'm laughing as I write this, but I wasn't laughing then. All these thoughts thumped around in my head as though they were coconuts, and I was shaking the tree to be sure they would hit — and hurt.

I phoned the number for the group, still expecting to be rejected for something — I didn't know what. I was prepared to peek in the door marked "disabled lesbian," then shut it quickly without entering; to reject before being rejected. But this was not the 1940's, with the isolation and lack of support that existed then for lesbians. I was interviewed by a young woman who had been disabled by polio. No, I wasn't too old; the group had been informed of my age. Heart disease was an "acceptable" disability. She smiled broadly, (how could she help it?) at the idea that I might not be "lesbian enough." She was sure I would fit into the group.

And I did fit in. My first realization was that the ageism I had feared was absent from that setting. I was not even seen as a mother figure, as I had envisioned myself. In fact, I found myself leaning on and listening to the younger disabled members. We had much to share with each other: tears, giggles, and anger at our status, or lack of it, in society.

In one of the first sessions I shared with the group my reactions to a "hulk" in a truck who parked in the handicapped space for "just a minute." With the opportunity to vent my anger in the group session, I learned to tell him to get out of my space. It was easier to try to get across the street before the WALK turned to WAIT, knowing that I had a friend who made it even though she couldn't see the sign! I even reached the moment when I could take my medication in front of other people, when it was time to take it, rather than suffer until I could swallow the pills without people seeing me.

One day I sat among my disabled friends with a very silly grin on my face and some news I wanted to share with them. I was in love! At sixty-two, with one heart problem, I now had another heart problem — Lorraine! I told the group that she had so many problems of her own that she made me forget I had any disability. Her parents didn't understand nor support her when they discovered that their daughter, newly graduated from convent school, was gay. Lorraine was everything new and wonderful in my old heart-burdened life. She needed my love and, oh, I loved her. I needed her emotional disability. Oh yes! She was twenty-two. I'm sure someone in group warned me that there might be pitfalls. Someone else cautioned me to be prepared to be a grandmother as well as a lover. But I didn't hear anyone until the forty-year age gap, and her healthy young heart, began to interfere with the health of my 62-year-old heart. Then, my tears began to flow, my energy to go, and my angina to show. I also learned that there had to be more than sexual attraction to hold Lorraine and me together, and that was all we had going for us.

About that time, Jana entered our disabled group. On her first day there she told us, tearfully, of her dilemma. She was forty, disabled by a rare disease, and couldn't cope with her young lover, who was in her twenties. Jana and I became friends. When Lorraine "found herself" (and someone else), it wasn't as bad as it would have been without Jana. Her young lover moved back east, and left the two of us with our arms around each other in sisterly affection, being upheld by women who understood. The group was such a comfortable place to be.

. . . Well, almost comfortable. It had, in fact, become a sort of disabled lesbian closet for me, until our facilitator entered one day carrying a paper. She told me, in front of all my friends, about a group called Gay and Lesbian Outreach to Elders (GLOE), made up of gays and lesbians over sixty — and they didn't have to be disabled. "Not me," I protested. I didn't want to go out there. I wanted to stay where I was: the old woman among people as impaired as I. "Please don't ask me to take this step," I pleaded.

But the group members betrayed me. They encouraged me to go to a GLOE Women's Party. At first, I was angry at the facilitator. When the group supported her, I became angry at the whole group. I looked around at their smiling faces and grew angry at myself. Then I returned to the memory of the beginning of my heart illness and I became angry at Life. The stubborn closet door wouldn't close; I was pushing on one side, but the whole world was pushing on the other side, against me.

As I walked into the room to attend that GLOE women's social event, I saw very few lesbians over sixty. They all looked very healthy. No one looked disabled. I turned and started back out the door. It was blocked by a young woman, smiling, with an outstretched hand. She introduced me to another young woman, JoAnn, who was to be my helper. I was shaking with fear when a familiar voice behind me made me wheel around and face Lynn. I had admired her for a long time. She was active in sports, and we had danced together several times. We hadn't seen each other since my heart attack. What would I say to her? Then I noticed her cane. Only a few years had passed since we had seen each other — and we were both disabled! But she looked just as beautiful as ever. "You look just as beautiful as ever," she said to me and, somehow, fear fell away. Being alive looked better than it had for a long time. There was lots to tell the group that next week. There were also lots of grateful tears and hugs.

This year, I made plans to attend my first Gay Freedom Day Parade since my bypass surgery. GLOE arranged to have a float in the parade, and I signed up to ride on that float without giving my handicap a thought. By that time, I had friends I wanted to ride with. I'd be proud, I thought; I'd laugh and we'd wave at . . . But then I considered the obstacles. How would I take my medication, riding on a float? Without it the pain would incapacitate me. And since I was no longer steady on my feet, the crowds might jostle me until I fell over. I phoned JoAnn and told her my problems and that I wouldn't be able to participate. I explained to the group of disabled women that I was there again in my familiar pattern: pulling back, tired of trying. Aging, disabled lesbian. Jill, our co-facilitator smiled that all-knowing smile. She was on the parade committee, in charge of the Disabled-Aging section. JoAnn and Eddie, young women from GLOE, would meet me after the parade and see that I got back to public transportation safely. There *was* a place for me at the parade. How was that for an answer?

I attended the Gay Pride parade — as a disabled, aging, *cared for* dyke! The gay community needed me to scream as each contingent went by! I cheered, I waved, I laughed and cried, and that's what I was doing when JoAnn and Eddie came to pick me up. Instead of only accompanying me to the public transportation, they boarded with me, and we all held hands and chattered about everything that had transpired. At the end of the line, we held each other in a three-way hug, kissed each other, and waved until we couldn't see each other anymore. I was GLOEING with happiness.

* * *

When I started to dance today, I felt no pull of death, nor fear of the chest pains. I felt all the things I have written here. I felt the life, the love of the lesbian community. There is a women's newspaper to which I can turn to find the group(s) where I belong. I can purchase that newspaper at a women's bookstore, or subscribe to it, openly. There are disabled rap groups, groups for aging lesbians. There are places where we can network, to help each other. We fight together for our place in the sunshine.

Young gerontologists are reaching out to the aged. Today there is a National Association of Lesbian and Gay Gerontologists. More and more urban areas are realizing the importance of organizations for aging gays and lesbians.

But perhaps my words sound too optimistic. There are still lesbians from the 1940's aging in closets in the 1980's. There are still women-identified women crying alone with their disabilities and dying alone of their fatal diseases. How does the community reach out to them? How can they reach out to the community? It was so impossible for Trudy and me, long ago.

I don't have many answers. I only know I am grateful for the help I have received. Perhaps now I can pass on that help to other "old and heart-weary" dykes.

DR. EILEEN

A Charmed
and Lucky Life

My first gay encounter was in medical school in 1941. After
that I never really questioned that I was gay. I had never felt attracted to men nor they to me. Being "unpopular" with men
was not something to which I gave much thought. The reality
was that being gay created for me, for the first time, a community — a place where I could actually belong.

For the rest of the world it might have been a sub-culture,
but my experience was that it gave me an identity, a self-iden-
tity and for the first time a community identity. This was
much different from my growing up. My father worked in
China. I was sent to a missionary school in Korea. I was one of
the few at the school who wasn't a child of a missionary. I
returned to China but at the end of 1940 the American government requested that all American women and children leave
that country. When I arrived in the United States they came on
board ship and took our passports. I arrived in New York an
American, but with no sense of belonging; I was still an outsider. But with my first gay encounter I met people who were
like me. It was something I had never felt.

And then I met Ann. I had actually met her many years
before in Korea when I was twelve years old and she was six-

teen. When I "found" her in New York it completed my sense of having found a home community. In those days the gay community was much different than it is today. It was a large community that was almost entirely closeted to the outside world. We were not openly gay — it didn't seem like an option to us. I think we all felt that it would be a mistake to "broadcast" that we were gay. I don't remember ever talking to anyone in those years about being gay — not to gay friends and certainly not to straight acquaintances. But we did have a gay identity.

In those days, during the fifties and sixties, there were large parties. Because I was a doctor I met many different and interesting gay people in my practice. Ann and I would get invited to dinner parties or Halloween parties. There would be fifty gay men and women. It seemed fantastic to us. Everyone would dance and drink — we drank a great deal. They were wonderful parties where we could be ourselves. People were vital; you could see they were involved in the world. We were informed and concerned about the world as a group, though we weren't too involved in politics.

Even though we were closeted, I felt support from my community. Gay men and women came to see me as a doctor, and I got many referrals from the people I met at parties. I felt like I was serving "my community."

Ann and I also had an identity together, a world we created for ourselves. Because Ann was a nurse, we had a great deal to share. After medical school Ann and I decided to open a practice. We worked side by side after it opened in 1955 on. In our practice we were never openly a couple — not many non-gays knew that Ann lived with me. But even though no one talked about being gay, I know they knew, because they sent me gay patients. I never felt comfortable talking about being gay, yet I was comfortable with being gay.

I was proud of Ann. She was the kind of person everyone liked, warm and outgoing. She was generous to everyone she met. She truly loved people and was always trying to find ways to help people who needed help. She shared many things with me: her love of art, music and literature. We loved to go skiing together. We met most of our friends in a lesbian investment club. (That club is not operating anymore but it was an example of how gay people used such organizations for social and personal support.) With Ann I had a family.

Our community was very present when Ann got sick. She smoked, and in 1976 she lost a lung to cancer. Eight months later she had a convulsion and became paralyzed. Toward the end, it became worse and she could speak only every once in a while. I knew she understood me, and was aware of me but she was not able to talk much in those last weeks. It was then that our gay friends stood by us; they came right to the end and took care of Ann and me. They gave us 24-hour care.

Ann died in 1977; we had shared thirty years together. I spent most of the next two years crying. It seemed like I could not stop. I was shattered. Everything I counted on was Ann. My grief was total. I had a hard time continuing my life, and even my work became a burden. I almost couldn't work, I often cried between patients. My work has always been important to me, so it helped pull me through this period of grieving. It gave me a way to keep going.

I was sixty when Ann died. I didn't feel my own aging until I was 65. I began to feel, "God, I *am* old. I'm a senior citizen." My hearing got worse, my joints ached more. I had a lot of patients calling in about that time asking, "How old *is* the doctor?" Some of them came in and they wanted a doctor that was going to be staying in practice another ten or fifteen years. I began to realize that I had to face the fact that people weren't going to come to me because I'm old.

The type of practice I've had, my patients got old with me, so now it is more of a geriatric type practice. I gave up OB's; I didn't have any more babies. I began to realize that I was feeling the wear and tear of being sixty-five, even though I never thought I was getting old. I don't think you ever *do* really. One time when my mother was 78 she was telling me about a party. She said, "You should have seen all those old people there!" Then she laughed. The only reason she felt old was that she couldn't do all the things she did before. But with the mind functioning, you don't realize it — you don't put yourself in somebody else's place looking at you.

Lately I've been thinking about retiring. I think, "Well, my dad died when he was 78; that gives me eleven more years. Why should I sit here and worry about not making it? I might as well stop and do some of the things I'd like to do and spend the money I've saved. I've no one to save it for." I think it's time to stop and use the money I've earned. I actually would have liked to practice for another three years. It somehow had seemed appropriate to stop when I was sixty-nine! Actually I had always sort of thought I'd just practice till I dropped dead. But the climate of the practice of medicine has so changed now. The workload has gone down and the cost of insurance had almost doubled. I don't feel like I have to stick with the notion of working until I drop dead. Besides now I feel like there are others to take my place, other women to serve my patients. I am not needed in the same crucial way. I'm sort of glad; I feel like I want to spend time doing things I've postponed or not done as often as I would have liked — like visit the museums, walking and biking in the parks. I may join a gay retirement group that a friend of mine belongs to. They are mostly professionals who get together every month or so and help each other out . . . If someone has a fence down, they all meet and bring their tools.

But I am apprehensive about retiring because my new lover is twenty years younger than me. (I am only a little younger than her mother was . . . a few weeks.) We met in my office. She's an ex-patient of mine. I've tried to make my age an issue between us, but she won't let me. I think I am worried about what I will do with myself during the day when she's off at work. Knowing her, having this relationship, has made my life worth living again.

We seem about equal on wanting sex. We have a pretty reciprocal relationship. It's different when you start together and earn your money together as Ann and I did. Everything we owned was mutual; we didn't think, "Who bought this? Who bought that?" It was different when I moved into my new lover's house. She's used to splitting the cost of each thing. But it works out fine. It took a little getting used to — it used to be whatever needed buying, we bought. I'll just go buy things and then when she gets to dividing up the accounts, I've lost the slips. I've got to remember to keep them.

I probably have some regrets about my life . . . but I'd do it all over again. I'd go into medicine, I'd certainly pick Ann. I don't know if I'd stay as a GP — maybe I should have gone into one of the specialties. I probably regret being harsh with people sometimes — patients and friends.

Now when I walk down the street, I usually smile at people because I figure it's nicer than not saying or doing anything and they just go right by you and never see you. You're just not there when you're older. Your own age group almost always smiles at you.

I realize there's a whole new community of gays and lesbians out there, but I don't think about it much or what they do. Maybe I should look into it, but it's just not my style to join things. I've never been involved with the gay movement or the women's movement.

As a younger gay woman, I did not conceptualize my growing older. I just started and ran my life the way it seemed right for me to run it and it went its course. The fact that I was going to grow old didn't hit me at all until I got there because I don't feel any different; I still have my friends. I think it would be hard if I was in a social climate in which looks and bodies are very important . . . because I know they're going to go. For people who go to gay bars now . . . pretty soon, you'll be going and nobody's going to look at you. That can be hard. The physical is so important there. But I believe if the mind is what's important, you have no problem . . . because that's going to grow.

At sixty-seven, I'm not sure that I have the perspective yet on what it's like to get older. I have to get into retirement to find out about that. That's where my own resources come up. I think, though, that as you grow older, you don't feel any different than when you first started, except that you mellow, you learn more about coping and how to get along with people whether they're gay or not. I feel I've had a charmed and lucky life.

MARJORY NELSON

Flowersong

I bought flowers for my mother today, big bunches of chrysan-
themums, with double rows of long bright petals, golden as
the sun, and green and yellow centers, soft as moss and grassy
hills. The flowers are a symbol. On the eve of my 56th birthday, the flowers are a gesture to my mother that my lifelong
battle with her is finally over.

A life time is too many days, too many hours for so much
animosity, so much shutting down of love. I have deep crusty
scars and tender wounds that weep with touching.

I can't blame her for the interminability of our estrangement. She's been dead for years. With persistence and ingenuity
I have kept my resentments simmering and stewing, without
any help from her at all!

The pathetic part of this is that I didn't even realize what
was going on. Because Mother was dead I thought that I had
finished with her. I didn't think of myself as angry with her. I
simply didn't think about her. Because I have created a lifestyle
that is very different from hers, one that she disapproved of,
I had pretty much discounted her influence in my present life.

Because it had been she who had taught me so many
destructive myths about women, lesbians, and life in general, I
had come to see her way of thinking as a threat to my exist-

ence. In discounting these values, I negated all the positive aspects of her life.

But as I grow older, and particularly since I've been disabled, more and more I see my mother in myself. I see her in my fat aging body, in my gestures and, most especially, I see her in the ageism I experience from younger women. Their behavior toward me is so similar to the ways I treated my mother.

Lately my life has been so difficult, I've been thinking and writing about death. Mother has showed up all over the place, grabbing my pencil, crossing out words, knocking down my elaborate constructions like the walls of a sand castle. I don't mean I actually see her, or hear her voice. It's just that she has been everywhere demanding my attention, my thoughts. Clearly, I will not be able to come to any terms with death until first I come to terms with my mother. Perhaps it is the other way around: that I cannot come to terms with my mother until I come to terms with death. I'm not sure, but the connection is powerful.

Like most people in my culture, I learned to see death primarily in personal terms and to be terrified of it. We kids used to sneak up into the attic where Mother had hidden the illustrated copy of Dante's *Inferno*. Of course we found it. We poured over the pictures of bodies burning in hell, souls chained eternally to horrible fates. We did our best to scare each other with tales of ghosts with cold clammy hands popping out of dark corners, of ghouls who tried to steal our bodies.

When someone we knew — a playmate, or a schoolmate — died, we were "protected" from the experience and excluded from all the rituals. Needless to say, this kind of "protection," like the hidden book in the attic, only exacerbated our fears. When I screamed my terror of death into the night, my mother would laugh, "Nonsense. You have nothing to fear. You are young." Or she would tell me that I had "too much imagination."

If it was a grandparent who died, or any old person in the family or neighborhood, we'd hear that "Miss Baldwin died *because* she was old," as if to imply that old people *should* die, that no one young dies.

Ageism is the shroud our culture wraps around death, making it impossible for people even to acknowledge their fears, much less examine them. Ageism obscures our life-long affair with death, creating a false sense of security around life. Under the surface, most of us know how tenuous that security is. We know it is a lie, but we don't want to look at it. Ageism intensifies the line between life and death, creating the illusion that the newborn child has achieved a status outside of death. An ageist culture defines the infant as a blank mind to be imprinted in ways strictly age-graded as she beings to grow. From this perspective, death waits only at the end of long life, very far away, unseen, unthinkable.

There is general agreement among people in this culture that old women should die. Ageism says to old women, "Step aside now, you have lived your life. Step aside and make room for the young." We see death as acceptable for old women because we don't take them seriously. It is part of our ageism and part of our denial around death. We do not see how their lives might be connected to our own. Their deaths are as meaningless to us as their lives.

The reality is that life can end at any age. When I was 32, severe illness and a rapidly growing tumor on my throat diagnosed as cancerous forced me to look directly at death. For three awful months until the illness subsided and the surgeon could operate on the tumor, I lay in bed terrified, watching those closest to me back off, out of their own fears. Feeling my own life choke away out of my control. Nightmares found me suffocating in closed coffins.

My mother came to stay with us to run the household. She told me not to be so morbid, to think only of the husband and children who loved and needed me. I thought she was cruel, heartless, even stupid in her refusal to give credence to my fears.

The tumor was benign, my recovery from illness slow, but the experience turned my life around. I vowed that never again would I be so helpless before death. I began to look directly for the source of all my fear and found a mountain of illusion that was so tremendous I couldn't see the top. Directly blocking my path were all the myths about women. Step by step I started climbing. There was no path, only steep cliffs — a mudslide here and there, an avalanche or two, wildly swaying bridges over roaring streams that sometimes pulled me down and under. That was 1960. The quest led me out of the bourgeois world, away from those institutions that I'd found so oppressive — the nuclear family, church, academia — into radical politics and the arms of women. The quest led me away from my mother. And somewhere along the way, I lost my fear of death.

My mother suddenly appears vigorously shaking the leaf on my poinsettia plant. My struggle for authenticity is not over, she warns. There is something about being an old woman, something about dying that she has to teach me.

The thought is shocking. I have identified my mother with all the cultural oppression I wanted to flee. What could she possibly have to say to me?

I think about the way she died, so quietly. Cancer ate her guts away. There were two grueling operations, days of pure agony, months of chemo-therapy when her skin turned yellow and cracked and her mouth tasted like a burned-out motor, and then more pain and constant nausea. Yet never did I hear a whimper or a word of self-pity. I thought that was because she was just trying to ignore what was happening to her — to pretend it wasn't there. I made jokes to my friends about how she was dying the way she lived — as a lady. And you can be sure of the sneer in the enunciation of the word, "lady." (A "liberated" feminist, I called myself *woman* and rejected "lady" as a bourgeois affectation.)

It never occurred to me that Mother's way of dying was important to her sense of who *she* was, to what she called "character." In all these years I never stopped to think about the fact that it took immense courage for her to transcend her fear and all the pain and die in so much dignity and peace.

I sat with her and watched her die. I had not known that death could be so quiet, like the gentle falling of a leaf. Filled with my childhood images of violence and horror, I sat and waited for some cataclysm to occur, but all there was was stillness. On one corner of her lip a few flecks of foam gathered which I wiped away, blotting gently (as she'd taught me years before) with a lace handkerchief I found in her bedside table.

She'd arranged with her doctor to have no extraordinary measures, no tubes, no heroics, few if any drugs. She controlled her death completely.

In my early days as a feminist, I used to believe that this kind of quietness in the face of adversity signified assent to oppression, and consequent denial that the oppression exists. As I began to understand my life in political terms, it seemed that my mother's attitude was a "cop out." I would scream at injustice and hurl my pain back at my oppressor. Other women seemed to believe similarly. We all got very busy defining the ways in which we had been victimized and organizing to change the situation. It was important work and still is. But something is still missing.

Feminism has encouraged women to seek out the political dimensions of personal life. This subjective approach has brought us great insights into how power works. It shows the extent to which our lives are manipulated by those who oppress us. But there is a trap here. If we focus on how we are victimized, it's very easy to slip into the perspective of seeing ourselves only as victims, and to fall into the habit of blaming everyone else for what goes wrong in our lives. The prime scapegoat in this endeavor is Mother.

The room fills again with Mother's presence and the memory of her saying to me, "Just wait till *you're* old and sick and then you'll understand." The words were a disguised way of saying, "You stupid person, you think you are so smart, but you don't understand my situation at all. However, *someday* you will. Someday you will be old and sick — in pain. You will feel isolated from younger women who ignore you, discount your work, and you will remember me. And you will be sorry for the way you've treated me."

And she was right. I do remember her. For now it is I who am getting old and sick and disabled — and now I am surrounded by younger feminist women, lesbians, who have the same mentality toward me I had toward my mother. They do not want to hear about my pain. I feel them separate themselves from me, as though my weakness might contaminate them. And now I also understand how I was under the illusion that if I drove myself night and day, if I moved into the fast lane, I would prove my strength and *that* would prove my superiority to my mother. My strength would prove that no longer would I be prey to the traditional oppression I'd experienced as a child and young woman.

Such an illusion and such a destructive way to build a movement.

This fear of weakness grows out of our victim mentality. When someone is talking about severe illness, crippling disabilities, and death, it is very easy to switch into the victim mode. We do not know that we *can* act. We feel so helpless, and we see the person so afflicted as helpless, too. We close our ears to try to escape our own impotence. Wanting to think of ourselves as women who act, people who care, we grow angry with the person who shatters these illusions about ourselves.

Yet that is the essence of death, which not only threatens the loss of our physical bodies, but the destruction of all our illusions about ourselves. That can be terrifying. Death tears to shreds our fancies and our fantasies, bringing a consciousness of what and who we have lost, a sharp awareness of what and who we are. It takes great courage to face the awe-filled fact that we who live are stuck with the world that is here, with our own struggles, our own imperfections, and somehow to transcend our victimization. It occurs to me that this is what my mother meant by "having character."

I have daughters now who are adult, who are as ambivalent with me as I was with my mother. They make their paths away from me to find their strength and I struggle to acknowledge that my primary experience with them is of missing them, and not even being able to say that to them without somehow making them feel guilty, angry, or impatient with me. If I try to tell them of my pain, my fears about my weakness, I feel them pull away.

We all fool ourselves saying, "Yes. We want to hear." But when the telling starts, what cues do we give with our bodies, our sighs, the interruptions that say, most dramatically, "STOP!"

I believed that I encouraged my mother to talk about what was happening, but now I suspect that I also let her know in many ways, subtle or not so subtle, that I didn't really want to hear the difficult parts. No wonder she learned how to shine things on, to say, "Don't be morbid." If she thought that things go more easily if you don't look at the negative side, perhaps she felt less vulnerable that way. I'm sure that she *was* less vulnerable. How many jokes are there about complaining old women? Women who talk you to death? Such jokes are designed to shut the mouths of old women. The political strategy of speaking our pain and bitterness only makes sense if someone is listening.

Before she died, my mother asked me to promise that her body would be cremated instantly. She didn't want people standing and staring at her, making comments or jokes about her fat, or anything else. There was no fat liberation then, no one to tell her that her soft plushy body was beautiful and precious. No one came forward to stroke her softly, hold her, kiss her sweetly on her breasts. Certainly not me.

Mother's dying was so quiet that I sat by her side and wondered how I'd know that she was gone. And then an abrupt shock like an electric current touched my body and brought me to my feet. There was no doubt that it was her, leaving her body. And then the room filled with a profound silence, a thick sense of absence. I touched my lips to her forehead and then went to call the mortician to arrange for an immediate cremation.

I interpreted that shock to be an affirmation of my life and my new lifestyle, but it never occurred to me then to see that it was an expression of *her* life, her courage, her strength.

It takes great courage to live as an old woman in our society, and to die with dignity and self-respect intact. We expect old women to die; with few exceptions, we do not even expect that we shall miss them. In the same way, we expect those who are sick and disabled to get out of our way, out of our sight. I'm ashamed to admit that I believed that my mother's death would give me greater freedom to live my life as a feminist and a lesbian. I sat and watched her die and felt no great emotion. After all, I excused myself, wasn't she old and sick? Didn't she have cancer? Hadn't my father's death eight years earlier left her broken-hearted and depressed? (The implication being that if she had struggled to liberate herself from him, she would not have felt so much pain.) No, I didn't cry when she died. I was too "tough" and much too arrogant to be able to mourn the loss of one sick, old woman.

It only recently occurred to me that the way she lived her dying transcended all of her weakness, all of her depression, and certainly all of the traditional values which I had so despised. Her dying was completely her own. Refusing to become a victim of her circumstances, she did what she could to maintain her control of her life, even after she had drawn her last breath. Who of us can say we have done more?

My lover strokes my body and tells me that I'm beautiful, and I can see it in her eyes and feel it in her finger tips.

A new emotion touches me, and I am wrapped in sadness, all the anger gone. I am sad that Mother didn't know the woman whom I love now, or any of my friends. I think they would have liked each other, and the thought itself is startling. For so many years *I* needed to see them in opposition to each other. And now that notion only seems absurd. It occurs to me that more than anything else, I miss my mother. And now I can cry for her, for me, for all of the stupidity and arrogance we lay upon each other and ourselves.

No matter who it is who goes away — to die, to live across

the continent — we harden our hearts and that is all we do. Who understands before it is too late that our lives have been richer because of the fact that we have known each other? Life gives us relationships that need constant healing and attending, and death catches us short, in a state of being unfinished, imperfect, confused, and always on the edge of something. Feeling secure about life and death means trying to understand and accept the unfinished areas in every relationship and to heal those broken parts of ourselves. No matter how old the body is, regardless of how sick or how disabled, the self who lives there is always struggling to grow. I discounted that in my mother.

I bought flowers for my mother today. And on my way home I felt something stir in me in a place so deep, so lost, and so forbidden that I had thought that it had died; a part of me that was so hurt that I had tried to stamp it out like some dread disease.

I set the flowers by my desk, a reminder to me that strength is found in many ways, but particularly in the struggle to transcend the oppressive circumstances of daily life. The flowers recall my mother's victory over her own depression, her triumph over pain and fear and isolation. The flowers are to give me courage to live in this aging body and this imperfect world, even as I may continue to struggle to change it.

WILMA AND ROBERTA
Not Always
a Bed of Roses

Roberta: I remember how I first met Wilma. It was in 1949; we were stationed in Germany. She walked into the mess hall with this other girl. I thought, 'Boy, I bet she's a bitch to work with.'

Wilma: I was in my room later on that same day and Roberta came in. I hadn't gotten my trunk so I didn't have any dresser scarves and she said, "I have some extra ones, I'll bring them down." I thought that was pretty nice, that someone would offer me some dresser scarves. So she got two and gave them to me. That's how we started running around together. We became lovers — I'd go up to her room or she'd come down to my room at night. We'd take our leaves together.

R: It was very risky, two women in the service being lovers. I'm the more cautious type. She kind of liked the risk.

W: I can't honestly say whether anyone suspected anything of us or not. I don't think they did because that was too foreign to them in that day.
  I'm the one that was always doing things that might be

pretty bad if you got caught at it. But I didn't really think about getting court-martialed at that time. Did you?

R: Of course I thought about it. I hate getting caught. Morally speaking I'm not much better than anybody else, but I do hate getting caught.

W: I'd gotten out of the service before and lived with this other girl for a year. Even then, it never occurred to me that I'd get caught. But I'm the one that came closest to getting kicked out of the service for it. That was later.

R: I came home because of alcoholism in '51. They gave me a diagnosis of "Anxiety Reaction" but it was my drinking catching up on me. They put me on reassignment in '52 but I didn't quit drinking right then, I can tell you that. I spent some time at a military hospital in the psychiatric section and when I went back, I knew they were breathing down my neck with a court martial. I was offered the alternative of resigning so I took it. That's not dishonorable, but it sure isn't honorable either. I had a hard time with that for a while. In the first place, there were so many of them in the service that drank as much as I did and got by. I was in the wrong place at the wrong time. So I didn't think I was an alcoholic — I thought I got stuck in a bad situation. I knew I was going to do something about my drinking but it was always tomorrow — never today.

I continued to drink until 1954. I was living with my brother and his wife and children. My brother called our family physician about my drinking; the doctor said, "I can't do a thing for her but I have a friend who's running an outfit called AA." And so a woman from AA came out to see me — which is unusual, because we don't normally make third party calls in AA; the alcoholic has to take the initiative. I knew I had to get these people off my back so I went to the meetings.

I was impressed with the meetings and I felt comfortable in them. But I didn't do the first step; we have a first step in AA where we admit that we are powerless over alcohol and that our lives have become unmanageable. I could see that I was powerless over alcohol but I would never have conceived of my life as unmanageable. I thought I could manage my life just fine.

I was dry for ten months. At the end of ten months I decided that I'd go back to social drinking. That was a mistake because I never drank socially in my life. On my job, I was working for a fellow that was in AA and when he saw that I was drinking again, he saw to it that I got to a drying out place. And it was there that I saw a psychiatrist who asked if I wanted to talk to him about my sexuality. I did and his comment was, "It's neither wrong nor right. There's no wrong or right to it. It's whatever you're comfortable with."

That was the first time I'd spoken to a professional person about my sexual orientation. It had a real impact. I didn't feel guilty, but I did feel it wasn't normal. I said to him, "I under-stand that I probably have two choices — to continue doing as I am or sublimate." He said, "Yes, that's true. Whatever you're more comfortable with. Do you feel that you're doing wrong?" I said no. He said, "Well, it's your feeling about it that's impor-tant." It really made me feel better to hear that. I thought, 'I'm not doing anything wrong in my own life; if society doesn't accept it then I have to live with that aspect of it. I might be in the closet but I don't have to feel guilty about it.' Up until that time I'd never heard anybody say anything about it.

W: I'd never heard anything about it either. I'd read *The Well of Loneliness*. You just didn't hear anything. I heard one thing about homosexuality when I was in high school. My mother was a dressmaker. One evening we were over at the house of this lady who she sewed for. The woman brought out a picture of her daughter; she was with another girl and she was dressed in sort of a butch way (I didn't know that terminology then); she had slacks on and nobody wore slacks in those days. My sister, who was ten years older than me, later said, "Oh, that's that queer daughter of hers." I didn't even know what she meant. I had no idea what she meant about that "queer daughter."

R: But we both felt, when we realized that we were gay, that we were abnormal. It wasn't the socially accepted thing to be.

W: You just knew that there was something wrong with you.

R: I left Wilma behind when I left the service. Although we corresponded, Wilma was mad at me because I had left the service. I missed her like hell. I was in Georgia and she was still in the service. I wasn't holding a job long enough to make enough money to go anywhere — because of my drinking. By 1956, she was having some trouble with the gal she was living with. I was jealous, but I could understand it. I wasn't there and might not ever be there as far as I could tell. I knew I wasn't there because I was drinking.

W: But if she'd been sober, she wouldn't have been there. See, we were in the service. We knew in Europe that we would be separated eventually. We knew that I would be sent one place and she would probably be sent to another. The chances of our being sent to the same place were remote. We didn't know that we were ever going to live together. We had made no plans to live together; there was never that commitment. I had another eleven years; she had another fifteen years before we could retire. And at that time, I thought it might be longer than that. So we hadn't made any commitment of any kind. She had gone to Europe before me. On the normal rotation, she would have come home before me. But she got in trouble.

I drank, too. But I never knew I was an alcoholic until the day I called AA. I was in all kinds of trouble, too. But I always blamed it on the other person. I never accepted that I had a problem with alcoholism. So I never saw her problem either. We drank together in the service. We had a good time together. My advice to her was, "Just don't drink where they can see you. Get away." And that's exactly what I did. I came back to Los Angeles; I had a sister living there. And I'd drink at my sister's or in the city of Los Angeles, but not where they could catch you.

I was sent home in '52 also. It was alcoholism, but they called it "dementia melancholia". I'm no psychiatric nurse — I had to look that up. Then I got so mad I could have killed them because I was thirty-eight and dementia melancholia is a disease of senility. I thought, 'Well, you damn idiots.' I had the D.T.'s; it was pure and simple alcoholism. But they tried to be nice to me because an alcoholic diagnosis would have gotten me kicked out of the service.

I was lonely when I came up here to the military hospital. I was missing Roberta a lot. So I met this gal that was a patient on my ward. She was a WAC and I was an officer, which was forbidden to begin with. She got out of the service shortly thereafter. But God, what a mess that turned out to be. Anyway, we lived in an apartment right next door here. I got off the post and she'd gotten out of the service and with this money that she was going to inherit and the $875 I had in the bank, we bought this land and contracted to have this house built. But after we moved in, the contractor's wife called and said he was going to place a lien on my salary. I said, "What for?" She said, "Well, he didn't get that check from you." This gal had taken the check . . . Then things started coming to light. She wasn't working. I couldn't get her to move. I don't know how you put people out of the house that won't move.

So one night we were sitting there and here comes a knock on the door and the sheriff's standing there. And he says, "Are you Wilma Jaget? We'd like to talk to you down at the sheriff's office." I thought, 'My God, what in the hell is this about?' I hadn't done anything that I knew of that would involve a sheriff. When I got down there they said, "Have you been up to Forestville lately?" And I said no. And they said, "Well, you were up there a week ago." And I said, "No, I wasn't." It turned out that she had taken the car, dropped me off at work, and gone to Forestville and cashed a hot check with my name.

There were three checks she had cashed. I told them the truth and I never saw her again.

But two days later, I got a call from the CID — the Criminal Investigation Department of the Service. I knew that my military career was in jeopardy at this point because the police were going to report to the hospital that I was involved with somebody who had been cashing bad checks. I'd seen the CID railroad blacks out of the service; I'd seen them operate. So I went over to see them. They asked me a few questions about her and I said, "Yes, I knew her." And they asked me to take a lie detector test and I said, "Sure, I'll take the test." But I was worried that my being gay would come out. So I went to the chaplain and talked to him and he said, "Are you homosexual?" I said, "No, I'm not." And he said, "Well, if you are, then your sin will come out anyway."

When I went back there that day to take the test, I gave them my name, where I was born, the day I was born, and my rank. Every question they asked me after that I said, "My name is Wilma T. Jaget, 2121." I did that for one hour and a half — every question they put to me. I answered them with my name, rank and serial number. I figured if I answered one single question, I was in trouble. They said, "You know the Senior Officer will see this report." I said, "I'm aware of that." And they said, "Now, if she tries to blackmail you, be sure and let us know." I said, "What is she going to blackmail me for?"

So two days later, I'm walking down the hall at the hospital and the Senior Officer walks down the hall and says, "Well if it isn't Wilma T. Jaget, 2121." I said, "Yes, it is." And that was the last I ever heard of it. But there was no one I could go to. I dealt with it all alone.

After that gal got me into all that trouble, I decided that I wasn't going to take chances. I only knew one person that I'd take a chance on and that was Roberta. So I flew back to Atlanta in March. I wanted to see if I could get her to come out here. We talked about our drinking — I was still drinking and Roberta had stopped. She said, "This isn't going to be very mature of me if I go out there." And I said, "Let's take a chance on your maturity."

R: The story of my life!

W: So then she agreed to come to California. But before she got out here in June, I got into a driving accident. I came around a corner and hit a car. I was stoned, absolutely out of my mind. The police came and I blamed my little dog, said she jumped on me as I made the turn. But I was cited; I had to appear before a judge in August, soon after Roberta was out here.

That's when I called AA. It was going out to get Roberta and seeing her sober. That was a great influence on me. But I didn't understand it at the time. I couldn't understand why she was so damn happy and she wasn't making any money and living in a boarding house. And here I was — I had a car, my career, and the bank and I owned this house . . . And I was miserable. I was contemplating suicide very seriously. It was partially my drinking, and partially what I had been through with this woman and then with the military. The day of the hit and run, I went to the cupboard and got out this full bottle of Scotch. I was a Scotch drinker. Every time something happened to me that I didn't like, I just said, "Well, I'll show them. I'll just get drunk." And I always got drunk, too. When I got the bottle down, I opened it up and smelled it. I just smelled it and I thought, 'Well, you damn fool, you can't drink.' I called Roberta first. In Atlanta. I asked her if anybody out here would help me the way they helped her or would they think I was crazy. And she said, "Well, they'll know you're crazy and they'll help."

That was the end of May and she came out on the sixteenth of June. So I had only a couple of weeks in between to get on a program.

So our commitment didn't start in the military; it started in 1956 when she came out here and we were both sober. It was wonderful being sober together. In the service we'd gotten into some physical fights with each other when we'd been drunk. I don't know what Roberta thought, but I knew that somewhere I was thinking that those fights were all drink oriented.

It's only been in the last few years that I've reflected way back on my own life and realized that I've always been gay. In the eighth grade I fell in love with a teacher. I knew at the time that I thought a lot of her and I saved up money to give her a Christmas gift. I knew that I was probably in love with a girl in training and another one in the military. But you didn't hear about it, you didn't know about it. I don't know if my drinking had anything to do with how I felt about being gay. Maybe yes. Maybe no.

R: I never associated my drinking with being gay. But I had had two relationships before I went into the service. I didn't think my life would change that much if I stopped drinking; AA tells you that you have to make 180 degree turn in your life which is true as far as the physical aspects of drinking and to some extent in your thinking. But the program gives a wide latitude to individuals; they say, you can tell a drunk, but you don't tell him much. You cannot say to somebody, "You got to quit drinking. You've got to do it this way." You cannot tell anybody that. If they'd done that to me, I wouldn't have been in AA.

W: We wouldn't have each other without AA.

R: AA made all the difference in the world. Sobriety gave me my life back.

W: We have friends over here that are gay that we have known since 1964 — twenty-one years. It was only about seven years ago that it came out that any one of us was gay. Yet all of us felt that the others were.

R: But we never said anything, we never talked about it. When we first started going to AA here, we never wore slacks there or anything like that. There were no other gay women in AA. We were very careful not to let anyone know that we were sexual, but we always went together. We let it be known that we lived together. But women historically have lived together.

W: Women can get away with a lot more than men can.

R: But it was fifteen years before any of us said anything to the other.

W: It came up in a very strange way. Marge gave a birthday party for Elly. She took us all to dinner at a gay bar, Tuxedo Junction. And Elly said, "I hope we're not shocking you." And I said, "No not exactly." It was the first we knew. It never came up that they were gay. We've never discussed it since. We didn't have any gay friends before them. They did. They were our first gay friends, but we didn't know it. We never talked about it. There was no community the way there is now.

R: I still don't have that sense of community.

W: We have it a little bit. There's two girls that live across the street and they're gay. They're probably the first ones we met where we met them openly and acknowledged that we were gay and that they were gay. They're in their early forties. We went to a tea dance with them. Nobody initiated telling; it was just there from the start.

R: I see no long-term commitments in the community today. I see more promiscuity. What do they call it? . . . cruising. Gay meetings in AA dwell too much on their gayness. I don't dwell on my gayness.

W: One thing that's lovely about this community is that I like knowing if something were to happen to Roberta, there are people around who would understand my sorrow and it damn well wouldn't be my heterosexual friends who'd understand my sorrow. It's got to be somebody that knows how I feel. That's why it's important to have gay friends.

R: It is a support. There's no doubt about that. The community has become more important to us as we've gotten older.

W: A young person could adjust easier if something happened. I think as you get older it's important to know that there are people who understand. One of the girls that comes over there lost her friend of some number of years just last year. Though they had lived in the Castro, they had never, ever associated or let out in any way that they were gay. And she was devastated. The woman died very suddenly of a stroke. These two girls across the street were her sole support at the time.

We've had a large number of heterosexual friends and they don't know that we're gay. They would never understand the sorrow that we would have.

R: As far as illness is concerned, neither one of us has any family out here and it's written in our orders to our physician that if either of us gets sick, the other can get in. They get real fussy over who can get in. So we wrote that neither of us has next of kin out here.

W: These are the things that you run into sometimes. We have a power of attorney. But you need more than that. Only another gay can understand. Nobody else is going to understand the kind of sorrow that you feel. I wouldn't expect them to. What I don't understand is ... Why can't it be all out in the open all over? I'm not because you have to be careful. But I think the time will come for others and I think that's what it should be.

R: I think we have been too conditioned to being closeted to be totally out. We are out with a number of people, but I'm not totally out. I'm not out with what family I have left. But I think we were conditioned for too long to be comfortable with that. I don't think it's necessary. I'd like to see a time when it's an accepted form — when your sexual orientation is your own business and you move on from there.

W: Too much emphasis is placed on it.

R: Too much. You know, we've been together in sobriety for about twenty years.

W: And it has never gotten stale. Roberta loves gardening and I don't. I like craft work and she doesn't.

R: You're good at it, too.

W: Roberta does the wash and I'll sew. We used to do the shopping together but it seemed silly for two grown people to do grocery shopping together.

R: It wasn't anything we talked about — it just sort of happened. But we spent most of our time around each other. There was a time I spent a lot of time alone in this house. It made me realize how much I enjoyed being with Wilma.

W: That was the time I was sent to Korea in 1961 to 1962 for thirteen months and then to another base in California for 24 months.

R: We were busy. We got used to doing things on our own.

W: It's not always a bed of roses — there have been hard times in our relationship.

R: Yes, we've had words, angry words with each other. It's give and take.

W: Sometimes it's 70–30, and sometimes it's 50–50.

R: There's not as much sex in our relationship as there used to be. I don't have the energy! But we still have sexuality. It's not as frequent as it was.

W: I don't think that's any different than heterosexuals.

R: Sometimes it's pretty frequent, sometimes not. Maybe twice a month.

W: Other than frequency, there haven't really been any changes in our sexual relationship.

R: We've both been through menopause, thank God! And that didn't affect us. Shouldn't affect anybody's sexuality.

W: We haven't lost interest in each other. If you love somebody — and love isn't sexuality; it's part of it. . .

R: Some facets of life are more important to people than others and maybe in some people that isn't as important. But people who report that they aren't as interested in sex are usually in therapy. And what are they in therapy for? To find out what's wrong with the relationship.

Sexuality has always been important to us. It's not the only thing, but it's an important part of the relationship.

W: If you love somebody more, then it's probably more important and it's probably more enjoyable than one night stands.

R: We don't set aside time to be sexual. It just happens. I never made enough time when I was working, but we've got time now.

W: We had times when we weren't sexual, but we always came back to it. I'm seventy-one. I'll be seventy-two in June.

R: I'm sixty-eight. I don't feel old in my head, but sometimes when you start to do stuff like out in the garden, you can't lift the loads. So physically, I realize that I'm older than I like to be. But I don't think it. Of course it's frustrating.

W: When you know you used to be able to lift these damn rocks and now you can't even pick one up. But I don't feel old other than that. I don't hide my age. If somebody asks me, I say "I'm seventy-one." Nothing I say is going to make that change.

AA has helped a lot because you have to let the other person have their space. You have to learn not to take their inventory and to take your own inventory. Now this doesn't always make it ideal because you can know these things but you don't always do them.

R: We do yell sometimes, but we never go to bed mad. We make up by saying we're sorry. We talk about it. We hug . . . it's affectionate though, not sexual. You have to have genuine affection for the person. And you have to give them their space and you have to know that they're not perfect and neither are you.

W: I don't think we'd have been together if we hadn't been in AA. We'd have been drinking. Or even if one of us was drinking . . . . It's taught us ways to deal with each other. Every so often I'll say, "We are lucky people." And I think we are.

RUSTY BROWN

Always Me

When I was eight-and-a-half years old I was sent to Five Points Home For Girls because I was always running away from home. My parents and I just never got along. Strangely enough those were the happiest years of my childhood — largely because the idea of homosexuality just never occurred to the people who ran the home. If two of us were holding hands or had our arms around each other, they thought we were "just buddies." Although some of my relationships were more than "just buddies," they never questioned us about it.

But when I was about thirteen, I was a little indiscreet and got caught in bed with another little girl who was eight years old. Naturally, they said I wasn't right in the head and they sent me to Bellevue. I shocked the psychiatrist with the high score I got on the I.Q. test. He concluded on further examination that I had homosexual potential.

I was sent back to Five Points, but they transferred me to a cottage of older girls. They thought the older girls wouldn't be as susceptible to my advances as the younger ones were. Then I really had fun! I was in that cottage until I was sixteen. Two of the eighteen year olds were gay. I had affairs with both of them. Being older, we had the brains to be more cautious, so we never got caught. I tried to stay in contact with them, but our letters got waylaid.

I was sent home at age sixteen. Since I wasn't menstruating yet, my mother took me to a doctor to see if I was pregnant. He said the hymen was broken which meant I wasn't a virgin. My mother blew a fuse; to her that meant that I was playing with boys. Nothing could have been further from the truth. The doctor said since I was very much a participant in strenuous sports, it could have broken that way. I was a broad jumper in more ways than one!

But my mother couldn't be convinced that I'd broken my hymen in sports. She took me to juvenile court and they sent me to Florence Crittenton. Boy, what an education I got there. The women there had been picked up for everything from pickpocketing to prostitution. In the month and a half I was there, I got all kinds of job offers. They were going to teach me the ropes. Then I wound up in a home run by the Salvation Army. Most of the girls were prostitutes or unwed mothers, which made me quite out of place.

I got out of the Salvation Army home in March of 1941. I went to work on a chicken farm in New Jersey.

Pretty soon I could see World War II coming; I knew it was just a matter of time before the United States was in the middle of it. I decided to sign up for the Army. I got called in for a physical but I wasn't taken for two reasons: One, I'd been in a home for delinquents; two, I had a heart defect. However I was able to pass the physical to become a civilian employee for the Navy and they sent me to San Francisco so I could go to welding school on Treasure Island at the Navy Base. I learned welding and some machine shop work and got acquainted with ship's engines and different parts of ships and how to do repair work on them. I got my welding certification and we were sent to Hawaii.

On December the 6th, 1941, we were aboard ship; we were going to be sent to the Philippines. We were out in the middle of the Pacific on Sunday morning when we were all suddenly awakened with the news that the Japanese had attacked Pearl Harbor. We did go on to the Philippines; I guess I was there about ten months and I had a pretty good time.

I got to meet a lot of the Navy women. The ones who were in the service had to be on the discreet side, and since I was a civilian, we always met in bars or other places — so-called coffee houses or a friend of a friend of a friend's house. They were called coffee houses, but lesbians hung out there — some civilians, some military.

We had strict butch and femme roles in those days. Take this one coffee house in Manila. You could tell when you walked in who was butch and who was femme. At some tables, one was butch and one was femme. At other tables the women were either all butch or all femme. I automatically went to the table with the butches. I wouldn't sit with the femmes. By sitting with the butches I'd find out who was going with who — I didn't want to get my head knocked off. I figured there were plenty of fish in the sea. I'd pick the one I liked the best and I'd start talking to her.

I never did go for one night stands. I didn't know how long I was going to be stationed there and I wanted somebody I could count on to be there a while. I always like to get to know somebody before I have sex with them. Jumping into bed and having a grand old time and not being able to communicate afterwards is not my cup of tea. Sex is not that important to me.

In fact I picked a woman I ended up being with the whole time I was there. She cried when I left; she was in love with me. I was fond of her, but I knew that with the war on, nothing could be permanent.

Next our ship was sent to Seattle. During the ride down, I got involved with a Navy woman who was also being shipped to Seattle. It was hairy. Keeping secrets on ship isn't the easiest thing to do. If word had gotten out she would been thrown out of the military. So we met secretly. It took a lot of negotiating to figure out how to make sure no one knew.

Since I was a mechanic, sometimes I'd say I was needed in the engine room — a big area with a main corridor with turbines out to the side. We would meet behind one of these turbines. We could never spare enough time to really have a real sex act, which aggravated both of us. As it was, we were both taking a big chance. Mostly we just hugged and kissed and had a little foreplay. We never did get down to brass tacks.

I got off the ship in Seattle. She remained on board. We didn't try to meet again as we had no way to know where we would wind up. There were some gay people in Seattle. There were no lesbian places per se, only gay male bars. So if you didn't know somebody, it was very tough to find someone. Most of the lesbians were butch like myself. We strictly went with femmes; nothing ever happened between us. I guess we were too much alike. It's like if we danced, who was going to lead? We would both be dominant.

I came back to San Francisco, then I got shipped over to England. I found a lot of gay people in England, both in and out of the service, both American and British. There were lesbian places in London; one was called The Royal Queen and the other was The Four Dices. The military had to be careful so they went to the Phoenix, a gay men's and lesbian bar. It was less obvious. But I wouldn't go to the military bar because I didn't want to worry about someone getting caught. I didn't want that on my conscience.

Even in my relationships, at that time, butch and femme were strictly separated. I would be like the husband. My lover would be like a wife. I was lovers with two English women. One drove a tram, the other was a bus driver. The bus driver was so tiny. To picture her driving a truck was a kick. I liked Victoria. She looked so delicate and fragile. She was sweet and pretty.

Then in 1945, the war came to an end and our world started to collapse. I was working at the Navy base in Brooklyn when the Japanese signed the surrender; 150 of us were told that in two weeks our jobs would be through. The war was over, the military was all coming back (those that survived) and they were going to give them the priority on the jobs. I thought, "Well what in hell am I going to do now?" Temporarily, till I could figure out what to do, I went back to New Jersey and got that job back on the chicken farm. But I really couldn't see myself doing that all my life. So I tried getting a job in the factories.

But I ran into a little problem: I was female. Finally I went to a machine shop and pretended to be a boy. I told them I was sixteen — too young for military conscription — so they wouldn't ask for my papers or discharge papers.

I told them my father had a machine shop and that was how I learned. When they asked why I wasn't working there still, I said he was dead. They hired me. When I went to the bathroom, I'd go in to the one stall that had a door on it. I tried to go to the bathroom as infrequently as possible. I used my grandfather's first name, Henry, but kept my last name.

After work, I'd go have a drink with the guys. They would talk about women. They'd say, "Listen, kid, make hay while the sun shines. Don't let yourself get hooked by any one woman. You have plenty of time before you get married." They gave me fatherly advice.

But I couldn't get away with that very long, because after all a boy eighteen or nineteen should begin to grow a beard. That was the one thing I was unable to do, so eventually I had to quit. By then things were opening up a little bit better so I decided to use my papers from the Navy and get a job under my own name.

At the time I was living in New York City. I had a room in Manhattan for nine dollars a week, which was a lot of money in those days. It was a brownstone turned into a rooming house overlooking Riverside Drive. People at the rooming house thought I was a boy, too. It wasn't difficult to pass, as it was mostly men and a few older women. The older women didn't pay me any attention. I kept more or less to myself; it was safer that way.

There weren't many gay bars in New York in the late 40's. It was hard to meet other lesbians. I would go to gay male bars. But most of the women I met there were on the butchy side. That didn't do me any good.

Meanwhile I met a couple of gay boys that I had known and they introduced me in turn to another gay fellow who happened to be a dancer. He found out that I was a good dancer so he talked me into being his partner. Well, I figured, that beats the chicken farm, so he and I started dancing. He was a female impersonator and I was a male impersonator. That's what I was doing when I met Terry.

One night I had just finished our show and for lack of anything else to do I thought I'd take in a strip show. And it was Terry up there on the stage. She looked to me like she was straight, yet I knew from experience that a lot of the girls in show business were gay. Well, I figured, nothing ventured nothing gained. I decided to become a stage door Johnny that night and I waited outside for her when the show ended. She wasn't using the name Terry at that time — she was using either May Devoe or Cookie Castle; she used both of those names at one time or another. When she came out I spoke to her, and she turned and started to give me a retort. Then she took another look and she started to laugh. She said, "This beats everything. I'm used to guys being out here trying to proposition me after the show and I have to fight them off, but you're a first." She said, "What the hell, why not? Come on, let's go."

So we went to a restaurant and I ordered dinner for both of us and something to drink. We started talking. All of sudden it got to be 6:00 in the morning. So I took her back to the theater. We exchanged phone numbers and she told me where she was staying and I told her where I was.

That night, she took in my show. And then she turned the tables on me: *she* waited for *me*. And we took it off from there. Course it started out we were just friends; we started seeing each other more and more. Either she'd take in my show or I'd take in hers. We'd meet after the show, and we got to know each other pretty well.

We drew closer to each other over time. It was a slow seduction. I was afraid of getting too involved with her. She sure looked straight up on that stage. She had to keep reassuring me. We were exchanging Christmas presents and I asked if I could kiss her. I had dreamed of a million different ways of getting her into bed and then it just happened automatically. She took her time. She wanted to be sure of me — that I would be stable.

Shortly after our first sexual experience — about a year after I met her — we moved in together. I said, "How about us taking a place together? I suppose that would be impossible; you go on the road a great deal more than I do." She said, "Well, I'm thinking of not going on the road anymore. Things are getting a little rough. The show is closing anyway."

She quit show business and she went in for nursing. Then she talked me into trying it. I said, "I'm no good at this stuff." She said, "Well, give it a try. Come on, we'll both go to school." Since neither one of us had a college education and we were both over 30 by this time — she was 40 when we met — the only thing we could do was become practical nurses.

I tried my hand at nursing for about two years; finally one day I came home and I said, "Terry, I quit. I can't take this any more. I'm going back to factory work. I get along better with machines." She laughed. " But," she says, "you took all this training." I said, "Who knows, someday it might come in handy, but it's not for me. I tried it, it's been almost two years. I can't take it."

So I quit and I went back to factory work. That is predominantly the kind of work I did for most of the time we were together.

Terry and I were together for twenty-eight years. Literally until death did us part. I'm not going to say that our life was a bed of roses. No two people, gay or straight, can live together constantly without there being much friction. But we did learn to work around it. She'd go into some rages and so would I — different kinds. She'd rant and scream, scream and holler and stamp her feet. I would simply go on a cleaning spree or stick on my hat and coat and go for a long walk.

But by and large with some exceptions, everything seemed to work out all right. We went everywhere together and did a lot of things together. We moved around — went to Oregon, Washington, and finally moved to Los Angeles.

We had very few gay friends. There were very few places you could go to meet other lesbians. The gay bars in New York were mostly for men. We were more or less isolated. When we went out men would often say things and harass us. Our getting involved in the gay community did not start until we came to Los Angeles. I'm very grateful for the gay friends I have here. I've never been in the closet; I've never pretended to be straight. I've never looked straight. It feels good and secure to be surrounded by lesbians.

Also, when Terry got sick, those friends gave me a lot of support. I wasn't alone. Terry died in 1979. I have to say the years together were good until she got sick in 1976. Those were hard times. That's when things got really bad.

Now my life is pretty well settled. I still have a lot of gay friends. Things are much better now. It was Terry who liked all that traveling around. I always wanted to settle down in one spot and put down roots.

California is where I intend to stay for as long as I am going to live. It may not neccessarily be in Los Angeles. Eventually I'd like to get a small mobile home on a piece of land. My present girlfriend would be welcome to come and live with me if she wants to. But my ultimate goal is to have my own place — a place nobody can take away from me. Maybe have a goat and a few chickens of my own.

ELENA

A Retrospective View

I remember...

A brilliant October sun bathes the world in a cool golden light. I drive carefully along the Outer Drive of Chicago. Lake Michigan is a deep turquoise blue; its intensity hurts my eyes. I have a doctor's appointment that I don't want to keep.

The car exhaust fumes are raw and pungent, even worse than the hospital odors.

No matter how often I bathe, wash my hair, change my clothes — the hospital odors are like a miasma; little droplets caught in the lining of my nose. The nightmare of the surgery was in August, two months ago. Left radical mastectomy. Words vaguely understood not long ago are no longer some other woman's grief. It's what happened to me. It's me they talk about now, my friends, my lover, my family and colleagues.

Today is another of an endless series (so it seems) of post-operative examinations. I dread it. I am pounded incessantly by an obsessive train of thought. I can die. The cancer can spread. Maybe it has. But I want to live. I shall get better. Over and over, the thoughts drum in my head.

My automobile is transformed into a charging monster careening down the road. I grip the wheel to hold the car, to contain its speed. My mouth is full of cotton. I must concentrate. Since when has driving a car become such an ordeal?

My morning (and sometimes evening) ritual is to press my fingers gently down the long reddish scar etched onto my chest, searching for any unusual swelling or growth that's sprung up in the middle of the night. But who am I to diagnose myself? The doctor's hands are more knowing.

The horror of it all, and my obsessive mutterings echo in my head. Why isn't each passing day a little easier for me? I take faint hope when the nausea recedes and the coffee tastes good in my mouth in the morning. But I feel fragile, vulnerable. I marvel that I was ever able to summon the energy it takes to manage my life.

The left side of my chest, except for the scar, is unbelievably flat and barren. Replacing my breast, my comfortable little pink-nippled breast, are acres of pale white plains. The skin around the scar is tight. The scar looks angry and ragged. It is an alien creature sewn into me, moving up and down with each breath. Under my left arm the skin seems cold and numb. I try not to touch it. The nerves will heal, they tell me in the hospital. Most of the sensation will return. The left arm can be as strong and supple as the right one. Keep up the exercises. Move the arm. Often. Morning, noon, and night. Stand flat against the wall, chin and stomach flat against it and stretch the arm upwards. I try. My left hand inches painfully upward; my arm follows reluctantly. But I don't stop. Keep it moving! Move! I jam on the brakes, startled as a small truck in front of me barely misses my left headlight.

It could be a nightmare, I think. I'll just wake up, brush it away, and cup my two breasts in my hands. And I won't die the lingering obscene death. What an ugly word! Cancer. A word of doom, of torture and pain, of plague and pestilence. One of my doctors, a long-time personal friend, tried to be reassuring. They're working on it every day, all over the world, she said. Extensive research. The answers should come soon. The next year or two. But she made no promises about me. How could she without losing my trust? The endocrinologist spent much time examining the cancerous lesion under the microscope.

No signs of wandering vagrant cells — malignant evil crawling vicious little cells — anywhere else. None in the lymph nodes. That was the main ticket in the game. Nothing sinister in the lymph nodes.

Staying with the reality of this disease was not always easy. But I needed to do it. I knew that a mastectomy was not an appendectomy or a hysterectomy soon to heal and be forgotten. This was not pneumonia or hepatitis or sciatica. There were cures for those diseases. But cancer? Another world. Who knew?

Could I live with one breast? The plastic prosthesis, the pink silicon-filled plastic breast that fit comfortably into my bra, looked normal enough. At the specialty shop crowded with braces, crutches, steel-ribbed corsets, elastic jock straps, inflatable cushions and arm and leg bandages of every size, I was placed in the hands of a saleswoman, tall and burly, with apple-red cheeks and an ample bosom. She was very business-like as she deftly inserted my new possession into my new bra and quickly hooked me up in the back. "It looks real good, honey," she beamed. "Thousands of women wear them, and you never know." Obviously she loved her work, restoring the silhouettes of broken down women. Business must be good. But why did I have to be a customer?

My terror intensifies as I look for a parking place near the medical office building. I'm just too young to die. Forty is not that old these days. I want a decent career. I need all of my energy and a free mind. I know women survive mastectomies. A social worker in the out-patient clinic where I worked was in her fifteenth year of recovery. She seemed full of energy: vigorous, aggressive, and happily married. She reached out to me. She filled me with hope. I was comforted.

I find a parking place a block from the doctor's office. I force myself out of the car as I'm battered by images of death on one hand, and surges of rage on the other. No! I shout in silent fury. Not too long ago I was twenty, and forty seemed centuries away. When I was a teenager, women of forty were ancient, they were old grandmothers. They spent their days cooking, gossiping, quarreling, nagging. They were old and fat. And here I was. I had joined the club.

I announce myself to the doctor's receptionist. The doctor is an expert on lymph nodes and the rest of the endocrine glands. He does not make me wait, greets me warmly. A tall lanky man with a shock of sandy hair, serious blue eyes behind the rimless glasses. He examines me carefully, hands sure and certain along the scar and the other breast. I feel his calm seep into me. "Everything looks fine," he grunts finally. Then he grins, "It's a beautiful scar." I pretend to admire it also, secretly finding it ugly. "I think you'll be all right," he says as I prepare to dress and leave the office. He asks the receptionist, a slim dark-haired beauty who devours him with her eyes, to make another appointment for me in six weeks.

That evening, my lover Marge and I gazed at the wide green expanse of park in the darkening mists of Lake Michigan. I loved our living room with its thick rugs scattered on the polished wooden floor, the paintings on the walls, the feelings of warmth and comfort. Marge sipped her vodka martini. I cradled a cup of warm coffee. She was a lovely woman, slender, her skin golden in the evening light. Her large blue eyes contrasted charmingly with her silvery hair, cropped close around a beautiful head.

"So what did he say?" she asked eagerly about the doctor. I was warmed by her concern.

And her concern was real. How could I ever forget the day she drove me home from the hospital, a week after the operation? I thought a warm bath would feel good. She helped me step into the tub. The stiches on my chest formed a surreal image of black marks sewn tightly into white skin. I forced myself to look and was overwhelmed with fear and disgust. Her calm manner was soothing. I tried to see things her way. I must get over this. But who had done this to me? I washed carefully, crying to myself, and avoided touching the long scar.

That night, my first night home, we lay together. Her arm was gently and light, careful about the wound. "You'll be okay," she said. "I know it. You're a good fighter."

It was blissful to lie in my own bed, away from the noise and stench of the hospital. I tried to let the nightmare go and drifted off to sleep.

I knew Marge loved me. I think I was different from almost everyone else in her life. I was thoughtful and intellectually curious. She was fascinated by the patients I saw in my therapy practice, men and women struggling to keep their lives together. Marge was sympathetic, yet bewildered by so much self-destructive behavior. She was, at the same time, oblivious to her own.

We had both struggled in our lives: Marge with establishing her now-flourishing but very demanding business, I with the years of working my way through college and graduate school. The endless pressure and exhaustion that went into building business success was accompanied by her increasing dependence upon alcohol. Desperate, she finally responded to my encouragement and spent a year in psychotherapy. It did help her some; she became more self-accepting. But the drinking problem, under control for a few months, was not touched.

My emotional life was a mixture of despair on really bad days and simple resignation on other days. My life with Marge had become a narrow passage of pleasure and pain. Her endless little involvements and flirtations with both men and women whirled me around in torrents of jealousy.

One hot summer evening about two years after my surgery, Marge was on the phone for nearly an hour with a woman who I knew to be aggressive and blatant in her pursuit of my lover. My rage spilled over. I was told to mind my own goddamn business and I yelled back that I could not stand her flirtations and threatened to move out. She offered to help me pack. And that's how it ended. I managed to find a room temporarily in a friend's house, and packed my suitcase the next morning.

My pain and depression were severe. I searched for and found a therapist, a warm and understanding woman. Her support and reassurance were healing. We talked about me and about Marge. She acknowledged the validity of my anger and grief. Marge simply needed to be loved by everybody. Inside she was a hungry infant in an endless search for love to fill her emptiness.

After several months, Marge and I both calmed down and we were able to resume our friendship. It was a satisfactory arrangement. I was no longer tortured by who she saw or what she did. I reached out for new friends.

It was not easy for me. How could I make love to another woman, or be made love to? I was terribly self-conscious about the scar. Clothed, I felt all right. My special bra was a godsend. It provided the illusion of normalcy — two breasts, well balanced and properly shaped.

Eventually I ran into an acquaintance standing in line near me in the supermarket. She was attractive, cheerful, full of vigor. Her smile was warm. We left the store together, our arms filled with large paper bags stuffed with groceries. I suggested that she call me and she was very agreeable. In the coming weeks my inhibitions dissolved in a burst of passion. She was indifferent to my skewed body shape. Our love affair flourished for several months and my bruised self-image was soothed.

But I was restless. My job felt stale and repetitious. I was encircled by the same group of social workers year after year — prisoners of the state civil service. Little cliques formed; the older supervisors clung to their powers and privileges and patronized the new staff. I attended staff meetings, went to seminars, read the literature, consulted regularly with staff psychiatrists.

One December I was invited to visit some friends who had left Chicago and settled in Seattle. The day before Christmas we all lunched in a luxurious restaurant overlooking Puget Sound. I fell in love with the panorama of green hills, soft mists, the incredible beauty of the Northwest. Could this paradise be for me too? I was encouraged to try. Why not? It was time for a change in my life, and I knew it might very well be now or never. After all, there were cancer specialists in Seattle, too.

It was not easy to find a job that was appealing. I wrote letters, followed every possible lead. Finally after almost a year the break came: an interested response and a request for an interview. I grabbed the next plane and got the job. I was forty-three years old and had never lived any other place than Chicago.

The year was 1960. When my excitement died down and the packing and dismantling of my Chicago apartment began in earnest, all of my doubts and fears mocked me, doing a devil's dance in my head. I was afraid to leave the world I'd always known: the city of my whole life history, my family, my schools and my sicknesses. All of my friends and my family were locked in the safety of the vast city by the Lake. My mother was ailing and alone. My presence was a part of her life. My sister's children were young and I loved them.

I struggled with guilt but was pulled toward my fantasy of a new adventure. The new job sounded exciting. I liked the people who had interviewed me. I loved Seattle; I'd heard stories about the growing lesbian community there. And so I kept on packing doggedly, divesting myself of a lifetime collection of books, and arranged for a moving company to store my furniture until I found a place to live.

I took off one morning in a car jammed with possessions, and as they say in the Westerns, headed for the open spaces. Five days, two thousand miles, and one flat tire later, I drove into Washington and found my friends' house on Capitol Hill.

The first year in Seattle was tough, exhilarating and scary. The job was stressful and demanding. I had many things to learn. I was no longer a therapist in a clinic, sitting with a patient behind a closed door. I was now a community organizer and had to master the intricacies of social agency policy and budget. There were hordes of new people to get to know, professional colleagues to connect with. I made several new friends. A pleasant flat with a fireplace and a view of the Sound became my home and I settled in.

I was often lonely and battered by waves of homesickness. Had I made a mistake after all? Everything was gorgeous: the water, the beautiful hills, the sparkling Sound. Yet, who cared whether I lived or died? My deepest connections seemed lost. Weren't family and friends, after all, the meaning of one's life? No one had lived with me through the nightmare of my surgery. There was no one to talk to about how I felt about myself. I returned to Chicago for a week and was restored to some extent. Everybody was still there and wished me well. My mother had moved to Florida to live near her sister. My guilt lessened.

By the end of my first year in Seattle, I was in a relationship.

I saw Gail for the first time on a steamy muggy August morning. I had driven the fifteen or so miles from the foggy city to the small town where Dorie, a fellow social worker from Chicago, lived. As I drove up, Dorie's partner Gail was busily clipping the long hedge in front of a ranch style house in a neighborhood of tract homes, not far from acres of orchards. My quick impression was of a solemn, rangy, sandy-haired woman in her mid-forties, her glasses glinting in the sun.

Dorie, a petite attractive woman, greeted me with a charming smile. She and Gail were fairly new to Washington too, and we both enjoyed talking about mutual friends in Chicago, one of whom had asked me to check in with Dorie about job possibilities for her. I stayed about an hour in the cool, comfortable, well-furnished house. I left with the anticipation of seeing her again and becoming acquainted with Gail, who was still intent on pulling weeds as I walked down the driveway to my car.

I was hungry for "connections" in those days. I reached out wherever I could. I thought Dorie felt the same way. Chicago social workers shared a common history in their education and their agency experiences. I drove back to the city, planning a little dinner party with them during the next few weeks. The following evening I was immersed in a good suspense novel, munching on potato chips and enjoying the blazing fireplace. I knew it was hot and muggy everywhere else in the county, but in my Seattle the night chill stung your bones. The telephone interrupted my reading.

"This is Gail, Dorie's friend."

How nice, I thought. "Sorry we didn't have a chance to meet yesterday. You looked pretty busy."

"You're the woman who was here then?" she asked slowly.

"Yes." Why the question?

A few seconds of silence.

"Hello . . . are you there?" I asked.

"There's some bad news," Gail said.

"Bad news?" I echoed stupidly. "What is it?"

"Dorie . . . it's Dorie . . ."

I was astonished. What happened? Why was Gail telling me?

"Dorie died last night, about ten o'clock."

This must be some ghoulish joke.

"What are you saying?" I asked. "She was fine yesterday morning. Did she have an accident?"

"The doctors aren't sure what happened," Gail struggled to speak. "After you left yesterday, Dorie said she did not feel well. Maybe it was the heat. She took a nap. I let her sleep until about five, but she didn't want to get up. Later I tried to get her out of bed, but she wouldn't move. I called the Fire Department. They sent an ambulance and rushed her to the hospital. She wasn't breathing. The doctors tried everything. It was no use."

The news was monstrous. Several days later I called Gail and heard the rest of the story. The police had searched the house that night and discovered a large bottle of seconal in the medicine cabinet — about a thousand little red pills. The autopsy report indicated a high level of alchohol and seconal in her blood. There was no inquest.

During the painful unhappy weeks that followed I phoned

Gail, arranged to have lunch with her once or twice. She needed to talk. She was usually pale and depressed and felt very lonely. She wanted to talk about her fifteen years with Dorie: about Dorie's pills and drinking, many extravagances and purchases of high fashion clothes, and endless debts. I listened and I listened. I wondered to myself why Gail had been patient with Dorie. She said she'd been enthralled.

My own loneliness was echoed in Gail's depression. True, I had made some new friends — attractive professional women involved with their jobs, responsive to social conditions, interested in the arts. They loved to arrange little dinner parties. There never were any men present. I suspected several of them might be "closet" lesbians, but I never heard the words gay or lesbian when I was invited to the social gatherings. I was flattered at being included as the "new" woman in town. The time was the early 1960's; many single independent professional women were very conflicted about their sexuality — not wanting involvements with men, but fearing sexualizing women. It was fun and games — mildly flirtatious, casually but never overtly seductive. I wanted and needed more intimacy.

I became more and more responsive to Gail. I told her about my surgery, about my self-consciousness about my body. At that time five years had passed since the operation. I knew five years and no symptoms was a good sign. I also knew that ten or fifteen years without symptoms was better. She was very kind and sensitive. I had lost a breast; she had lost a lover. No equality in the losses — a whole person versus a part of a person. No contest with her pain. I remember she told me, "Be glad you're alive."

Eventually, as the lonely months of autumn and winter wore on, we saw more and more of each other. One rainy evening after dinner, we lay in front of the fireplace. The room was in shadows except for the burning logs. It seemed quite natural for us to lie close, our arms entwined, our mutual hunger passionate and intense.

Her death from lung cancer three years later was devastating. I still see her face, feel her pain and sadness, her quiet resignation, her courage as all hope and optimism faded.

I was with her in the early morning hours of a dismal February in 1964 when she died. I still wear the diamond ring she wanted me to have. "Diamonds last a long time," she said.

* * *

Now it is time for retrospection. I have made it to age sixty and beyond. I have lived with my one breast for many years; with each passing year, and with each symptom-free physical exam, I grow more accepting, more comfortable, less self-conscious. My days are full of activity. Life swirls and I am caught up in it. But, even now, at bedtime, when I unhook my brassiere with the plastic insert on the left hand side and stare at the reflection in the large bathroom mirror, I still hate it. I marvel that anyone could love all of me. The mood always passes, but is never entirely lost.

How has it been for me to fall in love, to undress in front of a new lover, to let her hands caress my body?

The long scar, red no longer, but pale like the rest of me, has to be reckoned with. It is not an abdominal scar that fades into insignificance. With me something is missing. The look of wholeness and completion, the balance nature intended, is gone.

The first time making love is the most difficult time for me. I am self-conscious, uneasy, and I struggle with the old shame. How stupid of me to worry so! But how will she react? I look for subtle signs. Do her eyes turn away too quickly? Is she surprised, frightened, a little repulsed? She has been prepared; I am careful about this. I take my time. I need to feel the temper of this person. We must have rapport. She must know me as I must have some knowing of her. We must care about each other's pain.

Since the mastectomy, now almost thirty years ago, I have experienced many episodes of despair — about an unhappy relationship, the loss of a friend or lover, or just the general uncertainty and malaise of existence. There are more times, however, when life seems to work well.

Can I ever forget Gail's words? Her wasted body was pain-wracked and fragile, but she clung to my hand. "Be glad you are alive," she whispered, her blue eyes flooding with tears, "Live for me."

I live with a woman now. I am blessed with her sensitivity and caring. This does not erase the scar or replace the missing breast. But there is so much more to me than what I have lost.

PAT BOND

Tapioca Tapestry

I went to high school out in the middle of Iowa, and somehow I got a copy of *The Well of Loneliness* and read it. And then a German film was being shown in my town. I just had a gut feeling that it was about lesbians so I went to see it; sure enough it was about lesbians. Of course it was disastrous — the lesbian kid kills herself. I had crushes on women so I decided, aha! That's what I am. I'm a lesbian. It was those crushes on teachers that convinced me. Not gym teachers; nothing so shabby as a gym teacher. I had to have a *French* teacher to have a crush on. Then I went to a Catholic college and I fell in love with a nun . . . so I knew.

I wanted to be an intellectual; therefore all lesbians were intellectuals. Dreadful mistake. All lesbians played baseball and football — in my generation — and they hadn't read a book in their lives. Until feminism, dykes weren't intellectuals at all because they were imitating men — the worst side of men — the truck driver man. Nobody ever thought of imitating a college professor.

I just knew the army was full of lesbians, so I ran off and joined the army. And to my horror, the army was filled with lesbians who hated the fact that I read a book once in a while. Terrible, anti-intellectual — like the rest of this country. It was awful. Not only was I rejected by the women I had fallen in love with and by my mother, but now all these fucking lesbians in the army were rejecting me.

I had hoped the army would provide me with a community of women, but it didn't. I felt like an outsider. I tried like crazy to be a good butch, a real dyke, but it wasn't my nature. I'd sneak and put Chanel behind my ears. I tried to do the walk, but I couldn't carry it off for long. I tried to put on men's clothes and I looked like Laurel and Hardy. My figure is just not cut out for men's clothes. I'm too round.

So, mostly I hung out with a lot of faggots I met in Davenport. I remember sitting in this park right by the Mississippi: while they cruised the park I would sit there and memorize Shakepeare's sonnets. They had me over for dinner. They liked opera and they liked the theatre and it was my milieu. These were people I could talk to about my interests.

I had joined the army in Davenport with the hope of being sent to Europe. I had this dream that somehow I could go to Paris and there would be Gertrude and Alice, you know, the whole enchilada.

I never got to Europe . . . but clever moi. The army put me in the medical corps, of all things. Me — with three years of college and a major in English lit. — in the medical corps! (It was worse for a friend. She was a linguist with a master's degree in languages — they put her in cooks and bakers.) I was stationed in Clinton Island which is right outside Davenport. All our officers were so gay it was unbelievable. My commanding officer then was Minnie the gym teacher. We called her Tick — she had a man's haircut, the whole thing. In fact when she'd check the barracks at night, the women would scream — they thought a man was loose.

I fell in love with a woman who was in with me. She was my own age, but she was in love with our first sergeant. So the three of us hung out together. The company was breaking up and we were all going to get transferred to Springfield, Illinois. I didn't want to go to Springfield; I wanted to go to San Francisco medical corps so I sat down at the typewriter and said,

"To the commanding general, Letterman General Hospital, Dear Sir, Could you use a medical technician WAC in your outfit, etc." Totally unheard of in the army. You go through channels. Well, I didn't. And the letter came back endorsed by three major-generals. My commanding officer was furious. She said, "I'm glad you're going. I hope I never see you again. Get out of my life." All the other officers on the post were saying to her, "Tick, did you get Bond to write a letter to Major Sherman?" So I came to San Francisco and 400 women went to Springfield, Illinois.

While I was stationed in San Francisco, they sent me to Japan for a little over a year. I got there just in time for the witch-hunt. I didn't know that it was going on — none of us did. Well, there we were in Japan, all these kids. We were twenty, twenty-one and MacArthur had said he wanted American women in Japan so that Japanese women could see what free American women looked like. I'm sure that what he meant was not the five hundred dykes who got off that boat. And I mean, *dykes*. We had an all-woman band and they were all in men's band uniforms. We had girl's night home, one week a night where we were all dancing and drinking, falling in love and out of love.

It was like there wasn't any risk at first because everybody was gay. The officers, all of us. Our favorite song was *Prisoner of Love*; "Alone from night to night you'll find me, too weak to break the chains that bind me. I need no shackles to remind me, I'm just a prisoner of love." And we drank like fish. It was nothing to polish off five or six quarts of beer a night. We were young. Hangover victims. We started in again the next night. Just lucky I didn't get to be an alcoholic. And the woman I was in love with ran off with a man. She fell in love with a man. God, I was miserable. I was going to kill myself.

Then they decided to crack down. After the war, when we were no longer needed, they decided to get rid of the dykes. So they had court martials. Every day you came up for a court martial against one of your friends. They turned us against each other. When I was living it, I didn't have any idea why they were doing this to us. I only knew they were throwing us out of the army with dishonorable discharges. One woman killed herself, for God's sake. She was twenty-one years old. Helen. Her family will never know why she died. And then they gave her a military funeral. It was just insane. And it was *our* officers who were conducting these summary court martials. Lesbian officers.

But I had married Paul Bond; in those days gays got married to protect themselves and their families. Paul was gay and wanted to marry to make his family happy — so that they would think he was straight. I did it for a lark. It was a marriage in name only; we divorced in 1955. But if you were married, you could get out of the military. I wanted to protect the woman I was involved with, so I went to my C.O. and I said, "I want to get out because I'm married." She said, "You're *what*?" And I produced my wedding license and I got out. The only way I could figure out to save my lover was to get out. If I had been there, they could have gotten us both because other women would have testified against us. If someone said, "I saw them dancing, I saw them kissing," — that was enough. We would dance and kiss at that WAC's night home.

There was a sense that it was never going to end, that it was OK. We were very good at our jobs. I mean how many ladies of that era could have taken a bus motor apart and put it back together again? Dykes could. How many women worked on syphilis and gonorrhea wards? I did. You know, we did one hell of a job. And then they decided they wanted to get rid of us.

So I was sent home. Which made me feel kind of guilty, like people who survived Buchenwald. So I waited and everybody came home. They sent the five hundred women home for dishonorable, but a lot of them got off because the Attorney General's Office looked at it and said, "Come *on*, five hundred??" What they didn't know was that all five hundred were dykes.

We were angry. Especially when Helen killed herself and they did that military funeral for her. We sat around, wouldn't go to our jobs, just sat and drank for days and days, crying and drinking, drinking and crying. And you suspected everybody. You thought your best friend was going to turn you in. The military does turn you against each other. I can remember thinking a woman I still know — she lives in Mexico now — that she was a spy. She was no spy. But you got paranoid. So everybody was a spy. There was no way we could work together. After Helen killed herself, my friend Bunny and a few other women got one of the officers and beat the shit out of her. Seemed to be the only thing we could do.

I hope those officers are miserable. I hope they live with guilt all their lives. I did a show called "Murder in the Women's Army Corps" because I consider that they murdered Helen, literally. And I can't do a lot with it, because I can't get it from my gut when it happens on the stage. It's almost like a lecture. So I stopped doing it because it was too hard on me. I would be miserable for days afterwards trying to get it out. And my friend in Mexico is trying to write about it. She's a writer and she can't do it either. It's very hard.

They were officers and gay . . . but they weren't busted because they were officers. You don't bust officers, you transfer them. None of them, as far as I know, ever got touched. And they conducted those summary court martials. They were the ones questioning you. And none of the women being questioned brought up the fact that the officers were gay. They were afraid to. I went to one of them once, drunk, and staggered into her office and said, "Why are you doing this? *Why?* What have we done? You're gay, too. Why are you doing this?" She said, "Go to bed. *Now.*"

I did, because they had the power. We didn't have any power. If any of them had been suspected of being gay, I suppose it could have turned on them, too. But in that era, when we were kids, it never occurred to us. I still hate those women. God knows. As I say at the end of that show I did, "Mildred Burgess, I indict you for murder in the Women's Army Corps." And she's probably dead; they were older than we were. They're in their seventies so who knows where they are?

We wound up being afraid of each other. One woman went out and got pregnant because she was so terrified.

We didn't think about therapy; the human potential movement had not happened. So you didn't go trotting off to a therapist or a support group. That didn't happen.

When I was flown back, I was miserable. I was leaving my true love behind. I was coming back to San Francisco, what was I going to do then? Again I was isolated and alone. I felt the witch-hunt was dastardly, unforgivable. It was totally unjust. We all thought so and we couldn't think of any way we could combat it. We even thought of writing Walter Winchell — really dumb things, but we didn't know what to do. Of course you're in Japan, you're in another country where there was no way you could get any help at all. Even the civil liberties union I don't think would — *then* — have been willing to take the case.

When I got back to the Presidio in San Francisco, I was too busy running around to the gay bars to do any of my allotted chores. It was wonderful. You got out of uniform and you went to the gay bars. Mona's club was right there on Broadway. They had male impersonators — women done up like men. Gorgeous women with silver hair at the temples and tuxes, and they sang and they entertained and they did all these hideous things that I do in my show now. Two of them would sing, "Two old ladies are home in bed, one turned over, the other one said, 'Stick out your can, here comes the garbage man.'" We thought that was just great.

You got to know everybody in the bar, so it was kind of a community. It was mostly civilian dykes and a few military out of uniform. It was right after the war. I joined the day President Roosevelt died, so it was 1944 and the war was still on in Japan, but it was over in Europe. Then when I got to San Francisco, the war ended in Japan. I was about twenty, twenty-one.

They wouldn't let military men in the gay bars because they caused so much trouble. They'd hang out outside the bar and beat up dykes and stuff like that. So they made the bars off-limits to military personnel to protect the women. And so there I was in the middle of it all, having a ball. God, I loved it. Every night we were in the bars. It was a sense of being somewhere finally where everybody was gay, not just you. I'd done that in the army, but it was very different. And in San Francisco, you drank, you got drunk, you cruised. You could flirt. And the entertainers were wonderful. It was just so exciting to have entertainment going on every night. There were about five gay bars in San Francisco then. You could go from bar to bar, and you did, every night.

You would stay all night in the bar, then at two there'd be a party somewhere. You'd go to the party. You're always in love, you're out of love, you're looking for a love, you lost a love. The hormones are doing an outrageous tap-dance. I was in and out of love a lot. I never met anybody that wanted to settle down with me.

We all knew we were gay. We all talked among ourselves about who we were in love with, what they were like. We also talked about what did we *do*, because we were just as puzzled as heterosexual women are when they're young. What do you do in bed? I have a spot in my show where I tell Bunny — she's six feet tall, a natural born dyke, shaves in the morning, and her vocabulary consisted of "No shit" — where I tell her, "Bunny, if we're going to be real dykes, you gotta make love to 'em with your mouth." And she said, "Down there?" I said, "That's right." She said, "No shit!" We were all terrified of that. I'm sure it's the same conversation heterosexual women have. So I said, "Don't worry, I've invented this periscope and it goes out around the covers so you can breathe while you're down there." So we talked about what you could do, what a femme expected, what a butch expected.

A butch expected you to be just lying there. You couldn't make love to the butch. That wasn't to be done. All the femmes asked each other, "Have you made love to your butch yet?" Because sooner or later they went down like sticks in the wind. "How do you do it, how do you manage that?" So they figured out a way. Every femme in the world figured out a way.

My friends were always gay — lesbians and faggots. It was

a rigid butch-femme scene. You had to be one or the other. I tried being a femme for a while. I didn't like that much because the femmes had to do all the work. Just like in heterosexual life. If your lover was a butch, she could hardly go to work in those outfits — you know, men's clothes. So the femmes would get office jobs and support the butches. There were a lot of prostitutes and a few femmes who supported butches that way. I didn't like the idea of doing all the work. I figured it was much more interesting being butch, so I tried being butch but I wasn't very good at it. So I finally just was me. I did the best I could with it. I went to this dinner party once; the hostess passed out blue napkins to all the dykes and pink napkins to all the femmes. She gave me both and said, "Pat likes dykes who wear black lace underwear." Of course with the feminist movement I finally came into style. Dykes don't have to look butch or femme anymore. We can now wear perfume *and* read books. It was difficult for my friends; they never knew really where I was coming from. Neither did I as a matter of fact.

We certainly knew everyone. If you went to the gay bars in San Francisco, you knew everybody who was gay in San Francisco. We were open in the bars, but when you walked outside . . . We used to say, "Don't ever leave North Beach. Don't cross the color line." We tried to stay away from it if we were dressed in certain ways, in drag. Of course, I was never in drag. It was unsafe to appear gay, but not *too* unsafe. San Francisco was never unsafe in spite of what people might tell you. I never saw one raid in San Francisco in all the years I was hanging out. I knew people who were harassed on the streets by cops. I knew people that were stopped on the streets by cops. When civilians stopped us — "Oh, look at that big dyke," — we'd just stick out our tongues. We *liked* that. It was like a confrontation. It was neat. And I think gays still like that — they're always trying to shock straights. Most of the time anymore it doesn't work, so it's kind of boring. You used to be able to shock them. It was fun.

The bars were really family; there was no community at all outside the bars. If you were a closet dyke then — there were lots of them, I'm sure — you stayed home. You had your own little circle of friends that you saw. That was about it. My family never knew and I was terrifed that they'd find out. Very often if you broke up with a lover, the lover would call your parents and tell them you were gay. Or they would call up your job and tell them you were gay and you would get fired. There were lots of stories of gays abusing gays. It went on all the time. I knew a lot of people who that happened to. I wasn't threatened by that because they always broke up with *me*. I was always the rejectee.

People weren't just afraid of the straight community; they were afraid of each other. There was a guy I knew who wanted to be in the FBI. And the FBI guys that were checking on him just went to the nearest gay bar and said, "Hey do you know Tom?" And they said, "Tom who?" And he said, "Tom Who-ever." And they said, "Well, he was in here last night. . ." And that did it. Out. No chance. So they tried not to do that. Like at Mona's — if someone phoned you there, the bartender would never say you were there. They would come and tell you some-one had phoned you, but they wouldn't tell the caller because it would give you away.

All the bar owners then were straight. They made all the money; gays didn't have any money. And there were five gay bars, so you can imagine the money those people were making. They didn't put any money back into the community — they had a sort of disdain for us really. We were just their money-makers. And they had rules that were unbelievably rigid. Like if you put your arm around another woman or held her hand you were thrown out. And if you were thrown out, you were out of touch with your world. I had a friend whose sister came in one night; they hadn't seen each other in a couple years and they embraced each other. They both got thrown out. And Roberta was saying, "But she's my *sister*." Didn't make any dif-ference. There was no dancing. No touching. In the male bars *and* the female bars.

I remember walking up Grant Avenue one night with a friend of mine and she said — I've never forgotten it — she said, "God, don't let me die on Grant Avenue." That kind of feeling stuck — like ghetto people must feel stuck. You know, I'll never have a prayer, I'll never get out of this, this is it for life, I'll be going from gay bar to gay bar.

By then the feminist movement was happening, and I made a few more women friends . . . but none were as close to me as my men friends. I'm very male-oriented; the men didn't betray you. It was the women, over and over, who betrayed you — other gay women. Like the army. Our officers who were gay themselves turned on us during that horrible witch-hunt in Tokyo.

I was in San Francisco for quite a few years. Then I moved to Sausalito. There I found a very different kind of dyke . . . the elegant dyke. You had to wear Irish knit sweaters and knee socks and a gold coin around your neck. They're still at it, the vestiges of the Sausalito dykes. My lover and I went to a party that one of them gave for Christmas last year and she was in a long plaid skirt with a wide leather belt with a cashmere sweater. That's how we always looked in Sausalito. I didn't like it because I didn't have the money, but that was the Sausalito look. Not intellectual, but ritzy-looking. The thing was to look as rich as possible. Like you were in college and you were the sorority girls. Some of them had more money than the women in the city, some didn't. A lot of them were teachers. They made good money teaching and then there were some who had inheritances. This was a more conservative and richer group.

I loved Sausalito; it was so beautiful. It was just hard; were you in the in-group or the out-group? It was like being in college again. The popular and the unpopular. And I was in between. I was sort of accepted, but not really because I didn't have any money. But I was educated and it was obvious that I was not lower class.

I had no lovers at that time. I would have affairs once in a while. Mostly we all got drunk and we'd go home with someone new. I had one or two friendships. Again mostly with faggots. They were the ones who seemed to *really* care. Like I had to move once, and I had to go to work and they moved me while I was at work. It was great. They got the whole place set up and I loved tapioca so they had a big bowl of it on the table. I didn't miss women; I saw them all the time in bars and knew quite a few. They came over to my house and I went over to theirs, but there wasn't that kind of a woman community feeling at all. So most of my very close friends were men. It was true for other women too.

I left Sausalito when I married another faggot. He was a performer and drag queen. Six-foot-four drag queen if you can believe it. Skip Arnold. We were both terribly lonely. We thought, what we ought to do is hang together since we don't have what we need in life. It's not easy for a man and woman to live together at *all*, let alone a gay man and a gay woman. In that era you thought of marriage, just like the straight community did. You didn't think of living together.

The marriage lasted less than a year. I was thirty-two, he was thirty-four. He got a job performing in a place called Alta Dena which is near Los Angeles. I was going to be his manager. So we went down there. Then we moved to Los Angeles and we got into fights. It was just impossible. I wanted to go out with a woman and he didn't like that. You know, all those marriage things click into place when you get married. We weren't sexual with each other at all, but we agreed to be celibate — to have a marriage and be together. Like a family. Well, it didn't work out, obviously. We lost a friendship as a result of it, which is too bad. We should never have married.

My thinking about being a lesbian began to change when I went up to Sonoma State and started taking some women's courses. One of my instructors — she's a friend now — said, "My name is Molly and I'm a lesbian." She was in slacks and a work shirt; she invited us over to her house for discussion groups and we'd all smoke grass. It was just unbelievable. None of our teachers in college would ever have let anyone know they were gay. Here was an authority figure saying that she was gay, and an authority figure who didn't wish to be an authority figure. She would merge in the background and let us take over the class and guide it. She was perfectly happy being a lesbian. And no one was firing her. She got her job as an open lesbian. I'm still incredulous that she got the job.

I moved back to San Francisco because I missed it. I missed the people I knew. And Sausalito finally out-priced me. So I moved here and eventually along came *Word is Out*: some friends were making a film about being gay. They interviewed me for twelve hours. It took me that long to get serious — that's me with the jokes. They asked me about my life and about being gay. What with the feminist movement and *Word is Out*, people wanted to see me. I worked up a little show I still do, called "Conversations with Pat Bond," which is about growing up gay in America. When I was in Chicago, Studs Terkel interviewed me on the radio; I'd always admired him. And he asked me a very good question. He said, "What was it like growing up in middle-America, a young girl feeling so different?"

Word is Out really did it. I became a celebrity. It was really great. I remember going down to the Castro after the film had opened to have coffee with a friend of mine and I had eighty thousand people around me, begging for autographs, cheering. We all came out on the stage on opening night at the Castro. They had spotlights, red carpets and all those balconies in the Castro were full of people standing and cheering. And gay parades where I was in a car, and being applauded. Accolade after accolade, flowers sent. It's still going on. I go perform, people want my autograph on a plane. It's unbelievable. It's great. And what's more, you have a certain conviction that you deserve it which makes it kind of nice. To live through all that shit . . . and I do deserve it. So it ain't like Lana Turner being discovered in a drug store.

The film gave me a great sense of community. Like when we all came out on stage at the Castro and they were all cheering. It wasn't like they were cheering movie stars. It was like we were cheering each other. It was that sense that the people on the screen are *us*. It was just us. And of course the director, Peter Adair, saw to it that the film played at only the best movie houses across the country. I got flown to New York. I, who couldn't afford a trip to Oakland if they were giving free trips, got flown to New York. And there were more people cheering. Rex Reed is sitting there with the tears streaming down his face. Peter and I taking a cab through Central Park . . . And meeting everybody else that was in the film and just feeling we knew each other.

Approval and accolades when I desperately needed it.

Since the film I've made some close women friends. Not so much faggots anymore. It's like the friends who were my friends before are still my friends, but it's more like women are interested in what I'm interested in. Which they never were before. Like politics, like getting together and defeating an issue. So I find it much easier now to be with women.

I'll be sixty soon. I like working; I don't want to retire. I just hope I can get some security together for my old age. Five years ago, I didn't worry about aging or growing old. After all, I've lived like a dyke so I'll die like a dyke.

At present I have no financial resources and no family resources. My situation will make me dependent on the community. I would like to see a senior home for gays . . . with a stage — so I can keep on performing.

FAITH REBOIN

Lesbian Grandmother

Three years ago my daughter Debbie had a baby, and as a result I became one of those people the world calls a grandmother. Grandmother? Me? Being a grandmother was alien both because of my image of myself as a radical lesbian and because of my personal feelings about motherhood.

Becoming a grandmother forced me to a recognition, through no decision of my own, that I am getting older — that I am an "older" lesbian. For me, that recognition was fraught with fearful and mostly-unexamined possibilities. Although age is an issue for all women, I believe it has a different significance for me as a lesbian.

Economically it is more threatening since, as a woman without a man, I can expect more than my share of poverty in my old age. As part of a sub-culture which has only in recent years become visible, I have few models of aging lesbians to guide me. The most visible and immediately accessible aspect of lesbian life is still the bar scene, which no longer appeals to me because it reinforces the associations of lesbianism and youth and lesbianism and alcoholism that I am no longer willing to accept for myself.

Age is one of several issues which have come up for me since becoming a grandmother that have specifically challenged my image of myself as a lesbian. There is a conflict of images inherent in the words "lesbian" and "grandmother." Our culture defines lesbians as sexual beings, which implies youth and activity. Grandmother means an old woman, and aging in this culture connotes asexuality and passivity. Even understanding the misogynist basis of these stereotypes, and as a lesbian struggling to create for myself new images of strength and beauty, it has been painful for me to discover how many of my feelings about myself as a grandmother were affected by these old rigid definitions.

Little Golden books say that grandmother has gray or white hair, is plump and matronly, wears aprons and dowdy print dresses, and sits by the fire knitting baby booties and comforters while she waits for the children, the doers of the family, to return to her. In real life grandmother often looks tired and worn, has a matter-of-fact attitude towards her children and their offspring who surround her like weeds popping up here and there, turning to her when they are in need, always tied to her by the bonds of family. It is difficult to reconcile either of those images with me — the grandmother who goes to the bar with my lesbian lover and slow dances with my leg between her thighs, stands up to my boss when he treats me disrespectfully, and changes my own engine oil.

It is equally difficult for me to reconcile my image of myself as a grandmother and as a "political" lesbian. Having come out on the wave of the women's movement, I was convinced that this patriarchal world was desperately sick and oppressive and I was always aware of the political implications of lesbianism. I separated myself from men in every way possible; I resolved not to participate in this culture they had created, and worked actively to destroy it through the education and agitation of other women. "Reform" was a dirty word to me, since I felt that only when men were forced to give up all their power could we women form a sane and egalitarian society. I rejected as opportunistic those women, straight or lesbian, who sought power or privilege within the existing system because I feared they would be co-opted by material success into believing in the political status quo. My political beliefs were not only radical; they were rigid, judgmental, and very dogmatic. Gradually I cut more and more people out of my life as part of my investment in my political persona. After years of political action I became tired and discouraged at the slow rate of change. My response to this frustration was to resign even further from the world through the use of drugs and alcohol.

The birth of my grandchild reminded me dramatically that I am a part of the continuum of life, and I began to want to be part of the world again, however imperfect it might be. Once again I began to feel, as I did when my own daughter was young, that my responsibility to the next generation does not end with changing their didies and keeping Gerber's in the cupboard, but extends to making the world a better place for them to live. I have accepted the reality that the vision I have cherished of a world in which "women's" values are predominant is a goal toward which to struggle; it is not a world which will magically appear in my life nor for which I can afford to wait.

Age has not made me any more accepting of the political status quo. But it has, combined with sobriety and therapy, helped me to accept my own limits and needs and to be more willing to live in the world that is now rather than in a dream of the future.

When I learned that my new grandbaby was a boy, I was surprised and disappointed. Having decided years before that men were my enemy — the bearers of privilege and the oppressors of all women — it was disturbing to have this male child suddenly thrust into the middle of my tidy analysis. Becoming a grandmother, Nathan's grandmother, forced me to begin re-examining my attitudes and feelings about men. These old fears and resentments that I had clung to from my childhood and my marriage were interfering with this new relationship in my life in very real ways.

My feelings about men and my lesbian political ideology dovetailed perfectly to convince me that the nuclear family is an inefficient and unjust social organization which is particularly oppressive to women and children and with which I choose not to be associated. It isolates them from the rest of the world, places too much responsibility on individual women, and provides them with far too little compensation in money, security, power, or prestige. Further, since no one woman can possibly fill all the physical and emotional needs of a child, much less several children, it creates for children a model of human relationships based on scarcity. With Nathan's birth I found myself emotionally invested in just such a family.

Facing my feelings towards men, I have recognized that I am no longer that powerless child or that frightened wife and I need no longer fear or hate those men who once dominated me. Letting go of that fear and anger, I can now afford to make room in my life for my grandson, and his father, and to respect them all as the family my daughter has chosen for herself.

With all the adjustments I've made the grandmothering part has been surprisingly easy. I am a traditionally doting grandmother in a way that I would never have imagined or anticipated, and yet the role fits like a comfortable shoe. An entry from my journal shortly after my first visit after his birth reminds me how I felt when Nathan was a newborn baby:

> When he woke from his nap I beat Debbie up the stairs to get him out of his crib. As I entered the room he was letting out little trial yelps, still half asleep, rubbing his fists in his eyes, staring sleepily at me as I picked him up, warm, damp, and relaxed. I think it's knowing that I have "rights," sort of an instant emotional investment in this relationship, that allows me to let all this out when I am with him. All those tender, motherly, loving, protective feelings well up inside me in a way that is exciting to feel and remember.

Shortly after his birth, I toasted the event with several friends. I vaguely recalled a childhood fairy tale in which the newborn baby was blessed by different witches with wishes for her future health, beauty, happiness, and other desirable attributes. As I named their wishes I made my own special wish for my grandson: that he would always know and understand what the women in his life had given him, that he would respect the uniqueness of that gift, and that through that knowledge he could relate to all women in a way of respect and caring. It was my own way of expressing the hope that I could keep this child in my life forever.

When he was six weeks old, I consciously memorized each part of him: the feel of his skin against my cheek, his weight in my arms, his baby aroma, his plump square feet, and his docile good humor. I knew then that the time might come when I could no longer like the person he had become, but I would always love this infant grandchild and be grateful for his presence in my life.

The rediscovery of joy has been one of the most pleasant changes I have experienced since becoming a grandmother. This has come mainly through the resolution of my personal conflicts about myself as a mother. I was seventeen and pregnant when I married and I soon felt resentful, trapped and very guilty. Twelve years later I came out as a lesbian and my confusion and mixed feelings manifested themselves in months of erratic and irresponsible behavior. Debbie's initial cautious acceptance of my lesbian choice soon changed to resentment at my inattention to her needs and after six months she decided to live with her father. The pleasure and satisfaction I had felt in watching my child grow and develop, and the special tie I had shared with her when she was young were lost to me. Those memories were lost in the guilt at having allowed her to leave me, and in my grim attachment to the concept of my own oppression as mother.

Imagining Debbie, my child, as a mother was frightening and depressing to me, but the reality of seeing her as a mother has proved immensely reassuring and healing. Seeing her with her own baby I have felt a reassurance that no words could have given me about the kind of mother I had been. I recognized her absorption, her patience, and her loving mothering style immediately and knew that through it she was recapitulating her experience with her own mother — me. Being with my grandchild I feel again the special uniqueness and pleasure that children bring into our lives. When I am with the two of them I am aware of the almost tangible bond between them, and I remember the glorious, imperative absoluteness which that bond of love gave to my life twenty years ago.

Accepting myself as a lesbian grandmother has required me to look closely at my own self-image and develop a willingness to change it. I discovered within myself depths of self-hatred, misogny, and homophobia that I had not realized existed. These ugly attitudes, fed by four decades of messages from the outside world that old women and lesbian women are not desirable, normal, interesting, active, and acceptable human beings, were ironically a part of me — an aging, lesbian mother. I had first to acknowledge these untruths as a part of my beliefs about myself in order to let go of them. Even letting go of such destructive attitudes is difficult, strange as it may seem, when change feels so risky and the status quo is, if nothing else, familiar.

But the rewards for this effort have been incalculable. Most important among them is that I have learned to know and love myself in ways I never dreamed possible. This process for me has meant getting clean and sober, one of the greatest acts of self-love I have ever committed. My relationship with my daughter has grown strong, healthy, respectful, and mutually supportive. After an emotional estrangement of eight years, stemming mainly from my inability to accept myself and so not wanting to face her, I have gotten Debbie back into my life. My grandchild (and his baby sister) have given me tremendous pleasure and inspiration.

Gradually I have come to incorporate all the conflicting messages about "grandmother" into my own self-image. Now when someone expresses surprise that someone like me (youthful? attractive? active?) could be a grandmother, I am able to respond, "But this is what a grandmother looks like!" It feels important to me to communicate this new reality to other lesbians. Only in this way can we demolish the stereotypes about us, re-cast the role in our own image, and help create the model of new possibilities for other women.

PAULA GUNN ALLEN

Indian Summer

But Grandmother, What Tiny Bones You Have

This week my grandmother died. My last grandmother.
My last grandparent. The one I grew up living next door to.
The one who spent the last six years of her life living with my
parents. The Presbyterian Laguna one. We buried her a couple
of days ago. I am not a granddaughter any more. What could
that mean?

My granddaughter Chelsea is almost a year old now. For
nearly a year I was a grandmother and a granddaughter. What
did, what does that mean? Is it important? Isn't it private, meaningless to others, not of general interest? Lots of people had no
grandparents that they knew. Lots of people have no grandchildren. Shouldn't I remember them and keep to myself my
wonderings about what granddaughter/grandmother means? Is
it too heterosexist to talk about my breeding relationships?
Those of my progenitors and descendants? Is it dykely to
discuss grandmotherhood on either end of it, the grandchild of,
the grandmother of? Is it too uncool to whip out my granddaughter's pictures and chortle over them to my friends, most
of whom are not and will never be grandmothers?

But Grandmother, What Big Ears You Have

An odd thing goes on for me in this phase of my life. I am often caught in a conversation with younger lesbians about mothers. Theirs. Each other's.

Oftentimes the women talking in dark tones about the horrors their mothers are perpetuating on them — especially regarding their lesbianism, or about how their hair looks, or about the clothes she buys them, or about why don't they ever call. And sometimes I join in, though not too convincingly, but I am uncomfortably aware that the conversation is about me. I am a mother. My daughter is in her twenties. Does she talk that way about me to her friends? Of course she does. Of course, I did, and do, talk about my own mother.

At Grammy's funeral I thought about the relationship between us, between her and all ten of us, her grandchildren. I was rather taken aback at what I discovered as I stood before her coffin, as I sat in the pew and listened to the minister, the music, and the words for her spoken by each of us grandchildren. She was important. To me, of course. To all of us, of course. We wept, or didn't, depending on our training. But crying or not, I could see what that woman, with her body, her hands, and her mind, had done: She had mothered three people whose children were actively engaged in many professions: theater, law, medicine, business, literature, art, dance, music and education. At least three of the grandchildren are gay. I realized how much of her is in all of my work, and I was amazed.

I was filled with a sense of humbleness before the intrepid spirit of my tiny halfbreed grandma, who never gave an inch, as far as I could see, in all of her life. Who made the land bloom and breed to delight and feed our spirits and our bodies. Who cooked and cleaned, smoked and drank (she was especially fond of Margaritas), scolded and giggled, demanded and accepted. Who loved fine things: music, flowers, china, relationships, rain, pure well water, the hills, dignity, courtesy, operas and symphonies, cats, dogs and grandchildren. Who knitted some of the first clothes I ever wore. Who played the violin, the piano, and, until she lost her sight, the organ. Who never depended on anyone for anything until the final years when she had to, and who hated every second of it, I'm sure. Who used to sneak food from mess at Indian School from her own tiny portion (they say they were always hungry there) to give to her younger sisters. Who never did eat much, but who loved butter, things cooked in butter, who set a good table until she was too arthritic and blind to do it any more, but who until her last stroke loved to eat. Jelly, coffee, chili, bread, meat. Who knew what hungry was, and never scorned the earth's blessings by refusing a good meal. Who was something special to so many of us at that burial, dressed out in a fine, solid oak coffin. She was Oak clan. Her last dress was exactly fitting, smooth and elegant, sturdy and gleaming with care, just like her life must have been.

And now, a few days later, now that all my connections to Cubero are done, who will bless the trees she planted? Who will take comfort and delight in her shade? And in time, what will my grandchildren have to say I gave them? I hope it will be worth as much to them as what she has given is to me.

The Better To Weave You With, My Dear

My journey into middlescence began in boredom. I was around thirty-nine when I first noticed it, but I decided to ignore it. Then I turned forty, and after the elation at becoming officially an old woman ("elder" is a more elegant but perhaps more sentimental and less vital way to put it), I noticed again how bored I was. I found that exactly nothing I had thought, done, wanted to do, or felt, was of interest. Come to think about it, boredom describes a chronic condition of my adolescence. I wonder if boredom and hormone changes go together? Anyway, I was bored.

My ambition for the past twenty years has been to grow up to be a dirty old woman. I wonder if I'll ever realize that ambition. I wonder if a country girl from Cubero, a convent school girl from the wilds of New Mexico, a half-breed, maverick girl from the wilds of society has a prayer of realizing such a coyote dream.

Let me tell you that I like being forties. I think I'm going to like being fifties even more. And I can hardly wait till sixties. My problem with writing this piece isn't my age, or even that no one loves an aging lady (as I certainly do — get turned on by gray-haired ladies, I mean). Rather it is that I've seen virtually nothing written by elder women for elder women that is connected to my own experience of this part of my life journey. For one thing, I don't have to cast about to find something to do with my life. I figured out years ago — when I was an adolescent — that middle age and old age would come and that I would need to have something to do other than sit around and gaze in despair at the lines growing on my face and throat. Since then I've directed my life away from the physical, away from the media images of self, away from putting my identity where my face and form is. My middle years are too damn full, if you ask me! I wake each day with more than enough to do for five days, and that's fine with me.

When I am old, I imagine I will sleep less and less, and I hope I will need the waking time as much as I presently need it; I also hope that I will have the mental/physical wherewithal to use it to write, think, talk on the phone, travel to readings and lectures, to visit with people I care about. I hope my eyes hold out, or that I learn to type accurately without being able to see; that I have someone to help me who I can depend on to proof-read. Or that I will have a computer that takes voice commands and then transforms them to type.

But what interests me about the space I'm crossing is its contours, its geography, its signposts, its highways, byways, and deerpaths. Who has been here before me? What did they see, feel, learn, do? Who were they after they'd passed through? No one's talking and it's difficult for me to write from the void their silence leaves . . .

Mirror Mirror On The Door

Then there's the problem of self-image. Am I really a dowdy old biddy? I am slightly over five feet tall and weigh around 200 pounds. I am a lesbian, and an unstylish one at that. My hair is merely graying, not fashionably grey or white; my skin is good, my eyes are clear, my hands and back are pretty strong (when not virtually paralyzed by arthritis). I usually wear corduroys, brushed demin jeans, or levis. I wear polyester shirts in bright or dark colors, sometimes with floral prints, sometimes with stripes. Because I am short as well as fat, with embarrassingly large breasts, I can't wear tailored jackets like blazers or suit coats, unless they're made by Levi company. The other brands hang over my hips and drape over my shoulders in a singularly unattractive way. I have found a couple of nice looking jackets in ladies wear at the department stores that fit my odd size because they are cut short, have ample room across the shoulders and boobs, but I feel like a matron in a nineteen-fifties movie in them. I think, "All I need is a pill-box hat with tiny veil and I'd be all dressed up."

The sad truth of it is that I'll never be stylish again. I had my chance years ago, and didn't enjoy it much then. Didn't have the money, the inclination, the lifestyle, the energy, the high sense of self-esteem, the whatever it took to be a sharp dresser. Now, even if I want to be one, even though I can at least think about affording it, I don't have the right looks for it. Or that's what I think. (Could be I think that because I always have.)

Self image, social image, public image. The problem is similar to the one I have in trying to write this: what images are available to me? Which ones apply? The first question is difficult enough, the second may be impossible. How many public socialized images can you think of that are suitable to a short, fat, huge-breasted, dykely, intellectual Semitic-looking half-breed aging convent girl cum grandma? I can't think of any at the moment!

That's not an unmixed tragedy, either. It may mean that as I have no socialized ideas to fall back on, no conditioned ways of judging how I "should" look, I can be open to whatever possibilities arise. Perhaps I should form an image — one that enables me to feel strong, functioning, satisfied, glorious — and then put it into action by whatever means I can find that gets me there. Maybe this time is when I discover that lots of options are open to me, that my years of experience and observation make it likely I can create choices for myself out of the available options and make selections from them as I go. If that's so, then this is the time when one discovers that growing pains are over and soaring pains have begun.

In the Native American world, middle age frees a woman for making choices congenial to her experience, circumstances and nature in many American Indian tribes. There she can choose who to be, now that her learning, practicing and nurturing tasks are accomplished. My Cherokee friend, another 40-er, tells me that among the Cherokee a woman of middle years could be a grandmother person, a healer-conjurer person, or a politician person. Certainly, the Native American women I know who are over forty do everything, and there seems to be no socialized built-in limit to their options. By that, I mean that their various social systems don't limit their choices, though their economic status, physical condition, educational level or legal status as tribespeople controlled by an alien set of laws and regulations often impose limits on them that their tribal ways do not.

It's been my experience that Indian women function in every capacity in their later years: they travel widely, take care of children, grandchildren, foster children, husbands, brothers, uncles, sisters, nieces, nephews, and assorted strangers; they are active in every profession, especially health and education; they are healers, shamans, traditional artists and dreamers; they serve as traditional leaders in their tribes, like on tribal councils, or as tribal presidents or chairs; they go to school; they lobby for tribal or national Indian issues at local, state and national levels, raise funds for children, elders, battered wives, destitute members of the community, and their own projects; they join in long walks, go to prison for political reasons, lead prayers and major dances at powwows, get on the radio, run businesses, farms, ranches, raise livestock, make rugs, blankets, pots — I can't think of anything they don't do in either the tribal world or the white world.

I have never been to any kind of public gathering in the American Indian community that was not graced with the directing and participating presence of women over forty, and women over sixty. Nor have I yet met a Native American woman of whatever age who characterized herself as old in the sense of incompetent, dependent, helpless and unable to function at some level. Many have complained of bodily limitations, but of those I have had an opportunity to watch, the limitations they experienced slowed them down as little as humanly possible.

In the white lesbian community women over forty are playing leadership roles, but the going is often tough as younger lesbians target institutions and organizations founded by and, after a decade or so of operation, owned and run by women over forty. It's the 'Young Turk' syndrome, I suppose, a dynamic common in the men's world but uncommon in organized form among women: younger adults, usually in their early thirties, make a concerted effort to dislodge the older adults from positions of leadership. Given the movement of political climate generated in communitites, the overthrow often succeeds.

I suppose the dynamic among white women is learned when the adolescent woman enters competition with her mother for most attractive woman. Separation of the generations is part of the maturation process in white America, and separation is usually achieved by denigrating the adversary in order to defuse the power mothers appear to have over daughters.

This is a far cry from the maturation processes among Native Americans, where older is valued and younger is valued and each takes the place proper to her age and life-phase. Trashing Mom — symbolically or directly — is not a common feature of Native American life. As a consequence of a system that positively values experience, the younger are not pressed to overthrow or trivialize elders, and 'palace revolts' are unheard of. Aging is seen as something that happens. It means whatever the particular aging woman makes it mean.

The connections between generations are so important. What I miss most in my lesbianism is just that. Most lesbians who are visible are between their mid-twenties and mid-forties — with the majority in their late twenties and early thirties. Where are my elders? Why is my lesbian community so bereft? And where are the youngers — the teenagers, the children, the babies?

My grandmother aged, but she did not view her aging as a humiliation. Nor did she see it as a reason to relinquish her connections to her obligations. She was tightly connected to her family — her siblings and their mates and their children and grandchildren, her children, granchildren, and great grand-children, her huge garden and music and books, her Margaritas and jelly and cookies and coffee — all through her old age. Not until severe arthritis and a stroke made self-care impossible did she give up her home where she had lived alone for twenty years. Not until her sight was all but gone did she give up her music. And not until her final, massive stroke did she accept hospitalization. And even then, all but brain-dead, she did not easily relinquish her grip on her body. Tenacious, she was. Alive.

Surely something goes on as we move through our life-phases. I have been through three and am in the early stage of the fourth, so I know something does change, something that is part of the body's change, that it tells us about. But what? The relationship of experience to world? The extent to which one's doing and being have greater and greater infuence over one's decisions, interpretations, understandings? Does 'old' mean in charge of one's life? I think that is so. Certainly the Native American women I have listened to and lived with give evidence of exactly that over and over by their words and more, by their gestures, nods, and habits, by their ever-more-evident being of just who they are and who they always have been. What changes is not identity but rather the degree to which identity determines choices and interpretations.

And that, if it is true, is the best most joyous reason I can think of to rejoice in the expectation and, for the lucky, the fact of growing old.

The better to die with, my dear.

JANNY

Crones, Commies, & Co's

I came from a well-to-do background. My father was the vice-president of *McCall's* magazine. He was always hoisting a Scotch and soda. I was his favorite but I adored my mother. Mama would bring us out and ask us to perform; to sing. I used to write songs when I was a kid. I'd sing off the back of a truck for Roosevelt. My voice is better now than it was then.

I'm sixty-two. I never was married. I'm pretty sure I've been gay all my life; I just didn't know it when I was young. I remember the first little girl I fell in love with, when I was nine. She looked just like Elizabeth Taylor. I slept with a hundred guys starting at the age of fourteen. Then when I was in my twenties, I came out here to California. Shortly after that I met Edie, my lover. We've been together for thirty-five years. I love her. We will always be together.

In the 1940's I was writing songs for the Communist Party, performing at the San Francisco Labor Theatre. Those people all persecuted Edie and me. There were a lot of guys around who were curious because we had a house and we were doing for ourselves. We always denied that we were lesbians; Edie still does. But somebody in the Party said they saw me at some gay place. I'd never gone there, but somebody testified they saw me in there. We always denied that we were lesbians, but I got thrown out of the Party for it anyway. That was in 1948. That's when I started drinking. I stopped writing music, and I started drinking.

I've been sober since I was fifty-seven. When I came out of alcoholism, I thought, "Screw it. I've paid my dues. I'm not going to go around with a big balloon saying I'm a lesbian, but I'm not going to hide anymore." I've always believed in what I thought whether society believed it or not. It was something I was proud of. I was proud of our love. I just wasn't going to hide it anymore.

Edie and I had some gay friends that we met about ten or twelve years ago. We'd go bowling with them, or to parties. But they weren't politically aware. I was always politically aware. I thought they were reactionary . . . these lesbian bowlers. A lot of lesbians then didn't want to identify themselves with anything political. They were persecuted enough. They would divert themselves in other ways, but they were not political. So I didn't have any close lesbian friends.

For years after I got thrown out of the Communist Party, I never wrote a song. Now I write for the women's movement, for the peace movement. I have a song about homosexuality that I wrote. I've written about being an alcoholic, about vulnerability . . . But for all those years, I didn't write at all.

I never thought about aging till my fifty-seventh birthday. The thought of aging and turning sixty bothered me. Edie thinks about it; she says, "Don't tell people how long we've lived together; they'll think we're old."

That's when I started going to SOL — Slightly Older Lesbians. I was always the oldest one. When I went to AA, it was a bunch of little kids. They kind of thought of me as a colleague, but I always felt like I was on the outside looking in. I felt lonely. And I felt old. I was old.

I was pretty active then, but I was tired all the time. I didn't know that I was sick. My body had started to break down. I had the flu, I had pneumonia, and then I got cancer. Now when people see me, they say "You look wonderful." My color is good. I've lost quite a bit of weight, but I'm not underweight. So I must have had cancer for quite a while before they found it.

For most people when they're aging, their accomplishments are in the past. But for me, having come out of an alcoholic fog, I'm now becoming more sucessful in the field I should have been in all my life. My aging is unusual. I'm better looking now than I've been in the last twenty years. I was fat. Then I got hypertension. Then I got sick and lost weight and kept it off. It's only been very recently that I've been taking good care of myself . . . trying to get enough rest.

How old people are treated makes me mad though. One time in front of Rainbow Grocery, there were some young women getting signatures and they bypassed me. They were looking for young people to sign their petition. They didn't even see me.

I have a show now on aging. I say that I was a communist. The communist party told me to get rid of Edie or they'd kick me out. I told them to go screw themselves. I was a rebel. Someone was always telling me I was doing wrong — the communists or my family. The Communist Party is down the drain and we're still here!

When I came out of the alcohol fog, I saw the women's movement. I saw these wonderful young lesbians who were militant. Just like I always have, they said what they thought politically. That's what my show is about. I come on the stage and I say, "I'm Janny and I write about what I believe in. I believe in women."

The song I wrote says that aging is a fact of life, and dying is part of life. I always pray to my higher power. And I have said to my higher power, "I know you gave me cancer. You must have given it to me for a reason." I know it's to help me deal with my stress, to deal with my "co" behavior . . . I'm always taking care of somebody else. It's really hard for me to do what's good for me. In the last year, not a week's gone by where I didn't have to see some doctor. I was afraid I was going to die until the last week . . . when I passed the test. So I prayed.

I remember when I first saw the press photo that went out

announcing my show. There were all these wrinkles in my neck. That was kind of a shock to me for a few minutes and then I chose to ignore it. I sometimes have a hard time seeing that my body has changed. I used to have arms. Before I had cancer, I was a big, strong woman. Now I feel I look diminished. You see this arm? That's like my mother's arm looked. It used to be a big arm. Now look . . . it's a skinny thing. It makes me mad to look at it. It's all dried up, too. My body looks like my mother's body looked when she was old. I look frail; I don't like to look frail.

Edie denies her homosexuality. It's so stupid. She says, "Are you going to sing that song in your show — the one about homosexuality?" I said, "I'm singing everything, Edie. I'm singing about what I believe in." And she said, "Well, I'm not coming." That's Edie for you. Of course, she came anyway. She's my biggest fan.

I think this is one of the best times in my life . . . or it's starting to be. I had thought I would be dead in the next six months, but I don't think I'm going to be now. I'm doing my own show and it's very sucessful. I remember before my first show saying to my higher power, "Just please give me a sign that I won't lose my voice, that I'm going to get through this." Just then the phone rang and the club said, "It's so crowded — would you consider doing a second show?" Now is that a sign or what?!

AGING IS NOT FOR SISSIES
by Janny

Aging is not for sissies
Aging is not for faint of heart
Aging is living's second part
Not for the quitter

Aging is for the fighter
Knowing just who and what you are
Courage will be your guiding star
Fear turns you bitter

Reach out to all
We love you too
Aging will call
On me — on you

Aging is not for sissies
Time's passage may diminish you
But you'll see the finish through
No fuss or glitter

You're born to do your bit
Aging is part of it
You're just a passing guest
And when you're gone
We'll know you did your best
AND YOU WERE STRONG.

FRANCES LORRAINE

Born-Again Lesbian

I'm a born-again lesbian, not one of those fortunate ones who have known since puberty that they love women. When I was growing up I never heard the word "lesbian," never knew there was anything other than heterosexual sex, and prior to my marriage I had never had a lesbian relationship.

I was brought up to grace a man's table, drawing room and bed. You know, dancing lessons, piano lessons, painting lessons, but just a little of each. I married because it was expected of me, and to get away from home. I chose my husband from among the contenders because he claimed to be an expert at deflowering virgins. When I walked down the aisle on my father's arm, a little voice inside kept saying to me, "Now you've done it, Frances! How are you going to get out of this one?" I was married for seventeen years; I've been very happily divorced for twenty.

When my first daughter was five, my husband and I were living in Washington, DC. My sister was in New York sharing an apartment with three other women. One weekend she came to visit with one of them. Her name was Sweeney and she was the first lesbian I'd ever met. Sweeney and I sat up late one night after the others went to bed and she told me that she was hanging around my sister because she was in love with her. I was flabbergasted, excited and intrigued. We exchanged a few kisses; when I went to the bathroom before going to bed I was astonished to find every indication of a high degree of sexual arousal — except I didn't put it in those words then. I probably thought something like, "Wow, I'm as wet as a dream."

About a month later when my husband was away I drove to New York and Sweeney and I spent some time in a dingy little room in Brooklyn. Sweeney gave me my first orgasm. It was 1950, and I was twenty-eight years old. Now I knew I had a clitoris, and where it was. She said, "I'm going to make you come seven times," and she did. We never saw each other again but I'll never forget her.

By that point in my marriage, I'd already begun to live two lives: the housewife, dutiful mother and charming hostess — and my own life: my creative-cultural-emotional life, which was separate and apart from my husband. I knew he didn't want anything more from me. So to this separate life of mine, I added sex.

I was pregnant with my second daughter when I met Ida. She was older than me by about ten or fifteen years and lived with husband, son and daughter in the apartment directly above ours. All through my pregnancy she courted me with out-of-season delicacies and exotic perfumes. I knew she was a lesbian but in the latter stages of my pregnancy I felt completely asexual. So I accepted her indulgences and kept her at arm's length.

When I came up out of the anaesthetic, I was filled with a raging lust that I must have been storing up for nine months. And Ida and I began our love affair. She used to say to me, "I'll fix your little red wagon." She did.

Our daughters started school that fall and they would go off hand-in-hand, the fellows would go off to work and she would come downstairs and we'd spend the morning in bed. Her love-making was a revelation to me. She was an experienced lover; and as she slowly and patiently awakened all the dormant, numb and neglected parts of my body, my sensations and pleasure in my sexuality grew daily. I was completely under her spell as she orchestrated our orgasms. I trusted her completely and was quite willing to be passive when the rewards were so great. She would arrange our bodies in her favorite positions, her arm here, my arm there and her thigh just so. After years of bony, bumpy men, it was exciting to discover how soft and gentle and sexy a woman could be . . . and how lewd and wanton two women could be.

I was blissfully happy and didn't care who knew it. But she was fearful of losing her children if she came out of the closet. So at her insistence we were discreet. I think both of our husbands suspected what was going on, but brushed it off as inconsequential. Two women, what can they do together? After all, without a penis it can't be serious. In the fifties no one had ever heard of lesbians anyway, except perhaps for Gertrude Stein.

We had nearly a year of close and voluptuous intimacy. On the weekends when we couldn't be together, she would play Mario Lanza's "Be My Love" at full volume till I could feel it through the floorboards. In time, inevitably, my husband and I moved across the river, and she and I would only see each other once or twice a week. A year later our husbands changed stations and my darling and I were separated. Maybe once a year we would manage to get together, but we were drifting apart. Then I didn't see her the three years I was in Alaska.

I loved Alaska. It was there I met the beauteous Shane, she of the high and elegant instep and alluring mouth. I didn't think about her sexually in the beginning of our friendship. Then one day we were on our hands and knees on the floor of my bedroom measuring lengths of organdy for something or other, and she was bent over and she had this wonderful back, and her shirt rode up and there was this space between her shirt and her jeans and I was looking at that back and I wanted to run my fingers along her backbone and kiss the hollows and then throw her down and I said, "Well, now, Frances, what's this?"

We had wonderful times together. We had all the same likes and dislikes. We would go for long walks, we painted together, we fished together, and picked berries and made jam. I got into the theater because she was a big theater buff and she played Vera to my Auntie Mame. And then one night, when our husbands were away, she called and said the tide was in, did I want to go fishing. We put on our rain coats and waders and went out and snagged some salmon. Then we came back to my house and had some drinks and dried out and she talked about how her breasts were growing. I said I hoped it might be because of me. And she said maybe it was. And I asked her if she had any idea what an effect she had on me, and then somehow we were showering together and in bed making love. Within a few short weeks she decided that she didn't want to cheat on her husband and our brief affair was over. After that, our friendship was strained. I lost track of her after we left Alaska and I've been unable to locate her since.

In 1959, my husband and I returned to Washington, DC, for yet another tour of duty. I got a job as a file clerk, having no previous work history. The woman I worked with was English and during the course of our budding friendship I related the tale of my sad and sorry marriage and how I felt that the children were being affected. She said, "Why don't you get a divorce?" I must have been waiting to hear that because everything came together in my head. I talked to a lawyer she recommended and then one morning after he had left for work, I took the two kids, half the furniture and the two Siamese cats and moved to an apartment in Arlington.

For three years my husband fought me with suits, countersuits, warrants, subpoenas — anything he could think of. He had achieved the rank of colonel by this time and he was damned if anyone was going to divorce him. My salary was very small and I was constantly sweating out the child-support payments. But a kindly judge had said that I didn't have to live with him so I was happy. No longer was I forced to endure his psychotic rages, the verbal abuse that I called his "monthlies." And in January, 1963, I was finally legally free. Divorced. Allowed by law to live without benefit of male authority. Hip-hip-hooray!

So here I was a single woman in Washington, D.C. There was no lesbian community to connect with, at least as far as I knew. Besides, I was still thinking of myself as a straight woman. And I was doing a lot of experimenting with straight men. I *did* know plenty of homosexual males — some carefully closeted and/or married — and they all knew each other. I worked for a gay man and most of the men in my office were gay. I gravitated towards the lesbian wing of NOW, stopped wearing makeup, wore blue work shirts with my jeans, gave up men and vowed to take control of my own life, take command of my sexual destiny and be responsible for myself. Finally, I was identifying as a lesbian — albeit a political lesbian, who was fighting the patriarchy.

And my daughters were growing up. The younger one transferred from George Washington University to U.C. Berkeley and I went out for a visit. I fell in love with San Francisco, came back to Washington and packed up some things, gave the rest away, and flew out to begin a new life. I was fifty years old. Parting words from my lesbian friends were, "There's some great women in San Francisco." I wanted to meet them all. I joined the Golden Gate chapter of NOW (which was formed by the dissatisfied and rejected members of the SF chapter whose president called them "lesbians and dingbats.") Since most of the chapter members seemed to be approximately thirty-five years old, I started the task force on older women so I could meet some women my own age.

So what happened? I fell in love with a younger woman. When we were first introduced, I was immediately attracted. On our first date, we went to Muir Woods on a rainy Monday, dropped acid and talked to the plants. She said she admired me very much and would enjoy a platonic relationship. That was certainly not the message I was getting and was not at all what I had in mind. When we got home and she started to sit down at a discreet distance from me, I hooked my foot around her and pulled her close and she fell against me. That did it. We didn't come up for air for six months. When we did, we realized that we had absolutely nothing in common except our mutual lust. And when that wore off, we parted.

So at this writing (as they say) I am sexually uninvolved and enjoying a period of heightened creativity. I am not monogamous — although I can get totally absorbed in one woman — and the older I get the more constraining I find the couple trap. As we age, I think it makes good sense for women to have two or three intimates, or just a warm circle of friends — or both.

I simply do not believe the negative articles about older women's sexuality that are mostly written by heterosexual men. What do they know? I believe women's capacity for sex increases until the day we die — the quality of orgasm, the duration, the excitement, the infinite variety of our sexual responses, the erotic pleasure in our own and another woman's body.

Yesterday I met a blithe spirit with wise eyes and tomorrow we are going to the beach and — who knows?

BARBARA TYMBIOS

A Free Spirit

I was born after the close of the nineteenth century in Sumter, South Carolina.

We lived in a bungalow on Liberty Street. I was the seventh of eleven children. In back of the bungalow was a forest. When I wanted to get away from the family I roamed in the forest and communicated with the trees.

We had two huge iron pots where we bathed and the servants washed our clothes and starched our petticoats and dresses, which were as stiff as cardboard. We had a privy, or outhouse as it is called today. We used newspapers to wipe our behinds.

My parents had a store on Main Street called "The New York Racket Store." It had a swinging shingle. Father employed two clerks: one black, Pinkney, and the other, Mr. Burgess, was white. I believe Father was the first white to employ a Negro clerk. Mind you, this was 90 years ago. We sold Hoyt's cologne at a nickel a vial, ginghams, clothing for men and women, spools of thread, needles — a general store. But thank heavens, no groceries.

Papa was an Orthodox Jew — actually a Rabbi — who did not believe in making money at the pulpit. He was strict all right — kosher food, and don't mix milk products with meat products. A separate set of dishes for milk products and for meat. At Passover, Mama had to sterilize her cutlery. How did she do this? By digging a hole in the earth and pouring boiling water over the knives, forks, spoons, etc.

During my childhood I loved girls and thought nothing of it. But as I grew older I knew I was different from my sisters, who all had beaux. I did not care for men at all. While in high school in Charleston, I asked my friend Harriet what she thought I was thinking and she said, "You want to put your head on my breast." I was shocked at her divination.

In 1917, I left home to live in New York with my sister Sarah. My real passion was dancing. I took dance classes at the Rand School with Bird Larson. We danced in large rooms with tall windows draped to the floor. It was primitive ballet. We danced barefoot to tomtoms and imitated animals. It was absolutely thrilling.

Through my sister Sarah, I met Herman Defremery who was a psychologist at Columbia University. We became friends. I confided in him how very perturbed I was at liking women. I thought I was insane. He assured me that I was not crazy, saying there were homos, bi's, and heteros, and that I was bisexual. You can imagine how grateful I was to him for straightening out my thinking about being gay. It was a time in my life when I was truly confused and in need of guidance.

Herman was always encouraging me to have affairs. I told him about this beautiful woman I had seen in one of my dance classes. With Herman's encouragement I was finally able to make friends and become lovers with Vi, the love of my life.

Vi and I had a private life. We didn't tell anyone how we felt about each other. But Vi was never comfortable being gay. One day she came to me and told me she had fallen in love with a man. Later in that same year she came to me and demanded that I burn her love letters to me. I did, right in front of her. What choice did I have? She wanted me to be her dark past. She married Art and she never spoke to me again.

After Vi married, I slept with every good-looking man at the Rand School. I got the reputation that I was promiscuous which I was not. I only slept with them; I didn't have sex with them. It was then that I met my Greek, Tony Tymbios. I was his ballroom teacher at the Rand school. He had a violent crush on me. I spent hours trying to explain my feelings for women, but he never understood me. Vi was married so I thought what the hell and I married him.

We moved to Greenwich Village and I tried to make a go of it. After six terrible months, I finally made him leave. He said he was madly in love with me and that I was his wife. At first he refused to give me a divorce, but finally he consented.

I started going to bars and parties. I met lesbians and had numerous affairs, primarily with married women. During the depression, I took any job that was available. For a while I worked as a water inspector in buildings. I got this job through the WPA. I would check toilets and waterlines.

After a while I made lesbian friends who introduced me to women with whom I was compatible. I met Joy Perry in the thirties. She was an administrator who sold to wholesalers. I fell in love the first time I saw her. I wanted her. Every lunch time, I would go to her office and we would neck. But we never had sex together. I felt like I could take the pillars of the Paramount Theatre and crush them, that's how much I loved her. We have remained friends for more than fifty years. We never talked about being lovers.

A friend of Joy's who worked for the *Times*, Maria Saurez, introduced me to Lorena Hickock at a party. I had an affair with her. I met a lot of newspaper people. She would take me to restaurants that literary people frequented. This was in the thirties. I had a job with AMTOG — the American Trading Organization — working on *The Economic Review of the Soviet Union*. We tried to explain what the Soviet Union was trying to do and to contribute to world industry. Hickock would come to the office for information. I was a clerk/secretary there. She would speak with one of the head people.

I never loved her but I found her extremely interesting. She knew a lot. I enjoyed conversations with her. She wanted me as a lover, not as a friend. When I ended the relationship, I never saw her again. I'm sorry for that as I admired her greatly.

I left her for a floozy — Ruth Morgan. This was an on-again/off-again relationship that went on for years. During that time I saw a lot of other women. I loved Ruth. I was fascinated with her. But she couldn't or wouldn't be faithful for very long.

It was difficult for me to have an orgasm until I met a fellow usher at the Century Theatre. Helen was her name. She had left her artist husband. She came to me on Cornelia St. in the Village, a woman about 5'10" tall, carrying a small overnight bag. She got into bed with me and proceeded to make love and within seconds I had my first orgasm. There were so many women with whom I had affairs, and I was rarely aggressive. But with Helen it was mutual love-making and I became a good lover.

But I grew restless. I needed something more. For the first time in a relationship, I had a clandestine affair. I shocked myself. I had never been unfaithful to my girls before.

In 1944, I went overseas even though my lover said she wouldn't wait for me. I wanted to help destroy Hitler and I needed to have adventures. Even though I cared for my lover, I needed to go. When I got back to New York, she was involved with somebody else.

In London I worked in the Movie Picture Dept. of the Office of War Information as a liason between OWI and the British Ministry of Information. While abroad I dared not do anything to jeopardize my job. You might say my celibacy was part of the war effort.

After the war ended I moved to Los Angeles where I tried my hand at running an antique shop in Hollywood. This shop was a dismal failure. I can't tell you how much of a blow this was to me — not to be able to be independent and work for myself.

In 1948 at the age of forty-nine, I moved to California and got a job as a clerk for the Army. Once I resigned myself to the job, I enjoyed the work and the people around me. I worked for the Army till my retirement in 1966.

You know I could go on with my list of lovers. I hope I proved that an old dame like me can be gay. Just because I'm old and sick and eighty-five doesn't mean I didn't have quite a gay life. You see I've loved a lot of women and a lot of women have loved me. In fact, if I weren't sick that would still be the case.

But let me tell you about my life right now. My health is very poor. I no longer have a physical feeling for anyone. And I should have it because it makes you forget yourself. I miss it.

I'm going into the hospital soon. They found a spot on my lung. These doctors drive me crazy. They found fluid in my lung. They're going to draw it off. I've been smoking all my life. I'm worried about having the operation; I'm so thin. I'll probably be going into the hospital at the end of the week. I had uterine cancer a couple of years ago and was in the hospital then. I'm a little worried that I won't come out of the hospital. I'm afraid of the operation; I don't really know much about it. I can ask my doctor about it on Thursday.

Every time I go to the doctor's, I've lost another pound. As I told you, I used to be a dancer. I studied dancing for years. I'm too weak to dance now . . . and in too much pain. I missed dancing when I stopped. But it has been so long now I don't think about it. When you are real old, everything hurts, everything is an effort. Every time I go to a doctor they say there is nothing they can do for anything — my neck, my eyes, all my aches and pains. I don't want to live another ten years, but I also do not want to die.

I think about dying a good deal right now. I think about who's going to get my possessions. I think about not falling in love anymore; I've been too ill for too long. A great deal of the time I think about my past. My family was very old-fashioned. My father was very strict.

The most important thing in my life now is to get my health back. After all I have my sister Rebeccah that I have to take care of. She was a genius but now she has lost her memory. Sometimes she's lucid. She's in a home. I sent the home two checks today. I'm responsible for her care.

The key word in life is "fight." I must be fighting unconsciously because consciously, very often I don't give a damn. Sometimes I think we all say, "I don't give a damn." But I don't know what's on the other side — I don't believe in life after death.

I'm still hoping my eyes will get better. I've been to twenty doctors; I've had operations and laser beams. I have an appointment with another doctor soon. I can't give up on my eyes. I have some days where it doesn't seem worth it anymore, but then I have to look out for my sister. My family is very important to me, but I'm not very important to my family. It's not because I'm gay; it's because they have children and they're preoccupied with them.

I need somebody most every day of the week. I have some people from GLOE [Gay and Lesbian Outreach to Elders], and a woman from Catholic Charities comes in once a week for $5.50 an hour. She does a good job. She cleans the house. The problem with that is that I have so many doctor's appointments. I tried to get her to call me first, because I might not be there. Now she doesn't want to work for me, because it isn't regular.

I have friends who come by and cook me dinner every now and then and I have friends who take me to my doctors appointments. These are new and younger gay friends.

At one point, I thought gay people were no good. But now all these gay people are helping me. It's not my family that is taking care of me; it's my gay friends. They have been wonderful to me.

My best friends are my oldest friends. Joy lives in New York with her lover and we speak on the phone regularly. I spoke with Joy just the other day and she said I musn't worry about my age. She's having a hard time health-wise but she still wants to live. She's as old as I am. She had plenty of aches and pains but she still wants to go on.

I speak with all my close old friends about aging and living and dying. That is one of the importances of old, dear friends. My other good friend, Thais, lives in Laguna Beach with her lover. I have known her for over fifty years. We were never lovers — just always the best of friends. She is younger than me by about ten years. I used to go down and stay with them. And now, I don't go because of my health. Thais calls me every Sunday and comes and stays here from time to time. But she whirls in here and takes over like Grant took Richmond. It always takes me several weeks to recover from her visits. She acts like I can't do anything. Of course, I appreciate all the things she does for me but it is important to do as much as I can for myself.

I took a bath all by myself today. I'm weak but I can still bathe by myself. You want to know about old age; that's old age.

I think the doctor will tell me I have terminal cancer. She wanted to examine my breasts but I said, "Leave my breasts alone." I'm certainly not going to let anyone operate on my breasts. They are little enough as it is.

* * *

You know, young gay people are a revelation to me. They participate in gay parades. One gal I know, she is a young person of thirty-five, is going to study politics. I told her, "For God's sakes, don't vote for a person just because they are gay. Be more objective in your outlook on life."

These young people flaunt themselves. They march in parades. They represent gay people on TV. I admire that but I don't do it myself. I've always been conservative about being gay. I can't imagine I could be any different. I have to be guarded but I think it's good that others reveal themselves.

I don't know what the present holds for me and I don't know whether there *is* a future. I do think about tomorrow and I'm hoping the doctors can help me. If they can help me physically, I'll be a new person. If I die, then I die. Sometimes it's very hard to take all this pain. It's hard to be dependent on people for everything. I still want to live, though. I'm going to try.

MARIE P.

New Adventures

I was born in Arkansas in 1921. I married for a brief time and had a son that I gave up. I've been gay all my life. I had a twenty-one year relationship and a five year relationship and a ten year relationship.

I married even though I always knew I preferred women. I married to get out of Arkansas and the hick town I grew up in. He was in the Navy so we moved around a lot. We had been married four years when he walked in on me and a woman in bed together. He left me and took my son with him back to Arkansas. He told the court I was a lesbian. I wouldn't have had a chance winning my son back so I didn't even contest the court's decision.

My first long-term relationship was with Lora. I moved in with her and just stayed. We raised her two kids through college. In 1972, they both went out and got good jobs and came home and informed their mother that I was moving out and they were going to take care of her. Lora sided with her children. So Lora and I broke up. The boy was going to be married and he didn't want his mother living with a lesbian, but he didn't think his mother was a lesbian — he thought I was the lesbian. We shared the same bedroom and the same bed for twenty-one years. They told me to go but since I owned the house, I told all of them to get out, including Lora.

We had friends who knew we were a couple. At Lora's job, they accepted me as her friend; we were both invited to all the parties — the company parties, the company picnics. We still have all those friends . . . I get Christmas cards from them, she gets Christmas cards from them. Something happens in their families, she'll get a call, or I'll get a call.

For many years after the break-up, Lora and I never talked. Now we are good friends and see each other weekly.

After Lora left, I stayed by myself for a year and a half before I got another lover, Jean. My relationship with Jean was a pretty good relationship, but she drank too much. So I started going out again and tried to drink right along with her. Working as hard as I was working at that time . . . things between us just didn't work too well. Jean was about fifteen years younger than me. So my niece just came along and took her away from me. She came to visit and walked off with her. And then my third lover came along. . .

Chris came into my repair shop to get her car fixed. She didn't have any money to pay for it after I fixed it, so she dropped out of college and came to work for me. She was twenty-one when I met her; I was in my late forties. We didn't hesitate because we knew a lot of other couples whose age difference was about as great. We used to have house parties where there'd be eight or ten couples where one of them was much older than the other. We used to do holidays with these couples, camping and fishing. Everything was done in couples. I never went out without Chris. I wanted it that way . . . probably because I didn't want her to have a chance to go out where somebody'd pick her up.

That's what happened anyway.

Chris and I went out together or we just didn't go out. We were always together — work and play. We enjoyed being together and being together with other people. The last year we were together, she would go to the bookstore on Sunday afternoons because she had started trying to write. I didn't go because at that time I didn't read at all. So usually when she did that, I would work on my shop's books or go to the shop and get something out of the way that was on my mind. And then we'd go out to dinner. I guess we just never thought about how much we were together. It never entered our minds. When I planned my retirement, I planned to spend it with my lover, Chris. But she met somebody else right in our very own life. We had a young lady who was living with us, sharing our house. She was in college and she couldn't find a place to live, so we rented her the front bedroom. She brought this straight friend of hers over. Her friend was on the fence. All she needed was a little push. So we all got in the hot tub and she and Chris fell in love. And that was that.

When Chris left, it was hard for me to maintain relationships with the couples we'd known because I'd had never spent any time alone with them. I didn't realize it, but when you're not with somebody, when you're not a couple, you don't get invited to those functions.

I would do it differently now. I would see that I had some single friends and intermingled with people a lot more. I know I wouldn't be as jealous as I was. I was a very jealous person. I shouldn't be so possessive. That's one reason why I'm holding back now — not trying to find anybody. Because I don't want to get involved. I want to do my own thing. I want to go on trips and I want to do a lot of things. I just haven't found anybody who wants to do the same things I want to do and the ones that I have found don't have the money to . . . and I can't afford to pay their way and my way, too. And it wouldn't be right if I did. So I've just kind of been dragging my heels. If somebody comes along that I can get along with, fine. I have a friend — we go out to dinner. We are sexual, but it isn't a couple relationship. I'm not looking for a couple relationship anymore.

I don't really know how to go about meeting older people, people my own age. I just have to feel that out. I have been invited to functions for older lesbians, but I just don't like to go someplace where I don't know anybody. I don't meet people very well. I never have. I think that's one reason I was so possessive of my lovers, because they would do the talking for me. They would do all the arranging and what have you and I didn't have to do any of that. That I miss an awful lot.

* * *

Lynne and Sandy are new friends. They have been two of the best friends I've ever had in my life. We have to be friends because we live in this small house together, but it's not a burden on any of us. We enjoy each other's company. They're happy living here. I have other friends who live up on Richmond Street.

I started talking more in the last three years than I ever did in my whole life. Except to talk to customers about a job, I never had anything to say. But I don't need a spokesperson anymore. I wished I had developed that skill earlier.

I try to get my couple friends to associate with single people and with straight people. They say, "Aw, we're going to be together till the day we die." And I say, "Yeah, I've heard that before." I think my generation is more isolated than younger generations of gay people. Sometimes you kind of feel like you're being left out, being an older gay person. Like I go down to the Senior Citizens luncheon once a month, just to talk to people and be around people my own age. But I go in and I feel like they don't quite know how to take me. I have a nasty habit of not wearing anything but slacks, and I don't feel like I fit in.

When I go down to this gay bar — Ollie's — every now and then, most of the people in the back room are young and energetic and they just don't have anything to do with me. And older people don't go there.

It gets scary thinking about getting older. What if this happens, what if that should happen? You don't want to be a burden to your family. But if you get sick, you get sick. If you don't have the money to take care of yourself, then your family has to help you out or be responsible for you. It's been very hard for me to accept the fact that I'm getting older. Until I got my first social security check — I threw it off that long. Now I'm starting to admit to myself that I am over sixty.

I do have the satisfaction of knowing that if I were to become bed-ridden, my son would help out and take care of me because we are very, very close. I would say that Jim and I are closer than any other mother and son I know of. I don't know if it's just because we're both gay or what. For the last twenty-five years, he has lived close to me. It is good to have him near. He didn't come to live with me until he was eighteen years old, but we understand each other very, very well. There is just that real bond of love between the two of us and I protect him as much as he protects me. I would rely on him as a person, not financially. I have enough money to take care of myself.

We've been discussing a Will. I just talked to my accountant last Tuesday. He suggested that I go to an attorney and put everything in a living trust so that if something happens to me Jim won't have to dispose of any property immediately to take care of finances at that time.

I've been very active all my life: jogging, biking . . . and working in the shop. Now I have arthritis pretty bad. I can't go jogging or play basketball anymore because of the pain. But I'm a jock kind of person so I have substituted other things. I work out three times a week: nautilus, sauna and the hot tub. I can walk three miles a day. Sometimes we make it and sometimes we don't. If we get tired, we come home . . . me and the dog. I don't like to carry her. I have to use my arms to come up the hills.

I retired a year ago, October. There's a lot of loneliness after you retire. There's not a lot of people around. I was in contact with at least fifty people a day when I was in business — telephone contact — constantly all day long, six days a week. I think that upsets me more than anything else, not having contact with people.

The good part about retirement is that my time is my own. When I get up in the morning, if I feel like going to Bakersfield, I go to Bakersfield. If I want to drive to L.A., I pack my suitcase and I take off. I'll call my sister and tell her I'm coming.

The fun is starting to compensate for the missing people.

Three months ago, I wouldn't have made that statement, but it is starting now to do a complete turn-around. I was still consulting at the shop. The retirement would be pulling me this way and the shop would be pulling me that way. And I knew that I couldn't go back to the shop. When I gave that up, when I washed my hands of it — 'OK, I'm through, that's it' — it lifted a load off me that let me relax more and enjoy what I thought retirement was going to be.

I thought when I retired I would be able to do as I pleased: go fishing, go on a cruise, go to Europe. At first I found it wasn't so pleasant traveling alone. I figure I got myself in this predicament by being alone, by being so busy in the shop and by being possessive about our relationship. But when I went on a trip by myself to Florida, everything changed. I enjoyed being alone. I drove from here to Florida by myself; all eleven thousand, six hundred and forty-three miles of it. All by myself. I enjoyed being in my car. I enjoyed the scenery. I hadn't driven back home in maybe twenty years. I just wandered around and visited relatives between here and there. Stopped in Texas and visited a couple of gay guys who used to live here. We're very close friends. Then I went on to Arkansas — I still have some brothers there — went to West Virginia and visited a cousin there. I went to South Carolina and visited a man who used to work for me many many years ago. He's a minister back there. I went there and found out that he's gay. I had known him twenty years. He knew I was, but I didn't know he was. He was married and secretly gay. He told me because I think he just had to have somebody to talk to. But he seems to be happy.

I really enjoyed that trip. There was a race at Daytona Beach in Florida. I went there and took pictures. Lived a memorable life for forty-eight hours. I got a hotel room on the top floor overlooking the race track. Cost me $184.00 for one night but I wanted to do that. I did everything I wanted to do that I hadn't had a chance to do. I went down to the tip of Florida and I chartered a plane and I went to all of the islands. I was only on the islands for forty-five minutes or so, then it came under storm so we had to get back in. And I told the guy,

"No, I'll stay here. We'll fly around." And we did. There's something called water spouts — a big thing of water that comes down, just straight down out of the sky and you can see them for miles and miles away. And we just kept flying around and flying around until we got back to Florida.

That trip was a turning point.

I'm learning to substitute . . . if I don't get to go to Alaska this year, I'm planning on going to Maine. I've never been back there. My sister told me to be sure and go in the fall.

This is the first time in my life I've been on my own. And I'm just beginning to enjoy it.

Appendix

KATHLEEN TAYLOR, M.D.

The Whole Picture: Our health reflects our lives

We who have been raised under the influence of Western culture tend to see health and illness as a set of circumstances outside our control — an external process. Somehow, we "catch" illnesses, or we think that heredity makes them inevitable. We expect that a specific cause can be found for a physical symptom, which can be cured by an external remedy. Western medicine's magic bullets are part of our health mystique; wonder drugs make headline news. This simplistic view fails to take into account the complex interactions between our bodies and our minds. The Chinese, in contrast, have recognized the flows of energy in the body for centuries, and include them in their systems of medical care. Only recently have we in Western culture begun to focus on stress, lifestyles, diet, habits, and emotional life as prime factors in health and illness.

By being aware of the influence of all these factors, we can take control of our health in a whole, new way. We must learn to look beyond the symptoms of illness to a better understanding of its causes. This holistic approach can also help us to prevent many ills, and to enjoy enhanced health as we age.

One important way to get and keep healthy is early recognition of the signs of stress on our bodies. We can then find ways to remove harmful stresses. Tension and stress can cause actual physical harm to various organs of the body: real ulcers, real blood vessel damage, etc. They also cause fatigue, irregular cycles, muscle and back pain, and other discomforts.

There are many ways to reduce or remove stress from your life. Enjoyable recreation, exercise and play are all good therapy for stress. Tai Chi and other Eastern disciplines help. If there are major emotional problems in your life, you may want to consider psychotherapy or bodywork, such as Lomi or Rosen massage therapy. Learn some basic relaxation techniques: deep breathing, chanting, meditation. These methods are 100 times more effective than Valium or alcohol in the long run. You'll find you have a healthier body, and a happier outlook on life in general.

Basics: We are what we eat.

The most important thing any woman can do to ensure her good health is to pay careful attention to her diet. How and what we eat becomes more crucial during and after menopause, as the assaults on our systems add up. The benefits of a good diet are enormous: more energy, improved appearance, prevention of pain and disability — and a healthy diet will actually save you money, both at the grocery store and in what you pay for health care.

A health-giving diet is a matter of good balance. High protein and high-fat animal foods should be kept to a minimum. Cholesterol-rich foods such as meat and shellfish increase the risks of high-blood pressure, stroke, and heart disease. A high-protein diet also increases the amount of calcium loss from the bone. Small amounts of meat, fish or poultry can be used in making delicious vegetable and rice or pasta dishes, but the emphasis should be on whole grains, vegetables, and beans. The high fiber and complex carbohydrates in these foods ensure the health of your digestive tract, from liver and pancreas to colon. In parts of Africa where diets are very high in fiber, bowel cancer is rare. High-fiber diets have also been shown to help lower blood pressure, control diabetes and hypoglycemia, aid in weight loss, and minimize hardening of the arteries. Oat bran is particularly effective, and causes fewer gas problems than regular wheat bran. Add some to cereals, breads, casseroles, soups; or just mix a tablespoon a day into juice.

A diet rich in dark green, red or yellow vegetables and fruits also contains needed vitamins and minerals. The best way to cook them is lightly, preferably steamed tender-crisp; boiling removes vitamins. If you don't eat three or four servings of veggies or whole grains a day, you should probably add a vitamin and mineral supplement .

Milk products can be included in the diet, but should be used with care. Many women, especially black women, lack the enzyme necessary to digest milk sugar; they can have cramping, bloating and even diarrhea after drinking milk. Cultured products such as yogurt and cottage cheese are usually okay. Use low-fat or skim milk products; whole milk is high in cholesterol, as are many hard cheeses. The low-fat products will add protein, calcium, and delicious variety to meals.

Foods with high sugar and fat content, such as rich crackers, desserts and ice cream, should be occasional treats, or eliminated. These foods add little nourishment, and cause stress on the pancreas and liver. They create a reactive drop in blood sugar, which may be experienced as feeling tired, shaky, or hungry again. Alcohol can do this, too: it also has many other harmful effects. In larger amounts, (three or more daily drinks), it can increase bone loss and osteoporosis, depress the ovaries and other hormone-producing centers, and slow the immune system. Many people enjoy an occasional drink with no apparent ill effect. But if you need alcohol daily, or take more than two drinks a day on a regular basis, you are adversely affecting your health in the long run.

Salt is also a bad actor, and should be used sparingly. Sodium not only increases blood pressure, but also increases calcium loss through the kidneys. Monosodium glutamate and chloride do the same. Try decreasing the salt you use, replacing it with other seasonings such as garlic, lemon, herbs and spices. Avoid processed meats such as hot dogs, ham and cold cuts. All contain nitrites, which have been linked to cancer of the bowel as well as being high in sodium.

Last, caffeine should be kept to a minimum. It has adverse effects on breast tissue, causing increased fibrocystic changes; over the long term, these become painful and may increase the risk of breast cancer. Caffeine also puts extra stress on the heart. There are very good decaffeinated coffees available, which are water processed. (The chemical process leaves traces of chemicals in the coffee.) Or, try caffeine-free herbal teas.

If you don't completely meet these guidelines with your diet (yet), you may need a vitamin supplement. These are also a good idea when you are under stresses such as illness or surgery. Such a supplement should contain about 500 mg. of vitamin C, 10,000u. of vitamin A, 150 I.U. of vitamin E, 400 I.U. of vitamin D, and the entire B complex. Trace minerals such as zinc or selenium should be included. It's fine to take extra C and B-complex when you are under high stress, or when camping (B-complex, taken daily, repels mosquitos): however, it's unhealthy to take too much vitamin A, D, B6, or trace minerals.

Calcium is a very important nutrient, especially for midlife women. It retards osteoporosis, maintains teeth, and can have a calming effect. Women need a total of 1½ grams of elemental calcium a day, from diet or supplement. Calcium carbonate, from oyster shell, is the most economical and easiest to take. Os-Cal 500, three a day, or Tums, six a day, supply the full daily requirement.

There are some excellent books on nutrition and diet which include recipes; see the list at the end of the chapter. You don't have to start off with a tofu and rice diet. Make small changes at a time, and get comfortable with a new way of eating. It's worth it!

Menopause: Before, during and after

Menopause, also known as the climacteric, is approached

with anxiety by the majority of women I meet. And no wonder: our society has given menopause a heavy negative emotional charge. Youth, slender bodies, and beauty are the positive attributes valued for women in all the media. Older women are frequently depicted as grouchy, unstable, and demanding. Jokes pin the blame on "going through the change." Some women fear menopause because they watched their mothers or aunts go through a difficult time. For many of these heterosexual women, menopause was a time of personal crisis, as their children left home and their life function was no longer clear. These *emotional* crises were blamed on the *physical* process of menopause. Old wives' tales are told about women going crazy because of "raging hormones."

All of these negative experiences and stories can naturally make us anxious about how we will handle menopause. A lack of clear information contributes to the problem. We're unsure when it will start, how long it will last, and what to expect. Should we take hormones? What about the risks of cancer? Will we lose our desire or desirability?

Fortunately, as lesbians we have already discounted many of the male-inspired values society has set for women. Our positive images are of strong women and natural appearances. We value older women for their experience and wisdom. I see women wearing "I like older women" buttons. We refer to a grey-haired woman as a Silver Fox. We have many wonderful role models such as Del Martin, Phyllis Lyon, May Sarton, Gertrude Stein, and a host of others. As lesbians, we certainly have the resources to make our menopausal years a positive experience. If we inform ourselves, take wise precautions, and draw support from our sisters, menopause and later life can be our richest time.

The Hows and Whys

Menopause is a natural process of change which means the end of only one thing: the ability to have children. Eventually it also means that menstruation or periods stop — no great loss for most women. This physical change is not a sudden event, but a transition which occurs over several years. The usual time is between age 45 and 55, although it can start as early as 40 or late as 60. The age of onset depends on heredity, climate, diet, habits such as smoking and drinking (these suppress ovaries earlier), and general health. To understand the process, it helps to review menstrual physiology.

A woman is born with all the eggs she will ever have already present in her ovaries — they remain dormant until the onset of menstruation. Each month from then on, several ova are stimulated by hormones from the pituitary gland to mature in egg sacs called follicles. One ovum reaches maturity and is released: ovulation. The follicle tissue produces our two female hormones: estrogen during the egg growth, and both estrogen and progesterone following ovulation. These hormones cause the uterine lining to grow, preparing it to recieve and nourish a possible pregnancy. The follicle, or corpus luteum, only lasts about two weeks; if no pregnancy occurs, it ceases to produce hormone, and the thick uterine lining, or endometrium, breaks down and is expelled from the body as menstrual flow.

During the reproductive years, we gradually use up the supply of ova until only a few are left. These are less responsive to the pituitary hormones, FSH and LH. We begin having cycles in which we don't ovulate; less hormone is produced by the ovary, particularly progesterone. The pituitary increases its production of FSH and LH to stimulate the reluctant follicles; they may mature faster, resulting in a shorter cycle. Or, their release may be delayed, with longer cycles. Many women find their periods vary in length as well as amount as their menopause approaches. This is due to the variation in timing and hormone output.

If no ovulation occurs, irregular bleeding may result from erratic estrogen stimulation of the endometrium without the stabilizing effects of progesterone. With prolonged stimulation, this can lead to endometrial overgrowth, or hyperplasia. Sometimes this hyperplasia becomes pre-cancerous, or even cancer. That's why it's important to have your doctor evaluate any irregular bleeding.

Eventually, the egg supply runs out, and ovulation stops occurring. Despite high levels of FSH and LH, estrogen production decreases. Usually, periods cease. Most of the remaining estrogen in the body comes from the changing of an adrenal gland hormone to a weaker estrogen, estrone, in the body's fat cells. Heavier women may continue to have enough estrone to cause bleeding for a longer time after ovulation ends. The uterine lining shrinks or atrophies until the weaker estrone can't affect it, then bleeding ceases.

Menopause and the Mirror

In this culture, whole industries are built around maintaining a youthful appearance. Advertising would have us believe that the decrease in hormones which accompanies menopause causes wrinkling and sagging.

A popular book published in the sixties, *Feminine Forever*, held out the promise that taking estrogens could retard the aging process, keeping us youthful and attractive. There are estrogen pills and preparations, as well as various diets and tonics promising to boost our hormones. What is the reality?

Many tissues of the body are sensitive to hormone changes, particularly the breast glands, genitals, and bones. The skin is only mildly sensitive, and does not respond to estrogen-containing creams rubbed on its surface. There are many tissue changes which have to do with aging alone, or with other factors. During mid-life, we may notice a redistribution of weight which is only partially hormone-related. The waist, hips and abdomen become thicker. This may be a survival response, giving us a reserve for the increased risks of illness. As time, weather, and gravity act on us, there is a gradual decrease in elasticity of support tissues. These effects can be magnified by smoking, poor diet and exposure to the sun and wind; all cause premature wrinkling and skin aging. A healthy diet, rich in vitamins and minerals and low in chemicals and preservatives, will help. Avoid overexposure to sun, and always use a sunscreen containing PABA. Exercise will help keep tissue supple and strong.

Weathering the Hot Flushes and Other Pesky Problems

For many women, the transition years of menopause are accompanied by a few side effects. They may be barely noticeable, or they may really be disruptive. The most common one is hot flushes: a feeling of heat over the neck and face, which may spread over the body, often accompanied by perspiration. These last anywhere from a few moments to an hour; the frequency also varies. They may occur at night, disturbing sleep. The loss of normal sleep is the main cause of the irritability and depression that some women experience during menopause. The flushes usually continue for over a year; in about a quarter of all cases they will last about five years. Sometimes they are accompanied by a sensation of palpitations, or of being short of breath. Other symptoms less frequently reported are feelings of dizziness, numbness or tingling, headache, and joint or muscle pains.

These symptoms aren't imaginary; heart rate and skin temperature both rise during flushes. They are probably caused by a pulsative release of the hormone LH from the pituitary gland. This hormone is produced in increasing amounts as estrogen production from the ovaries decreases. Somehow, this makes the body's thermostat hypersensitive. However, the severity is affected by many things. Hot meals and hot drinks can make them worse. Drinks containing alcohol also cause skin flushing, and may trigger hot flushes. Entering a warm room or going outside on a hot day may also start them. Having a cool drink, removing a layer of clothing, or using a fan will alleviate symptoms. Although flushes may feel intense and embarrassing, usually you are the only one aware of them. Make yourself comfortable by dressing in layers, so you can take off or add a jacket as needed. Keep a cool drink or a fan nearby. For most women, these simple measures will provide comfort — naturally. If your flushes make you too uncomfortable, or if they interfere too much with your sleep, you may wish to consider other alternatives. Some women find that taking an ounce of Aloe Vera juice — available in health food stores — each day reduces symptoms. Estrogen or progestin supplements will also reduce or stop them (see the section further on for a discussion of the pro's and con's). There are also Eastern medicine remedies such as herbal tonics or acupuncture therapy that you may wish to try. Some communities offer menopausal support and discussion groups where you can share feelings and information with each other. Just understanding the process as natural and self-limited will reduce the anxiety, and make the pesky problems easier to handle.

Sexuality after Menopause

It is untrue that we become less sexual, or enjoy sex less, after the menopause. Many sociologists believe that women don't reach the "peak" of their sexuality until their mid-thirties. Often, women find that they feel more sexual during and after menopause. This may be due in part to the increased levels of androgens (male-type hormones naturally produced by a woman's ovaries and adrenal glands). However, the strongest effects of menopause are likely to be on the number one organ of human sexuality — the mind! The increased feelings of self-confidence and self-awareness we experience as we mature are likely to result in sexuality that only improves. But stress from *any* source, including anxiety about our aging process, can decrease libido.

There are also some physical changes in our gentials after menopause. The vaginal and vulvar tissues may become thinner and form fewer secretions as estrogen stimulation decreases. However, women with an active sex life have fewer of these changes. This may be because a healthy sex life stimulates the production of androgens. The ovaries continue to produce low levels of androgens after other hormone production stops — well into the eighties. With some judicious precautions, the effects of the estrogen decrease can be minimized.

Be careful about cleanliness; the more delicate tissues are susceptible to infection. If you enjoy anal sex, be particularly careful not to enter the vagina after entering the anus without washing. If you find your vagina gets sore easily, or produces less lubrication, you may want to use a lubricant for sex, both externally and with penetration. Saliva works fine; any water-soluble lubricant such as Lubafax or Helix is a good choice. If used inside the vagina, creams and oils leave residues which can soften the thinner tissues, making them more susceptible to abrasion damage and infection.

For most women, particularly lesbians, douching is not really necessary. If you do, it should be kept to a minimum, not more than once a week. Use a mild solution of one tablespoon vinegar to a quart of warm water, or just plain water.

Because of the decrease in tissue elasticity, as well as thinning which can follow estrogen decrease, some women have increased problems with urination. There may be burning or irritation after sex. Sometimes there is loss of small amounts of urine with coughing or sneezing, or with exercise. Kegel exercises will help the dribble problem, as well as strengthen all the muscles of the vagina; this can also increase sexual pleasure. You can do them any time, anywhere, in any position: just contract the muscles of your vulva as you would to stop the flow of urine. Hold for a count of three, and release. Repeat this ten times. When you build this muscle's strength a little, you can add a series of ten rapid contract-releases. Do these ten times a day; in a few weeks, you'll notice a difference.

If these problems are severe, small amounts of estrogen cream used once a day may help. See the section on hormone therapy.

Osteoporosis

Probably the most serious effect of decreased estrogen after menopause is loss of bone density. There are many factors which affect how much bone is lost, and how fast. Black women are at lowest risk for osteoporosis, while very fair white women are at highest risk. Heavy women and tall women are slower to develop critical bone thinning than thin or petite women. Dietary habits have major effects on bone loss. In one study of lacto-ovo-vegetarians versus meat-eaters, the meat-eaters lost twice as much bone, even though they took in the same amount of calcium. A diet high in animal protein is high in acidic content, requiring increased dissolution of bone to neutralize it. The vegetarian diet is the opposite: low in acids. The average American diet, furthermore, is sadly deficient in calcium, and as we grow older, absorption is less efficient. As a result, an average postmenopausal woman loses 40 mg. of calcium in her urine every day! In a year this adds up to 1.5% loss of bone mass. If menopause occurs at fifty, she has lost 15% of her bone mass by age sixty. Another dietary problem which causes calcium loss is high-phosphorus intake. Most processed foods contain additives with large amounts of phosphorus, as do meats, cola-type drinks, potatoes, bread and cereals.

Smoking and alcohol consumption both decrease calcium absorption and cause earlier ovarian suppression, and so lower estrogen levels. Both habits increase the risks of osteoporosis.

OSTEOPOROSIS

High-Risk Factors	Low-Risk Factors
White, fair complexioned women	Black women
Slender women	Heavy women
Petite, small-boned	Tall, large-boned
Diet: high in meats, processed foods	Diet: lacto-ovo-vegetarian, no processed foods
Low calcium intake	Good calcium intake
Little exercise	Vigorous exercise three or more times a week
Smoking	Estrogen replacement therapy
Daily alcohol consumption	
Some drugs	
Surgical or early menopause	

Some drugs also increase bone loss. If you take steroids, antacids containing aluminum, anticonvulsants, some diuretics, or thyroid hormone, you may be at risk. Discuss this with your doctor.

What is the significance of osteoporosis? The effects of the disease are staggering, and — as more women live to their 70's — they get worse every year. By age 75, one in five American women breaks a hip. Fifteen percent die shortly after, and 30% die within one year, of complications of the fracture. Of those that survive, up to ⅔ are permanently disabled. Both hip and vertebral (spine) fractures cause chronic, severe pain, as well as loss of function. More than twice as many women are killed or disabled by osteoporosis as by breast cancer!

The good news is that osteoporosis is preventable! Every woman should carefully evaluate her diet, keeping the guidelines above in mind. Use a good nutrition book to estimate your calcium intake. You need at least 1 gram (1000 mg.) of *elemental* calcium a day before menopause, and 1½ grams a day during and after. Decrease or eliminate meat and processed foods. If you don't get these minimum amounts in your diet, then you need a calcium supplement. The best-absorbed and least expensive form is calcium carbonate; Os-Cal, Bio-Cal, and Tums all contain this form, as do others. If you don't get 30–60 minutes of sunshine a day, or drink a quart of fortified milk a day, you may also need Vitamin D to properly absorb the Calcium. Most multivitamins have 400 I.U. of Vitamin D which is all you need; don't overdose, as it can cause bone *loss* at levels above 1000 I.U. a day.

Exercise: All Pro's, no Con's

Exercise is the second major way to avoid osteoporosis. It also increases strength and energy, protects against heart attack and stroke, and improves your appearance. So how can you lose? Two ways: by overdoing it, and by not doing it at all.

You don't need to be a marathon athlete to promote good health — and have fun — with exercise. One hour of moderate exercise three times a week, or the equivalent, will prevent bone loss and benefit your cardiovascular system. Such activities as jazzercise or other dancing, aerobic and isometric exercises, jogging, biking, and racquetball are all effective. Swimming is somewhat less effective for the skeleton, but even a daily brisk walk of half an hour will work. Try carrying small hand-weights, or adding ankle weights as you increase your strength. If you are presently inactive, start slowly and build up. Watch your pulse rate; refer to the chart of maximum rates for age. Another beneficial activity is Tai-chi, which combines exercise with relaxation and stress reduction. In China and other Asian countries, Tai-chi routinely starts the workday in businesses and public squares. Exercise with a friend, a group, with morning TV — the main thing is to get moving!

Estrogen Replacement Therapy: Pro's and Con's

Deciding whether or not to take estrogens after menopause is not easy. If you maintain a very healthy diet (such as lacto-ovo-vegetarian), get adequate, regular exercise, and have none of the risk factors for osteoporosis, you probably don't need estrogens. However, if two or more of the high risk factors apply to you, or if you are having trouble weathering some of the symptoms of menopause, then you could really benefit from them.

Estrogen replacement therapy is the most effective known method of preventing osteoporosis. To be more effective, it should be started during the first years of menopause, and continued for ten or fifteen years. Bone loss will start again once the estrogens are stopped, but you will have saved 15–25% of your potential bone mass loss. This therapy should not be substituted for a good diet and exercise program, or for calcium intake, but used in addition to these measures. The dose of estrogen which is effective is low: 0.635 mg. of conjugated estrogen, or its equivalent. This is about one-third of the dose in low-dose birth control pills.

As with any drug, there are possible side effects. Unless

you have had a hysterectomy, taking estrogens alone will increase your risk of uterine cancer about six-fold. This is still a small risk: the risk of dying from endometrial cancer for women on estrogens alone is one in 200,000. (The risk of death from the complications of a hip fracture for menopausal women is one in 60!) This small cancer risk is eliminated when progestins are given for ten to fourteen days a month as well; this combined approach may actually reduce the cancer risk.

While on both estrogen and progestin, you may have a monthly period. This is expected. A small number of women have experienced increased blood pressure on hormone therapy. Blood pressure should be checked every few months at first, and therapy stopped if it increases. Other side effects are usually transient and minor. They are the same as those experienced with regular menstrual cycles: breast tenderness, swelling, or premenstrual irritability. They tend to decrease over time. With low doses of progestin such as Provera, there seems to be no increase in the risks of heart disease, stroke, or breast cancer. One recent, large study showed the death risk from *all* causes in women between ages forty and seventy who took estrogens was about one-third of that in women not using estrogens.

All currently available information indicates that taking combined estrogen/progestin therapy after menopause is both safe and beneficial for most women. Those who can't take hormone replacements are women with known breast or uterine cancer, previous deep vein thrombophlebitis, increased blood pressure due to estrogen, liver or gallbladder disease, or severe migraines. If you already have heart disease, previous stroke, large fibroids, diabetes or high blood pressure, you should ask your doctor's advice. During the years you take hormones, you should be checked by your doctor every six to twelve months. A yearly exam is important for other reasons as well, such as breast examination, blood pressure, etc.

This combined estrogen/progestin therapy is also effective for hot flushes and vaginal or vulvar effects of menopause.

If you can't take estrogens (or don't want to), progestin alone will help with hot flushes; it won't help the genital tissues, though. If you have itching, dryness, or urinary symptoms, a very small amount of estrogen cream will help to relieve them. A quarter of an inch of Premarin cream (on the measured applicator top), rubbed inside and out once a day, will usually give relief in one or two weeks. After that, half as much will maintain the effects for most women. The hormone does get absorbed in a very small amount into the bloodstream. Just be sure to have regular check-ups, and see your doctor if irregular bleeding occurs.

Other Parts

For many women, their breasts are tied to their feelings of femininity and sexuality. Finding a lump raises the specters of surgery, deformity, and possible death from cancer. For this reason, paradoxically, many women are afraid to examine their breasts; they would rather not know! Also there are many small, natural lumps: the mammary glands. Women feel them and become anxious, unsure about their ability to tell the difference between these and cancer. The truth is, eighty percent of lumps found are benign; and the majority of early detected and treatable lumps, which are brought to medical attention, are found by women themselves. Learn to do a thorough breast exam from your health-care practitioner, and start right after your exam. If you like, make a chart of your breasts, and mark where you feel your normal glands. You can refer to it the next month. After a few months, you'll know your own breast, and will recognize any changes. One in eleven women will develop breast cancer in her life. The best way to avoid a mastectomy and spread of the tumor is early detection!

What about mammography? This test is the most sensitive one available to pick up early tumors. It is not one hundred percent sensitive, though, so you still need to do breast self-exam and have yearly checks. The radiation from a modern mammogram is less than what you receive from a half-hour lying in the sun. The American Cancer Society recommends that all women have one by age forty, and that it be repeated every 1-3 years, depending on risk factors.

Keep a close eye on your skin. You or your lover should do an all-over check once or twice a year for any changes in moles or growths. Any rapid growth, color changes, or bleeding, non-healing sore should be checked by a doctor.

Take good care of your back. Ask your practitioner or exercise instructor for good back exercises, and include them in your daily routine. Learn to lift things with your leg muscles, not your back. Once a back injury occurs, you may have pain or limitation for a long time , even permanently, so treat it with respect.

Last, but not least, take care of your feet. As we get older, we develop more foot problems — they've been bearing our weight for a long time! Poor walking and posture habits begin to take their toll. If you start to notice calluses, corns, or aches and pains in feet and legs, visit a podiatrist who can nip a problem in the bud early, before it becomes expensive or disabling.

Our Most Valuable Possession

Middle-age can be the most fulfilling exciting part of life. We have gathered knowledge and wisdom; we have more time and money; we know ourselves better. The most valuable thing we can own, though, is good health. Without it all our other options are limited. Try this exercise: Make a list of all the things you would like to do by the time you're seventy. Now, eliminate things you can't do if bedridden; if heart disease or bone disease limit your activity; if you must spend large amounts of money on drugs and treatments. Now make a list of what changes you need in your life to insure your health. What does it cost, in time and money? What is it worth? Finally, make a plan for "health insurance": diet changes, exercise programs, a schedule for check-ups. A few minutes a day spent listening to our bodies can promote a long and healthy life.

Bibliography/Reference Books

Greenwood, Sadja, M.D., *Menopause Naturally*, Volcano Press, San Francisco, CA, 1984.

Gorbach, Zimmerman & Woods, *The Doctors' Anti-Breast Cancer Diet*, Simon & Schuster, New York, NY, 1984.

Weiss, Kay, Ed., *Women's Health Care: A Guide to Alternatives*, Reston Publishing Co., Reston, VA, 1984.

Notelovity & Ware, *Stand Tall! Every Woman's Guide to Preventing Osteoporosis*, Bantam Books, New York, NY, 1982.

Eshelman & Winston, *The American Heart Association Cookbook*, David McKay & Co., New York, NY, 1984.

SHERYL GOLDBERG

GLOE:
A model social service program for older lesbians

"I have nothing more in common with the people at the neighborhood senior center than my age. At GLOE, I have been able to meet women who, like myself, have been lesbians all of their lives. What a welcome alternative to the traditional senior agency or the bar scene. Thanks to GLOE, I have met a new group of supportive peers, and my life begins again."

— a 62-year old-woman

Gay and Lesbian Outreach to Elders (GLOE) is a social service program designed to meet the needs of the estimated 20,000 lesbians and gay men aged 60 and over who live in San Francisco. The program provides a safe environment in which this mostly "hidden" group of elders can meet others who share similar life experiences and interests. Within, one's identity as a lesbian or gay man is not only out in the open — it is supported, honored, and accepted. For some participants, this is their first experience of such acceptance.

Since 1982, the GLOE program has received funding from the San Francisco Commission on the Aging. Funding was awarded as a result of extensive lobbying by gays, both young and old. The program receives additional funds from private grants and donations.

GLOE also offers intergenerational support through its

corps of volunteers, who are primarily men and women in their thirties. Volunteers are active in all facets of the program: organizing social events, doing friendly visiting to homebound seniors, and performing administrative tasks within the office.

The program also serves as a link to other senior service agencies and groups within the lesbian and gay communities. Patricia, a 78-year-old senior living in a low-income section of the city, called the GLOE office inquiring about transportation service to her regular medical appointment. Pat learned about the services of GLOE while reading a women-identified publication. GLOE staff responded to Pat's request by putting her in touch with the Senior Escort Service in her area. She will now receive rides to her medical appointments free of charge. During the course of Pat's phone conversation with the GLOE staffer, it became evident that Pat was not eating well. To rememdy this, Pat was made aware of the neighborhood senior meal sites and the Meals-on-Wheels program.

Characteristics of GLOE Participants

Currently there are approximately 250 participants in the GLOE program, two-fifths of whom are women. Lesbians have proven to be more difficult to locate and attract to the program for reasons including the following:

• Older lesbians are not as public in their lifestyle as are older gay men. Women tend to socialize in more private spaces rather than in the public places like bars, political institutions.

• Many lesbians relate to and gain support from the women's community and the feminist movement, where it is not necessary for them to make identifying statements about their sexual orientation.

• Because there are fewer lesbians in the San Francisco community, they are less powerful politically and socially, and may have more to lose (job, social status) by being identified as a lesbian.

Many of GLOE's participants fall in the category of the "young-old" (ages 60 to 75) rather than that of "old-old," persons 75 and beyond. Approximately 52% have been identified as socially needy according to the San Francisco Commission on the Aging, which labels as "socially needy" people who meet any two of the following criteria: 75 or older, disabled, living alone, language communications barrier. Thirty-two percent of GLOE members are defined as low-income because they are receiving Supplemental Security Income (SSI) checks.

Despite their lifelong primary sexual and social relationships with others of the same sex, the term and identification as "lesbians" were alien to many women. Others have begun to live and enjoy a gay lifestyle in their later years. Many of these "late-bloomers" were previously married — reflecting the strong social pressures of the early 1900's which forced many lesbians and gays to marry in order to fulfill family obligations.

Large numbers of GLOE members are not currently relating to members of their biological families, in some cases due to non-acceptance of their sexual orientation. For this group of lesbians and gay men, friends have replaced nuclear families. GLOE helps older lesbians and gay men increase their base of support in later life by enabling them to form and develop a network of peers and other friends who care and will be there when needed.

Mary is a 71-year-old participant in the GLOE program. She is also a political activist in the larger community. Her children, two daughters who live on the East Coast, have not been very accepting of Mary's lesbianism. Mary came to GLOE in its earliest days. She has witnessed the development of a program which has increasingly been able to provide her with social and emotional support. As she said in a recent interview, "I feel very close to many of the people in GLOE, and I know that whatever happens, I won't be all alone. It's like having an extended family. That means a great deal to me, and I'm speaking from the heart."

The majority of GLOE participants are white, but outreach is being made to members of ethnic and racial minority groups. It is particularly difficult to locate minority persons to GLOE because minority cultures are often hostile towards members of their own culture who are gay or lesbian. Members of such groups may therefore be reluctant to openly identify as living the lifestyle of a gay or lesbian person. Those who do "come out" and join the GLOE program may feel somewhat uncomfortable and unsupported in a predominantly white group. This situation is slowly changing as more persons in the community learn about the program and trust develops.

GLOE Program Components

The GLOE program's components are as follows:

• Social Events: Luncheons, tea dances, open houses, picnics, parties, involvement in community events.

• Groups: Men's rap, neighborhood rap (meets in a senior housing development in the city's Tenderloin area), women's drop-in rap, writing workshops for women and men (publishes a quarterly journal and does community presentations), cooking class (meets in a neighborhood senior center) and AWOL (Alternative Ways of Living — a committee which looks at housing options for older lesbians). With the exception of the men's rap, all groups are facilitated by GLOE members who serve as older volunteers.

• Life Skills Workshops: Presented topics have included health, legal and mental health issues as they relate to older gays and lesbians; these have been held on a quarterly basis.

• Friendly Visitor Program: Trained volunteers are matched with homebound or socially isolated lesbian and gay seniors for a contracted one-year relationship.

• Outreach: This is an on-going, never-ending process and the backbone of the GLOE program. We have found the most successful method of outreach to be "word-of-mouth" or personal referrals. Also utilized to reach GLOE's target population is media publicity including television, radio, newspapers and other periodicals; presentations at lesbian and gay community agencies and social service programs for the elderly; representation at fairs and conferences. The GLOE program also sends out a monthly newsletter to 500 persons and agencies and will soon have a brochure to distribute.

• Volunteer Program: Volunteers are required to complete

a formal training session before working with the program. Trained volunteers serve the program in various capacities. Some perform administrative tasks in the office, some are friendly visitors in the community, others help at social events or facilitate groups. Volunteers are provided with support and continuous training by GLOE staff and by attending regular scheduled meetings.

Women's Component of GLOE

In the beginning GLOE was a mixed group program whose social functions included both women and men. These events were attended by close to fifty men and less than a handful of women. Where, we wondered, were all the older lesbians in San Francisco?

A year into the program's existence, GLOE staff and women volunteers made a decision to plan women-only events. Fifteen older women were invited to an afternoon tea held at an elegant downtown location. Four older lesbians, the GLOE Women's Coordinator, and nine younger women volunteers attended the program's first women-only social. The main objective of this meeting was to gather together and brainstorm about ideas to reach more older lesbians for the GLOE program. This effort was only minimally successful. The resulting mood of women in the program was one of disappointment and frustration related to the difficult task of locating and soliciting the interest of older lesbians.

In the following months, attendance at GLOE functions continued to reflect the preponderance of gay men in the program. Then, during a conference sponsored by the National Association of Lesbian and Gay Gerontology (NALGG) held at San Francisco State University during the summer of 1983, an older GLOE volunteer attempted to start a support group for older lesbians. After publicizing the group at the conference, through the local press and word of mouth within the community, it still seemed impossible to elicit interest in this group.

In an all-out effort to locate older lesbians and consequently to provide service for them through the GLOE program, an extensive outreach campaign began in the fall of 1983. Flyers describing the program and inviting women to an informal afternoon meeting were distributed by mail and delivered directly to neighborhood congregate spots. In addition, press releases were placed in local lesbian and gay and women's publications. The response was encouraging. Twelve older lesbians, four younger women volunteers and myself, the GLOE Coordinator, attended the "social planning" meeting.

Women were asked to introduce themselves and their reasons for attending the group. Some of the following statements were made:

"It's nice to know there are this many of us."

"How can we find more of us?"

"There aren't any role-models for older lesbians. We are it."

The most exciting outcome of the meeting was the scheduling of a "Fall Harvest Tea Dance" for older lesbians and their women friends. Another social-planning meeting was set for the following month to make provisions for the upcoming dance.

During this next meeting, outreach and planning efforts continued with an even larger group of women present. Flyers were handed out to all for distribution in their neighborhoods. Publicity for this event was expanded to include women's businesses and women's centers. The consensus of the group decided the plans and actions necessary for the dance: site location, refreshments, music, fees, and so on. Job responsibilities were delegated among the group members.

The flyer for the event was worded as follows, "GLOE of Operation Concern invites women over 60 and their women friends who *love* socializing with women to join us for a tea dance." By not using the word "lesbian," we hoped to attract some women (at risk of alienating others). The Fall Harvest Tea Dance was a tremendous sucess. Out of the 60 women in attendance, more than half were in their later years.

The ensuing plan of action set forth by women participants was to have one day each month designated as women-only time for GLOE participants. These events have taken the form of brunches, social meetings, additional tea dances, and events integrated within the larger community (e.g. attendance at a neighborhood cabaret or restaurant).

A GLOE Women's Interest Sheet was distributed to collect information about the types of programs women wanted. Options consisted of mixed or women's-only socials, trips, classes, workshops, and groups. Every one of the twenty women who responded to this survey expressed interest in women-only dances; more than half wanted women-only support groups, backpacking trips and brunches. A number of these requests were soon put into action.

Tea Dances

Tea dances for women are now held on a monthly basis. The word spreads throughout the community via monthly press releases to mainstream, lesbian and women's publications, flyers to community groups, and personal networking. The dances are held in a neighborhood senior center facility, where the rental cost is minimal. GLOE volunteers and participants help with publicity, registration, set-up, music, and clean-up. Transportation is coordinated and provided volunteers. Birthdays and holidays are celebrated at the dances. Special programs have included sing-a-longs and face painting.

Support Groups

Members wanted GLOE to provide not only social events such as dances, but also opportunities for members to become better acquainted with one another and more aware of themselves. This was especially important to those whose earlier social connections had been broken by the death of a partner or friends. Many members had been socially active primarily with women twenty to forty years younger than themselves; they were interested in meeting and befriending peers.

Under the leadership of two older volunteers, an eight week support group for women over 60 years of age was started. The group provided a safe, supportive atmosphere for women to share their herstories and gain support for present-day life situations.

Alternative Ways of Living (AWOL)

The AWOL committee had its beginning during one of the social planning meetings, where women were expressing fears about housing as they become older and more dependent. Those who were interested in creating alternatives to traditional accommodations for the "frail" elderly (i.e. long hospital stays, nursing homes, living alone) began meeting twice a month in an effort to create a supportive older women's living space. Gathering relevant information, sharing hopes, dreams and methods to accomplish this, have been some of the work efforts of the committee. At this time the group is working on a proposal to fund a consultant to help guide the committee. The group continues to meet and strategize around attainment of their ultimate goal: the establishment of housing for older lesbians in the Bay Area.

Friendly Visiting

For women who are homebound or socially isolated, GLOE offers a friendly visitor program. Trained volunteers (most often women in their thirties) are matched with needy seniors in the community. The relationship takes on the characteristics of the individual personalities and needs of both the client and the volunteer. Volunteers are encouraged to have contact with their clients on the average of once every ten days. The relationship, if satisfactory, is contracted to last for at least one year. Outreach efforts of the GLOE program seek to identify more at-risk women who could benefit from the support of the friendly visitor program.

Throughout the program's three-year history, twelve matches between women friendly visitor clients and volunteers have been made. The majority have been satisfying and successful for both people involved. Joanne, a 64-year-old woman, had been alone and isolated since her lover died fifteen years ago. With the addition of Shelley (GLOE volunteer) to her life, she is now part of a support system of peers that she met through her involvement with GLOE. I asked Joanne to comment on the program.

"My experience with the friendly visitor program within GLOE has been tremendous. When I was in the hospital having my knee operated on, Shelley, my friendly visitor, didn't miss a day. Other GLOE volunteers and members also came to visit. When people visit, say hi, and give love and caring, that's important. I wouldn't trade my relationship with my friendly visitor for anything in the world. She calls me regularly. We go out to eat once a week. I was invited to their home (I am great friends with her lover too) for Christmas and Thanksgiving. Shelley's a beautiful and most caring person. I still keep asking her, how come you pick an old dame like me to visit? We joke. We kid each other. When I was released from the hospital, they both took a day off from work and were there waiting for me when I returned home. I couldn't hope for any nicer people."

Elsie, a woman in her early sixties, is suffering from Parkinson's disease. She describes herself as a person whose "young, active mind is trapped within an old, stiff body." Rose, her 25-year-old visitor, has the energy and expertise to help Elsie continue her creative process. They are both involved with putting together a slide presentation of Elsie's world-wide travels as well as taping stories she will later have transcribed and hopes to publish. Elsie commented that, "My relationship is working out very nicely. Rose is helping me with my slides. We work on other projects together. She has a friend to type my manuscript to help me save money. We have dinner together and talk about a lot of things. It's nice to have someone who cares to listen and share."

Evaluation

A final aspect of the program that deserves attention is its evaluation component. Evaluation occurs in a number of ways. The first is through the personal communication between staff, volunteers and GLOE members. Ongoing feedback from members is solicited and provides a basis for developing and expanding the services provided through GLOE.

A survey of thirty randomly chosen GLOE participants (14 women, 16 men) was conducted in the fall of 1984. Focusing specifically on the women respondents, the results showed that most learned about GLOE through a friend, had been with the program for one year and were involved in social events and educational workshops. All felt that the program was meeting their needs. Most women liked the dances best. They found the people friendly and the social aspects enjoyable. They felt a great need for a program such as GLOE and found that it filled a personal and community need. Additional programs suggested by women respondents included one day outings and a woman's rap group. To answer to the latter, the program is in the process of organizing an informal drop-in rap group for women.

In addition, the GLOE Advisory Committee, which is composed of GLOE participants, volunteers and interested service providers for the elderly, meets twice a year to review activity plans and to brainstorm regarding future directions for the GLOE program. With the encouragement of members of this committee, we are now in the process of exploring the reality and need for a senior center for older lesbians and gay men.

Creating a GLOE Program

Following are suggested steps to take in developing a program designed to serve older lesbians in your local area, using the GLOE program as the model.

Step 1: Educate the public: Begin with the gay and lesbian community, women's community, and elderly service network. Explain the existence and special situations and needs of older lesbians (including isolation, invisibility, limited involvement in mainstream services for seniors, etc.)

Step 2: Lobby for funding: Public and private grants, individual donations.

Step 3: Spread the word: Publicize in local lesbian, women's aging press. Conduct outreach; flyers word of mouth.

Step 4: Work with participants to develop, plan and organize the program.

Step 5: Repeat the procedure.

Similar services are much needed throughout the country to meet the needs of lesbian elders.

ABBY ABINANTI, attorney at law

Utilizing the Law for Our Own Protection

The law can and should be used as an ally by women who have chosen to spend their lives in loving relationships with other women. Too often we let fear of the law interfere with using it to maximize our own protection. The "law" and its role in the lives of women must be confronted by women. The issues of illness, disability, retirement and death must be assumed and prepared for. Most of us will need the assistance of a lawyer to actually protect ourselves and our lifestyle commitments.

Selecting a Lawyer

In order to select a lawyer, you can check various sources: friends, local legal services to the economically disadvantaged, women's centers, gay and lesbian associations, and local Bar Associations. When you actually have your first contact, i.e., call to make an appointment, ask what the consultation fee is, telling the receptionist or the lawyer that you wish to discuss having a will and attendant documents drafted. (Wills and accompanying documents are explained and discussed below.) You can then determine whether this lawyer is financially an option for you.

In your first meeting, set out your goals and ask if the attorney can secure those results. If you find a resistance to goals, such as leaving property to a lover, do not continue with this lawyer. Trust your instincts! Remember, you are a consumer of a service and if you are not pleased with services you are receiving, you may select another service provider. It may also happen that you have a very willing lawyer, but one who admits that she has limited experience in dealing with lesbian relationships, particularly in ensuring that our wishes as to dying and distribution of property are carried out. If this occurs or if you think the lawyer could use some assistance, tell her that the definitive source to consult is *Sexual Orientation and the Law* by the National Lawyers Guild Anti-Sexism Committee of San Francisco Bay Area Chapter, Roberta Achtenberg, Editor, published by Clark Boardman Company, Ltd., New York, New York, 1985.

A difficult question is, when can I proceed without an attorney? If you have sufficient funds, I believe that the best course is to consult an attorney. And before you decide that you don't have sufficient funds, take the steps outlined above to see what resources are available at what costs. If finances or other factors prevent you from consulting a lawyer, you have other options which will vary depending upon your state of residence.

Bequeathing Assets Without a Will

Prior to your death you can ensure that distribution of assets after your death is consistent with your lifetime desires and without the necessity of probate. First, you may choose to provide for your lover and primary family by the purchase of life insurance. On any such policy you may leave all the proceeds to one person or, if you choose, "fractionalize" or divide the sum to be provided among friends.

Second, if you have a bank account — either checking or savings — which contains the major portion of your actual cash assets, you may wish a lover or friend to have direct and immediate access to such funds in the event of your death. (If you dispose of such funds by will, there may be a delay in the use of such funds while your estate is probated or until special orders are signed to allow access to this money.) In order to accomplish such an immediate transfer, you need to inquire at your bank, savings and loan company, or credit union about how they make such transfers. Most institutions allow for either joint accounts or designees who can only take charge of your account in the event of your death. Such a transfer will avoid having access to your funds restricted while your estate is being settled, as the transfer actually takes place "outside" the estate.

(If you use a savings and loan company, you should also be aware of the risks involved. In the 1980s, an unprecedented number of these institutions have failed. They are often attractive to savers because of high interest rates offered in comparison to other institutions. However, in making such decisions, you should determine what type of insurance these institutions carry, i.e., which depositors/deposits are protected. Federally insured institutions offer the maximum protection.)

Third, if you own real property, you can insure its automatic transfer after your death in the language utilized in the deed by which you take possession of the property. Escrow officers or attorneys can assist you with the proper language. The terminology must be very specific, as there is a current bias against such transfers.

Power of Attorney

At the same time you consider having a will drafted you should decide whether or not you want protection in the event of incapacitation. This protection can also cover burial instructions and instructions for care in case of terminal illness. Many states have adopted "durable" powers of attorney statutes which provide these protections. These durable powers of attorney are documents by which the intent of the person who signed the document gives certain powers to another. Unless a termination date is fixed in the document, this power exists until it is revoked.

Generally, such powers of attorney can allow another person to take care of your business, i.e., signing checks, insurance forms, managing your business, selling stocks, collecting monies due you, etc. It is an open question, one not decided by law in many states, if such a Durable Power of Attorney will allow health care decisions to be made by the one given the power of attorney in the event of incapacity. In California, that ambiguity has been resolved by a statute which specifically provides a "Durable Power of Attorney for Health Care." In states were no durable power of attorney statutes are in force or where the force of such states may not be clear, it would aid the enforcement of your wishes to execute an Authorization for Medical Treatment.

Wills

The final and perhaps the most important document which must be considered is a will. A will is a legal expression or declaration of a person's mind or wishes as to the disposition of her property, to be performed or take effect after death. The first issue to face when contemplating a will is to overcome the resistance many of us have to admitting our own mortality. That resistance alone is often enough to delay for years the drafting of a will. However, failure to draft a will may leave your lover or other close friends without the support and guidance they need in ensuring your wishes during what will be a very trying time for them.

A will should contain a listing of all your property, land, vehicles, investments, bank accounts (not jointly held) and personal items to be specifically allocated.

Additionally, just so a list exists somewhere, you may wish to list items such as life insurance policies which name beneficiaries. This will create a record of those items so survivors can check this list. They should not be mentioned in the will but a record is helpful to the survivors.

In preparing a will list, you will want to list all items specifically to be given, with the person to receive each gift, and then you must decide who shall receive the item if the first person you choose does not survive you. This is an important list, and you should work with it until it accurately reflects your wishes.

The second concern of a will is who is to administer the will so that the property is actually distributed as you have decided. This person is called the executor. You should select a person who you believe will be committed to your wishes and who will be sympathetic to your friends in their grief. Again, you will need to have a second choice should your first choice not be available to perform these duties. The duties are ensuring the legal distribution; a fee is proscribed by law for these services, and is based on the value of the entire property being passed.

A third concern of a will may be burial instructions. Many wills set out our preferences as to a funeral or memorial service and a burial or cremation. Such instructions can serve as guidelines to grief-stricken survivors.

Finally, the will should address what is to be done with any property and funds not specifically allocated, i.e., who will receive them. Again, a first and second choice is required.

I often will add a clause in wills of lesbians confirming their love for their "blood family," noting that their failure to provide for such family is specific, but not intended to indicate any diminishment of love or affection. This is intended as a reflection of our non-traditional families as a priority, but serves as an acknowledgement of our dual family status.

Preparing the above lists will put you in a position of being "ready" to see a lawyer and get down to business. Or, if you are choosing to not see a lawyer, you may choose, depending on your state of residence, to draft a holographic will. A holographic will traditionally is defined as one that is entirely written, dated and signed by the hand of the person writing the will. However, now states allowing for such wills have specifically set forth requirements for them. At this writing, the states which allow such a will are: Arizona, Arkansas, California, Colorado, Alaska, Iowa, Kentucky, Louisiana, Mississippi, Montana, Nevada, North Carolina, North Dakota, Oklahoma,

South Dakota, Tennessee, Texas, Utah, Virginia, Idaho, West Virginia, Wyoming, and Puerto Rico. If you live in one of these states and wish to draft such a will you should consult a law library, legal service, or similar resource to find out your state's specific requirements.

For an extensive choice of legal forms, you may consult *Sexual Orientation and the Law*, mentioned above. Or seek out the closest law library; courthouses usually have libraries, as do law schools. They are also listed in the telephone book. Then ask the librarian to see "Form Books" on wills or whatever you are interested in. Such books have models or suggested forms for you to copy. Also stationery stores may have forms for you to use. In using forms be sure you conform to the statutory requirements of your state, e.g., holographic wills have special requirements.

As a final word of caution, this article is meant to familiarize the reader with various legal options; but is not designed to be utilized as a primary legal source. Further, state laws may change. My hope is that this article will build your confidence so you can approach an attorney with the knowledge needed to be an informed consumer or begin the work to draft the necessary documents discussed in this article.

The author wishes to acknowledge the legal research necessary for this article which was conducted by Donna DeMatteo, of Bayside Legal Advocates, San Francisco, California.

Power of Attorney

Know all persons by these presents that I, _____,
a legal resident of _____, California, hereby
appoint _____, whose present address is
_____, my lawful attorney to act as follows:

I grant to my said attorney full and sole power to do and
execute all or any of the following acts, deeds, or documents
as fully as and in the place of any spouse, parent, or other
relative.

1. To authorize my medical treatment if I shall be
physically or mentally incapacitated or otherwise unable to
make such authorization for myself, including authorization
for emergency care, hospitalization, surgery, therapy and/or
any other kind of treatment which she shall, in her sole
discretion, think necessary.

2. To be given first priority in visitation should I be a
patient in any institution and unable to express a preference
on account of my illness or disability.

3. To receive into her possession any and all items of
personal property and effects that may be recovered from or
about my person by any hospital, police agency, or any other
person at the time of my illness, disability, or death.

4. To authorize the release of my body from any hospital or any other authority having possession of my body at the time of my death and to make all decisions necessary for and incident to the removal and transportation of my body from the place of my death.

5. To make all decisions necessary for the performance of funeral and burial services, if any.

6. To have published in any newspaper an obituary notice containing whatever information she may choose.

7. To contract with any competent person or company for the rendering of professional services by any funeral director of her choosing.

8. To make all decisions necessary for the interment or cremation of my body, including but not limited to, the selection of a casket or urn, selection of a grave site, and selection of a gravestone and the inscription thereon.

9. To contract with any person or company for the provision of care and tending of my grave site.

10. To execute all necessary instruments and to perform all necessary acts required for the execution and implementation of the aforesaid authorization.

IT IS MY EXPRESS INTENTION that no powers granted by this instrument shall be revoked, terminated, or otherwise limited in any manner whatsoever by my death or mental or physical incapacity. And I declare that any act lawfully done hereunder by my said attorney shall be binding on myself and my heirs, legal and personal representatives, and assigns.

In witness thereof, I have hereunto set my hand and seal this _____ day of _____, 1984.

_____

We declare under penalty of perjury under the laws of California that the principal is personally known to us, that the principal signed or ackowledged this durable power of attorney in our presence, that the principal appears to be of sound mind and under no duress, fraud, or undue influence, that we are not the persons appointed as attorney in fact by this document, and we are not a health care provider, an employee of a health care provider, the operator of a community care facility, nor an employee of an operator of a community care facility. We are not related to the principal by blood, marriage, or adoption, and to the best of our knowledge we are not entitled to any part of the estate of the principal upon the death of the principal under a Will now existing or by operation of law.

_____
Witness

_____
Witness

State of California
County of _____

On this _____ day of _____, in the year 1984, before me, _____, personally appeared _____, personally known to me (or proved to me on the basis of satisfactory evidence) to be the person whose name is subscribed to this instrument, and acknowledged that she executed it. I declare under penalty of perjury that the person whose name is subscribed to this instrument appears to be of sound mind and under no duress, fraud, or undue influence.

_____
Notary Public

Last Will and Testament

The following is presented here as a model to help an attorney who is drawing up a will; it is not intended to be used as is, without the advice of an attorney.

LAST WILL AND TESTAMENT
OF

_____

I, _____, a resident of the County of _____, State of California, being of sound and disposing mind and memory, do hereby make, publish and declare this as and for my last Will and Testament, hereby revoking all former Wills and Testaments and Codicils previously made by me.

FIRST: I am unmarried and I have no biological children.

SECOND: I give all my clothing, household furniture and furnishings, and other tangible articles of a personal

* Testator must sign the bottom of each page.

Page 1 of 4   _____

                              _____

nature, or my interest in any such property, not otherwise specifically disposed of by this Will or in any other manner, together with any insurance on the property, to my friend, _____, of _____, California, if she survives me for thirty (30) days, and if she does not, to my friend, _____, of _____, California, if she survives me for that period.

THIRD: I make the following gifts of money or property: 1. I give my interest in my real property situation in _____ County, and commonly known as _____, together with any insurance on the property to my friend, _____, of _____, California if she survives me for one hundred eighty (180) days, and if she does not, to my friend, _____, of _____, California, if she survives me for that period. I give the property subject to any encumbrances on it at the time of my death, including any mortgages, deeds of trust, and real property taxes and assessments.

FOURTH: I give the residue of my estate to my friend _____, of _____, California, if she survives me for one hundred eighty (180) days, and if she does not, to my friend, _____, of _____, California, if she survives me for that period.

If neither _____ nor _____ survives me for one hundred eighty (180) days, I give the residue of my estate to those persons who would have been my heirs if I had died one hundred eighty (180) days after my actual death, their identities and their respective shares to be determined according to the laws of the State of California in effect at the date of my death relating to the succession of separate property not acquired from a parent, grandparent, or previously deceased spouse.

FIFTH: If any person under this Will in any manner,

Page 2 of 4

_____

_____

directly or indirectly, contests or attacks this Will or any of its provisions, any share or interest in my estate given to that contesting person under this Will is revoked and shall be disposed of in the same manner provided herein as if that contesting beneficiary had predeceased me.

SIXTH: Except as otherwise provided in this Will, I have intentionally and with full knowledge omitted to provide for my heirs. I have not intentionally omitted my heirs because of feeling illwill toward them, and reaffirm here my love for each and every one of them. If any person who, if I died intestate, would be entitled to any part of my estates, shall either directly or indirectly, alone or in conjunction with any other person, claim in spite of my Will, an intestate share of my estate, I give that person One Dollar, and no more, in lieu of any other share or interest in my estate.

SEVENTH: I ask my friend _____ to make arrangements for the cremation of my remains and the distribution of my remains over Hawaii, if possible, and direct my Executor to pay for the expenses of my funeral, cremation, and distribution of my remains.

EIGHTH: I nominate my _____, _____, _____, as Executor of this Will, to serve without bond. If _____ for any reason fails to qualify or ceases to act as Executor, I nominate _____, of _____, as Executor, to serve without bond. The term "Executor" as used in this Will shall include any personal representative of my estate.

I authorize my Executor to sell, with or without notice at either public or private sale, and to lease any property belonging to my estate, subject only to such confirmation of court as may be required by law.

I further authorize my Executor either to continue the operation of any business belonging to my estate for such

Page 3 of 4   _____

_____

time and in such manner as my Executor may deem advisable or for the best interest of my estate, or to sell or liquidate the business at such time and on such terms as my Executor may deem advisable and for the best interests of my estate. Any such operation, sale, or liquidation by my Executor, in good faith, shall be at the risk of my estate and without liability on the part of my Executor for any resulting losses.

NINTH: If any provision of this Will is unenforceable, the remaining provisions shall remain in full effect.

I subscribe my name to this Will this _____ day of _____, 1985, at San Francisco, California.

_____

On the date last above written, _____ declared to us, the undersigned, that this instrument, consisting of four (4) pages including the page signed by us as witnesses, was her Will and requested us to act as witnesses to it. She thereupon signed this Will in our presence, all of us being present at the same time. We now, at her request, in her presence and in the presence of each other, subscribe our names as witnesses.

We declare under penalty of perjury that the foregoing is true and correct, and that this declaration was executed on _____, 1986, at San Francisco, California.

_____ residing at _____

_____

_____ residing at _____

_____

_____ residing at _____

_____

Page 4 of 4

_____

_____

Other books of interest from
ALYSON PUBLICATIONS

☐ **DEAR SAMMY: Letters from Gertrude Stein and Alice B. Toklas,** by Samuel M. Steward, $8.00. As a young man, Samuel M. Steward journeyed to France to meet the two women he so admired. It was the beginning of a long friendship. Here he combines his fascinating memoirs of Toklas and Stein with photos and more than a hundred of their letters.

☐ **THE MEN WITH THE PINK TRIANGLE,** by Heinz Heger, $6.00. In a chapter of gay history that is only recently coming to light, thousands of homosexuals were thrown into the Nazi concentration camps along with Jews and others who failed to fit the Aryan ideal. There they were forced to wear a pink triangle so that they could be singled out for special abuse. Most perished. Heger is the only one ever to have told his full story.

☐ **THE HUSTLER,** by John Henry Mackay; trans. by Hubert Kennedy, $8.00. Gunther is fifteen when he arrives alone in the Berlin of the 1920s. There he is soon spotted by Hermann Graff, a sensitive and naive young man who becomes hopelessly enamored with Gunther. But love does not fit neatly into Gunther's new life . . . *The Hustler* was first published in 1926. For today's reader, it combines a poignant love story with a colorful portrayal of the gay subculture that thrived in Berlin a half-century ago.

☐ **WORLDS APART,** edited by Camilla Decarnin, Eric Garber and Lyn Paleo, $8.00. Today's generation of science fiction writers has created a wide array of futuristic gay characters. The s-f stories collected here present adventure, romance, and excitement; and maybe some genuine alternatives for our future.

☐ **ONE TEENAGER IN TEN: Writings by gay and lesbian youth,** edited by Ann Heron, $4.00. One teenager in ten is gay; here, twenty-six young people tell their stories: of coming to terms with being different, of the decision how — and whether — to tell friends and parents, and what the consequences were.

☐ **DANCER DAWKINS AND THE CALIFORNIA KID,** by Willyce Kim, $6.00. Dancer Dawkins would like to just sit back and view life from behind a pile of hotcakes. But her lover, Jessica Riggins, has fallen into the clutches of Fatin Satin Aspen, and something must be done. Meanwhile, Little Willie Gutherie of Bangor, Maine, renames herself The California Kid, stocks up on Rubbles Dubble bubble gum, and heads west. When this crew collides in San Francisco, what can be expected? Just about anything. . . .

☐ **LEGENDE,** by Jeannine Allard, $6.00. Sometime in the last century, two women living on the coast of France, in Brittany, loved each other. They had no other models for such a thing, so one of them posed as a man for most of their life together. This legend is still told in Brittany; from it, Jeannine Allard has created a hauntingly beautiful story of two women in love.

☐ **WANDERGROUND,** by Sally Miller Gearhart, $7.00. Here are stories of the hill women, who combine the control of mind and matter with a sensuous adherence to women's realities and history. A lesbian classic.

☐ **TALK BACK! A gay person's guide to media action,** $4.00. When were you last outraged by prejudiced media coverage of gay people? Chances are it hasn't been long. This short, highly readable book tells how you, in surprisingly little time, can do something about it.

☐ **CHOICES,** by Nancy Toder, $8.00. This popular novel about lesbian love depicts the joy, passion, conflicts and intensity of love between women as Nancy Toder conveys the fear and confusion of a woman coming to terms with her sexual and emotional attraction to other women.

☐ **THE PEARL BASTARD,** by Lillian Halegua, $4.00. Frankie is fifteen when she leaves her large, suffocating Catholic family. Here, with painful innocence and acute vision, she tells the story of her sudden entry into a harsh maturity, beginning with the man in the fine green car who does not mourn the violent death of a seagull against his windshield.

☐ **THE TWO OF US,** by Larry Uhrig, $7.00. The author draws on his years of counseling with gay people to give some down-to-earth advice about what makes a relationship work. He gives special emphasis to the religious aspects of gay unions.

☐ **LIFETIME GUARANTEE,** by Alice Bloch, $7.00. Here is the personal and powerfully-written chronicle of a woman faced with the impending death of her sister from cancer, at the same time that she must also face her family's reaction to her as a lesbian.

☐ **IRIS,** by Janine Veto, $7.00. When Iris and Dee meet in Hawaii, they both know that this is the relationship they have each been looking for; all they want is to live together on this island paradise forever. But the world has other plans, and Iris is forced to flee to a desolate Greek island. When they are united, Iris and Dee find that their love must now face a formidable foe if it is to survive.

☐ **A FEMINIST TAROT,** by Sally Miller Gearhart and Susan Rennie, $7.00. The first tarot book to emerge from the women's movement, with interpretations of tarot cards that reflect women's experiences in contemporary society.

☐ **THE LAVENDER COUCH,** by Marny Hall, $8.00. Here is a guide to the questions that should be considered by lesbians or gay men considering therapy or already in it: How do you choose a good therapist? What kind of therapy is right for you? When is it time to leave therapy?

☐ **THE LAW OF RETURN,** by Alice Bloch, $8.00. The widely-praised novel of a woman who, returning to Israel, regains her Jewish heritage while also claiming her voice as a woman and as a lesbian. "Clear, warm, haunting and inspired" writes Phyllis Chesler. "I want to read everything Alice Bloch writes," adds Grace Paley.

☐ **BETWEEN FRIENDS,** by Gillian E. Hanscombe, $7.00. Frances and Meg were friends in school years ago; now Frances is a married housewife while Meg is a lesbian involved in progressive politics. Through letters written between these women and their friends, the author weaves an engrossing story while exploring many vital lesbian and feminist issues.

☐ **REFLECTIONS OF A ROCK LOBSTER: A story about growing up gay,** by Aaron Fricke, $6.00. When Aaron Fricke took a male date to the senior prom, no one was surprised: he'd gone to court to be able to do so, and the case had made national news. Here Aaron tells his story, and shows what gay pride can mean in a small New England town.

☐ **DECENT PASSIONS,** by Michael Denneny, $7.00. What does it mean to be in love? Do the joys outweigh the pains? Those are some of the questions explored here as Denneny talks separately with each member of three unconventional relationships — a gay male couple, a lesbian couple, and an interracial couple — about all the little things that make up a relationship.

☐ **YOUNG, GAY AND PROUD,** edited by Sasha Alyson, $4.00. Here is the first book ever to address the needs and problems of a mostly invisible minority: gay youth. Questions about coming out to parents and friends, about gay sexuality and health care, about finding support groups, are all answered here; and several young people tell their own stories.

☐ **GAY AND GRAY,** by Raymond M. Berger, $8.00. Working from questionnaires and case histories, Berger has provided the closest look ever at what it is like to be an older gay man. For some, he finds, age has brought burdens; for others, it has brought increased freedom and happiness.

These titles are available at many bookstores, or by mail.

— — — — — — — — — — — — — — — — — — —

Enclosed is $_____ for the following books. (Add $1.00 postage when ordering just one book; if you order two or more, we'll pay the postage.)

1. _____ 2. _____

3. _____ 4. _____

5. _____ 6. _____

name: _____ address:_____

city:_____ state:_____ zip:_____

ALYSON PUBLICATIONS
Dept. B-74, 40 Plympton St., Boston, Mass. 02118

After Dec. 31, 1988, please write for current catalog.